TWAYNE'S WORLD AUTHORS SERIES
A Survey of the World's Literature

RUSSIA

Charles A. Moser, George Washington University

EDITOR

Fedor Dostoevsky

TWAS 636

Fedor Dostoevsky

FEDOR DOSTOEVSKY

By WILLIAM J. LEATHERBARROW
University of Sheffield, England

TWAYNE PUBLISHERS
A DIVISION OF G.K. HALL & CO., BOSTON

Published in 1981 by Twayne Publishers,
A Division of G.K. Hall & Co.
All Rights Reserved

Printed on permanent/durable acid-free paper and bound
in the United States of America

Library of Congress Cataloging in Publication Data

Leatherbarrow, William J.
Fedor Dostoevsky.

(Twayne's world author series ; TWAS 636 :
Russia)
Bibliography: pp. 177–81
Includes index.
1. Dostoevskii, Fedor Mikhailovich, 1821–1881—
criticism and interpretation.
PG3328.Z6L36   891.73′3   80-28318
ISBN 0-8057-6480-1

Contents

About the Author

William J. Leatherbarrow is a Lecturer in Russian at the University of Sheffield, England. He graduated from the University of Exeter in 1969, and was awarded an M.A. at that university in 1972 for a dissertation on the works of N.S. Leskov. His interests are mainly in the area of nineteenth-century Russian literature, and he has published articles and reviews in several scholarly journals, including *The Slavonic and East European Review* and *The Modern Language Review*. He has also written occasionally on twentieth-century Russian authors. He is married and has two children.

Preface

To examine in even moderate detail the total literary achievement of an author as prolific and significant as Dostoevsky in a book of this nature and length would clearly be impossible. Consequently this work makes no claim to be comprehensive. Fortunately, the English-speaking student has been well served by Dostoevsky's biographers and critics, and there is no shortage of studies providing a full account of Dostoevsky's literary career.

In the present study my chief aim has been a modest one: to provide detailed readings of the four great novels which Dostoevsky wrote in the last two decades of his life—*Crime and Punishment, The Idiot, The Devils,* and *The Brothers Karamazov.* The readership of Twayne's World Authors Series includes nonspecialists, and for this reason I have tried to avoid analyses which are eccentric, recondite, or likely to appeal only to the advanced Dostoevsky scholar. I have tried throughout to write for the student and general reader approaching Dostoevsky in earnest for the first time; but equally I would hope that many details of my interpretations—such as the discussion of esthetics and point of view in *Crime and Punishment,* the function of apocalyptic imagery in *The Idiot* and *The Devils,* and the importance of biblical analogy in *The Brothers Karamazov*—might also be of interest to the Dostoevsky specialist.

Space has not allowed me to deal adequately with Dostoevsky's lesser works, and some novels which deserve attention (*The Village of Stepanchikovo, The Gambler, The Eternal Husband,* and so on) have been omitted from the discussion altogether. Neither have I been able to acknowledge as fully as I would have liked the work of other scholars. The Notes and Bibliography give only a partial impression of how richly Dostoevsky has been served by his commentators.

Studies of this kind often ignore the works Dostoevsky wrote before the great novels. In an effort to avoid this, I have devoted the first two chapters to the phase in Dostoevsky's career which ended with *Notes from Underground.* These two chapters, which examine Dostoevsky's early novels and tales as a retreat from the Enlightenment view of man, also introduce the themes which bind together the subsequent discussions of the great novels: Dostoevsky's religious, rather than utopian, vision; his opposition to the dream of paradise on earth; and his view of the discordant and chaotic nature of contemporary reality, perfectly caught in the discord and uncertainty of Dostoevsky's artistic world.

My emphasis throughout has been on close textual analysis, as detailed as space permits. Biographical information is introduced only where it facilitates discussion of the novels. The biographical chapter, which precedes the critical discussion, is intended only as a descriptive outline of the main events of Dostoevsky's life for the benefit of the reader who might require such information before tackling the examination of the works. It is in no sense an evaluative or analytical biography, and the reader who wishes for scholarly guidance through the labyrinth of Dostoevsky's life must turn to one of the many excellent biographical studies. The Conclusion also stands apart from the main body of this study: it is rather more adventurous, speculative, and perhaps incautious, but it is intended primarily as a basis for further thought and discussion.

All translations from Dostoevsky's works are my own, and textual references are to the current thirty-volume Soviet edition of Dostoevsky's writings: *Polnoe sobranie sochinenii v tridtsati tomakh* (Complete Works in Thirty Volumes, Leningrad, 1972–). Publication of this splendid edition is still in progress, having now reached volume 19.

I should like to express my gratitude to two scholarly journals, *Modern Language Review* and *Forum for Modern Language Studies,* for allowing me to use some material originally published there in article form. I am also indebted to the University of Sheffield for allowing me study leave to complete this project, and to my family, who have borne with exemplary stoicism the Jekyll and Hyde personality which is, I suspect, Dostoevsky's gift to all his serious students.

W.J. LEATHERBARROW

Sheffield, England

Chronology

1821   October 30: Fedor Mikhailovich Dostoevsky born in Moscow at Hospital for the Poor, where his father was a doctor.

1833–1837   At school in Moscow.

1837   Death of mother.

1838   Enters St. Petersburg Engineering Academy.

1839   June 8: father murdered by his own serfs.

1843   Finishes engineering course and is enrolled in Engineering Corps.

1844   June-July: first published work, a translation of Balzac's *Eugénie Grandet*, in the journal *Repertuar i Panteon* [Repertoire and Pantheon]. October: leaves military service.

1845   May: finishes *Poor Folk* and meets Belinsky.

1846   January: *Poor Folk* published in *Peterburgsky sbornik* [Petersburg Miscellany]. February: *The Double* published in *Otechestvennye zapiski* [Notes of the Fatherland]. October: "Mister Prokharchin" published in *Notes of the Fatherland*.

1847   April-July: "Petersburg Chronicle" (a series of feuilletons) published in *Sanktpeterburgskie vedomosti* [St. Petersburg Gazette]. Begins to attend Petrashevsky's gatherings. October: "The Landlady" published in *Notes of the Fatherland*.

1848   "A Faint Heart" and "White Nights" published in *Notes of the Fatherland*.

1849   January-May: *Netochka Nezvanova* serialized in *Notes of the Fatherland*. March-April: attends Durov circle. Falls under the influence of Nikolay Speshnev. April 23: arrested for subversion and imprisoned in the Peter and Paul Fortress. April-November: trial. December 22: mock execution. Sentence commuted to four years at hard labor, followed by four years of exile as a common soldier.

1850   Arrives at Omsk penal settlement.

1854   Posted to Semipalatinsk as a private in the army.

1857   First marriage, to Maria Dmitrievna Isaeva.

1859   *The Village of Stepanchikovo* published in *Notes of the Fatherland*. December 16: returns to St. Petersburg.

1860   Publication of early chapters of *Notes from the House of the Dead* in *Russky mir* [Russian World]. Two-volume collection of Dostoevsky's works published in Moscow.

1861   Dostoevsky and his brother Mikhail start publication of the journal *Vremya* [Time]. Emancipation of the serfs in Russia. *The Insulted and Injured* and *The House of the Dead* published in *Time*.

1862   First journey abroad. Friendship with Appolinaria Suslova.

1863   *Winter Notes on Summer Impressions.* Suppression of *Time* by imperial decree. Second trip abroad with Suslova. Gambling compulsion begins.

1864   Launching of new journal *Epokha* [Epoch] with Mikhail. *Notes from Underground.* April 15: death of first wife. July 10: death of Mikhail.

1865   Becomes acquainted with Anna Korvin-Krukovskaya. *Epoch* closes. Third trip abroad. Starts work on *Crime and Punishment*.

1866   *Crime and Punishment* serialized in *Russky vestnik* [Russian Herald]. Engages stenographer, Anna Snitkina, in order to write *The Gambler*.

1867   Marriage to Anna Snitkina. The Dostoevskys flee abroad to avoid creditors. Visit Dresden, Baden (where Dostoevsky meets Turgenev), and Geneva.

1868   *The Idiot* serialized in *Russian Herald*. Death of infant daughter Sofia. Passes through Basle, en route to Milan and Florence, in order to see the paintings of Hans Holbein.

1869   Returns to Dresden. Plans for "The Life of a Great Sinner" and "Atheism." November: murder of student Ivanov by Nechaev.

1870   *The Eternal Husband* published in *Zarya* [Dawn].

1871   *Russian Herald* begins serialization of *The Devils*. Returns to St. Petersburg.

1872   Publication of *The Devils* completed.

1873   Becomes editor of *Grazhdanin* [Citizen] and starts to contribute *The Diary of a Writer*.

1874   Leaves *Citizen*. Starts work on *A Raw Youth*. Travels to Ems and Geneva for treatment of emphysema.

1875   *A Raw Youth* serialized in *Notes of the Fatherland*. Again in Ems for treatment.

1876   *Dairy of a Writer* begins again as a separate publication.

1877   "The Dream of a Ridiculous Man" published as part of *Diary of a Writer*.

1878 Son, Alexey, dies from epilepsy. Visits Optina Monastery with Vladimir Solovev.

1879– *The Brothers Karamazov* serialized in *Russian Herald.*
1880

1880 Delivers Pushkin Speech as part of the Pushkin celebrations in Moscow.

1881 January 28: dies in St. Petersburg after lung hemorrhage. February 1: funeral in the cemetery of Alexander Nevsky Monastery, St. Petersburg.

CHAPTER 1

Fedor Dostoevsky: A Biographical Sketch

I   Childhood and Education

FEDOR Mikhailovich Dostoevsky was born on October 30, 1821, the second of seven children born to Mikhail Andreevich Dostoevsky and his wife, Maria Fedorovna. Fedor Mikhailovich's elder brother, Mikhail, with whom he was to enjoy close friendship, intimate correspondence, and a variety of literary activity until Mikhail's death in 1864, had been born the previous year. After Fedor came Varvara, Andrey, Vera, Nikolay, and Alexandra, before the frail and sickly Maria Fedorovna died in 1837. Dostoevsky's father was an ex–army surgeon, employed at the Marinsky Hospital for the poor in Moscow, and his mother was the daughter of a Moscow merchant, so that the family—although technically of noble status according to the Table of Ranks introduced by Peter the Great in 1722—was of a social position corresponding more closely to the lower middle classes of western European countries. Mikhail Andreevich seems to have been an austere and strict *paterfamilias*, devout in his observance of Orthodox ritual and expecting nothing less from his family. The family regime revolved about religious reading, elementary mathematical education, and invigorating walks. Social intercourse was limited, so that the Dostoevsky children, deprived of conventional friendships, drew largely upon their own resources and developed among themselves bonds of friendship which today we might consider unusually intense. Certainly Dostoevsky's correspondence with his brother reveals a startling emotional honesty and spiritual affinity which it seems reasonable to ascribe to the enclosed world of the writer's childhood. E.H. Carr has suggested that the self-containment of the Dostoevsky family inhibited Fedor Mikhailovich's social abilities for the rest of his life:

Human intercourse was always conceived by Dostoevsky in later life in terms of the intense, intimate relations of the family hearth. A friend must be a

13

brother or more; no lesser tie was tolerable to him. His singular childhood made him incapable of ordinary social intercourse, of those casual and partial relationships which add to the amenities of life without going far beneath the surface. In such relationships, when they were forced upon him, Dostoevsky was jealous, exacting, hypersensitive; he both gave and expected too much . . . .[1]

Dostoevsky's early education neglected broadly cultural interests in favor of religious instruction, and in this respect, as well as in the dourly middle-class nature of his family background, the circumstances of Dostoevsky's youth contrast sharply with those of his later literary rivals, Lev Tolstoy and Ivan Turgenev, both of whom enjoyed the cultural privileges bestowed freely upon the children of aristocracy. Dostoevsky was, in modern parlance, a self-made man: the cultural drought of his early years left him with a keen literary thirst which he slaked rather indiscriminately when he left home. Throughout his life he felt keenly his "cultural" inferiority, for no amount of reading could in his own view compensate for the excellent French and civilized ease denied him by his bourgeois origins. In characteristic outbursts of inverted pride Dostoevsky in later years would often emphasize the difficulties he had had to overcome in order to stand alongside Tolstoy and Turgenev at the very forefront of Russian literature.

Between 1833 and 1837 Dostoevsky and his brother Mikhail were educated in Moscow, first at a second-rate establishment run by a Frenchman and then at the academically respectable boarding school of Leonty Chermak. Dostoevsky has left a fictional memoir of his school years in *Podrostok* [A Raw Youth, 1875], which suggests that he was unhappy and unable to make contact with his fellow pupils. But the loneliness of his schooldays must have been tempered by a sense of emancipation: he had escaped the stern regime of his father's household, as well as the atmosphere of pain, poverty, and disease associated with his father's profession, and which one is tempted to see as a root of Dostoevsky's subsequent morbid preoccupation with suffering humanity.

In May 1837, still grieving for his mother, who had died earlier that year, Dostoevsky set out for St. Petersburg, accompanied by his father and Mikhail, in order to prepare for entrance into the St. Petersburg Academy of Military Engineering and, ultimately, a career in keeping with his father's middle-class expectations. The death of his mother was not the only grief he carried with him, for in January 1837 the great Russian poet Alexander Pushkin, "the father of

Russian literature," had been killed at the age of thirty-seven in a duel over the honor of his wife. The light of Pushkin illuminated every stage of Dostoevsky's own literary career, and reached its greatest intensity in his passionate speech in the poet's memory at the Moscow Pushkin celebrations of 1880. The sixteen-year-old Dostoevsky was so moved by Pushkin's death that he contemplated wearing mourning for him as well as for his own mother.

In January 1838, having passed the entrance examinations, Dostoevsky entered the academy, but now he was truly alone, for Mikhail had been denied entrance on medical grounds, and it is from the date of this separation that their remarkable correspondence, so revealing of the emotional development of the future author, begins. The young man who entered the academy must have struck most who knew him as singularly unpromising material for a military life. Sensitive, sickly, withdrawn, and emotionally volatile, he was depicted in the memoirs of several of his contemporaries as socially inept and disinterested in the pleasures which conventionally distract military trainees of his age. One contemporary remarked:

He was so unlike his other colleagues in all his actions, preferences and habits, and so eccentric and peculiar, that at first this all seemed odd, unnatural and enigmatic, and gave rise to curiosity and bewilderment. But later, when it became clear that this was hurting nobody, the authorities and his colleagues ceased paying attention to his strangeness. Fedor Mikhailovich conducted himself modestly, performed his military and academic tasks irreproachably, and was very religious, diligently discharging all the obligations of an Orthodox Christian . . . . Imperturbable and quiet by nature, Fedor Mikhailovich appeared indifferent to the pleasures and amusements of his comrades; you never saw him at the dances held in the academy every week . . . .[2]

Another of Dostoevsky's contemporaries has provided a vivid and evocative physical description of this remarkable recruit:

At that time Fedor Mikhailovich was very thin, the color of his face was a sort of pale grey, his hair was light and sparse, his eyes sunken, but with a penetrating, profound expression.

In the whole of the academy there was not a single student with less military bearing than F.M. Dostoevsky. His movements were somehow clumsy, but at the same time impetuous. His uniform sat awkwardly on him: his knapsack, cap and rifle were like chains he was periodically condemned to wear and which burdened him down.

In his nature too he stood out distinctly from all his other, more or less frivolous, comrades. Always self-absorbed, he spent his free time continually walking back and forth on his own, lost in thought, neither seeing nor hearing what was going on around him.[3]

On the other hand, the various reminiscences of Dostoevsky at the Engineering Academy emphasize also his meek and kind nature, which clearly did much to offset his eccentricities and aloofness. Nor was he totally without companionship: he enjoyed artistic and metaphysical discussion, and an intense friendship with Ivan Shidlovsky, an ecstatic Romantic poet five years Dostoevsky's senior, whose fate as the victim of an unhappy love affair had captivated the younger man's imagination. Later he was to write of Shidlovsky: "Often he and I would sit up whole nights, chatting about God knows what! What an open and pure soul! My tears are flowing now as I recall the past!"[4] It was through discussion with Shidlovsky and other, now unremembered congenial spirits, that Dostoevsky's self-education proceeded apace during his years at the academy. Aside from religious writings, he now satisfied broader and more secular literary tastes. In addition to the works of Pushkin and Nikolay Gogol, Russia's strange prose-poet, Dostoevsky had read the great European classics, Shakespeare, Goethe, Corneille, and Racine. He was also fond of the adventure fiction of Walter Scott, the fantasies of E. T. A. Hoffmann, and the social melodramas of Honoré de Balzac, George Sand, Victor Hugo, and Eugène Sue. His literary appetite, like his temperament, was disposed to the Romantic. But one figure towered above all these other literary giants, in the opinion of the young Dostoevsky: this was Friedrich Schiller, whose works he knew by heart and who remained a persuasive influence over him for the rest of his life.

Dostoevsky's dreamy and romantic nature during his years at the academy was reinforced by the city of St. Petersburg itself, so different from the Moscow of his childhood. The unnatural, fantastic beauty of the capital, with its mists, white nights, floods, and austere architecture, formed a perfect complement to the adventures, romances, and melodramas which were Dostoevsky's staple literary diet. It is hardly surprising that this remarkable city, forever on the point of being swallowed up by the natural elements it constantly defied, should have penetrated so deeply into the young writer's imagination and provided an organic backdrop to the social and psychological melodramas of his later novels.

In 1839 an event occurred which in a quite different way was to cast a shadow over Dostoevsky's life and reemerge in his fiction. On June

8 his father was murdered, under circumstances which have remained mysterious, while on his way to his estate at Cheremoshna. After the death of his wife, Mikhail Andreevich, now retired to the country, had become cruel and dissolute, abusing his serfs and seducing their women. It seems that on June 8 a dozen or so of them took their revenge in a particularly brutal way, although the precise details of the killing remain undisclosed and those responsible for it were never brought to justice. We cannot be certain of the impact of this tragedy upon Dostoevsky, but legend has it that the epilepsy which so blighted the rest of his life originated in the events of that traumatic summer day. Certainly Dostoevsky hardly alludes to the death of Mikhail Andreevich in his correspondence, and many biographers have seen in this evidence of a sense of personal guilt for his lukewarm feelings toward his father. Contact between them during Dostoevsky's academy years had been limited to ingratiating letters written by the son in order to extract money from his father. The evidence of his fiction, unreliable though this is as a source of biographical fact, does suggest that Dostoevsky felt himself to be in some measure responsible for the death of his father. In his final novel, *Bratya Karamazovy* [The Brothers Karamazov], written shortly before his own death, Dostoevsky wrote disturbingly of parricide and filial responsibility. All of the Karamazov sons are implicated in their father's murder, which occurs when they are variously distracted from their duty to watch over the old man's safety. Ivan Karamazov in particular advertises his indifference by going away to a neighboring village called Chermashnya, a barely disguised echo of Cheremoshna, where Mikhail Andreevich met his violent end. In any case, there can be little doubt that Dostoevsky's preoccupation in his later novels with the idea of the mutual responsibility of sons and fathers may be traced back to that fateful June day in 1839.

On August 12, 1843, Dostoevsky completed his course at the Engineering Academy and subsequently entered the Engineering Corps, but his years of study had done little to attract him to a military career. His heart was in literature, his imagination was inflamed by his years of solitary reading, and he wanted to be a writer. His life outside the academy was burdened by financial uncertainty, occasioned largely by his own chronic inability to handle money sensibly. It was partly in order to relieve his financial difficulties, and partly in order to instruct himself in the mechanics of writing, that he undertook a translation of Balzac's *Eugénie Grandet*, which appeared in the journal *Repertuar i panteon* [Repertoire and Pantheon] in July

1844, his first published work. Soon afterwards he left military service in order to devote himself exclusively to literature.

II *The Literary Debut*

Dostoevsky's taste for the romantic and exotic in his reading at the
academy had exercised his imagination, but it had also impaired his
capacity for real life and his potential as an artist. A huge and daunting
abyss separated the delicate fancies he had sustained in his life of
romantic solitude from the realities among which he found himself as
a young man trying to make his way in the world of literature. But he
was alert to the dangers of romantic escapism, and in two of his early
tales, "Khozyayka" [The Landlady] and "Belye nochi" [White
Nights], he both exposed the inadequacies of the idealistic dreamer
and documented his own retreat from naive romanticism. In effect
Dostoevsky woke up to the realities of life after his period of bookish
insularity at the academy. He was now in his early twenties and
emotionally naive, so we can perhaps put this revolution in his
personal development down to the processes of romantic disillusionment normal in late adolescence. For Dostoevsky the aspiring
novelist it proved a major emancipation. In the real world, not in the
realms of gothic romance, he found the themes and characters for the
works with which he began his career, although Romantic attitudes
colored his work throughout his lifetime. Later he was to describe an
experience, a sort of mystical vision on the Neva River, which he felt
marked the real start of his life. The "vision" discloses the dawning of
Dostoevsky's awareness that nothing is more fantastic than reality
itself, in particular the realities of the "unreal" city of St. Petersburg.
He then continues:

Suddenly a strange thought began to stir within me. I shuddered, and it was
as if my heart was flooded in that instant by a hot surge of blood, which had
boiled up with the onset of a mighty sensation, hitherto unknown to me. It
was as if I had understood at that moment something which until then had
merely stirred within me, but had not been fully comprehended. It was as if I
saw clearly into something new, a completely new world, unfamiliar to me
and known only through dark rumors and mysterious signs. I suppose that in
that very moment my existence really began. (XIX, 69)

Immediately after this passage Dostoevsky describes the onset of
inspiration in the form of a particular image, far removed from the
excesses of his Romantic past, but which matured into his first novel,

Bednye lyudi [Poor Folk], and became the main thematic concern of his early works:

I began to look around me and suddenly I caught sight of some strange characters. They were all strange, odd figures, completely prosaic, in no sense Don Carloses or Posas, but quite ordinary titular councillors, yet at the same time sort of fantastic titular councillors.

. . . And then I saw another scene: in a dark corner somewhere, the heart of a titular councillor, honest and pure, moral and devoted to his superiors; and along with him a young girl, wronged and sad, and their story tore deeply into my heart. (XIX, 71)

Gogol's influence was significant in alerting Dostoevsky to the strangeness of reality itself, and *Poor Folk*, which expands this image of a downtrodden clerk and a humiliated girl into a work of genuine social naturalism, owes much to Gogol's St. Petersburg stories, in particular "The Overcoat." Dostoevsky worked on his tale throughout 1844 and the early months of 1845, describing it to his brother as "a novel of the same dimensions as *Eugénie Grandet*."[5] The work was completed in May 1845, and although it was not published until January of the following year, it sent massive tremors through the Russian literary world for several months before it came out in print. Dostoevsky's literary debut was the stuff of which authors' dreams are made: he showed his freshly completed manuscript to Dmitry Grigorovich, a friend and budding author. Grigorovich was so impressed by the work that he took it to Nikolay Nekrasov, a young poet already making a name for himself. Nekrasov and Grigorovich read it aloud throughout a single night and proclaimed its author a genius, visiting him in the early morning hours to tell him so. Nekrasov then took the manuscript to Vissarion Belinsky, the most influential literary critic of the day. Upon reading *Poor Folk* Belinsky demanded that its author be brought before him. Toward the end of his life, in *Dnevnik pisatelya* [The Diary of a Writer], Dostoevsky recalled this awesome encounter, when he was enjoined by the great Belinsky to value the talent with which he had been entrusted: "Truth has been revealed and proclaimed to you as an artist," said Belinsky. "It has been apportioned to you as a gift. Value your gift and be faithful to it, and you will become a great writer."[6]

As a result of Belinsky's approbation, Dostoevsky was lionized by St. Petersburg intellectual circles. But sudden fame conspired with his innate social awkwardness to produce in the young man a mixture of inordinate arrogance and nervous anxiety which few of his new acquaintances could tolerate for long. His instantaneous rise to fame was matched by his precipitate fall from favor; the potential genius became an actual laughing stock. By the autumn of 1846 Dostoevsky's relations with Belinsky were also becoming strained, but the matter that came between them was not so much Dostoevsky's personal failings as irreconcilable differences in their attitudes toward art. Belinsky was displeased by Dostoevsky's second novel, *Dvoynik* [The Double], which had appeared shortly after *Poor Folk*. At that time Belinsky saw art unambiguously as propaganda to be used in the struggle against the stifling social and political conditions of Nicholas I's Russia. He insisted that literature should be naturalistic, should draw attention to the shortcomings of the present, and should contain a clear social message. *Poor Folk* had met these requirements, but *The Double*, with its preoccupation with grotesque psychology and apparent fantasy, clearly did not. Dostoevsky could never accept Belinsky's austerely utilitarian view of art, for his own esthetic views always owed much to the Romantic esthetics of Schiller. The short tale "Gospodin Prokharchin" [Mister Prokharchin], published in October 1846, served to confirm Belinsky's doubts about his young protégé, and by the following year the rift between them was more or less complete. When "The Landlady" appeared in October 1847, Belinsky dismissed it as "terrible rubbish."

Dostoevsky, however, was already beginning to move in different circles. In 1846 he joined a group of young intellectuals gathered around Alexey Beketov, a former colleague at the Academy of Military Engineering. Politically the group was quite harmless, for its stimulating discussions were confined for the most part to art and literature. But Dostoevsky was about to be drawn into a whirlpool of intrigue, the consequences of which were to transform his life totally. In the spring of 1846 he had met Mikhail Petrashevsky, an eccentric scholar-socialist, who ran a Friday-evening discussion group at his home. Dostoevsky began to attend these gatherings in the spring of 1847, and there he found the conversation decidedly political and potentially dangerous, given the reactionary climate of the time. The proliferation of such discussion groups was a characteristic feature of the age of Nicholas I, when political activity was practically impossible under the watchful eye of the secret police, and talk became a substitute for action. At Petrashevsky's Dostoevsky was introduced to the teachings of Charles Fourier, Louis Blanc, Saint-Simon, Pierre Leroux, Proudhon, and others, although he made no systematic study of socialist thought. He was in no real sense a revolutionary, but he did see in utopian socialism an ethical and political system which seemed to embody the values he held as a <u>Christian.</u> Long conversations with Belinsky had already tempered his deeply held Christian beliefs with the conviction that something had to be done for suffering humanity in the here and now. Utopian socialism seemed to him a form of practical Christianity which he was prepared to espouse, although he could never accept Belinsky's harsh materialism and revolutionary ideology.

The Petrashevsky circle came under intense police scrutiny in early 1849, following the widespread European revolutions of 1848, which both incensed and alarmed Nicholas. At about the same time, and possibly out of a sense of political self-preservation, Dostoevsky began to spend more time among the moderate and less political members of the Petrashevsky group, who met at the house of Sergey Durov. Here the conversation was confined for the most part to literary topics, but there was a wolf in the very midst of this flock of sheep. Nikolay Speshnev was a young man of aristocratic demeanor, mysterious and attractive, with a highly colorful past. A Romantic figure in the Byronic mold, he had recently returned from abroad, where he had fought in foreign wars, and attached himself to the Petrashevsky group. As Dostoevsky himself acknowledged, Speshnev was more than a match for the impractical dreamers of the discussion circle, and he manipulated the Durov group to his own ends, that is, the fomenting of revolutionary disorder. In time he initiated plans for a secret printing press to be set up. Dostoevsky became financially indebted to him and also succumbed to his charismatic personality. Almost against his will he was drawn deeper into political intrigue. His friend and physician S.D. Yanovsky recalled in his memoirs, published in 1885, how Dostoevsky appeared to lose his willpower and became listless:

The cause of all this was, as he later told me, his intimacy with Speshnev, and more precisely, his having borrowed money from him . . . . About Speshnev he would either say nothing or would dismiss him laconically: "I don't know him very well and in all truth I don't want to know him better, since that gentleman is much too powerful and Petrashevsky is no match for him." I tried to reassure him that his listless disposition would pass, but on one occasion Fedor Mikhailovich replied to my assurances: "No, it won't pass. It will torment me for a long, long time, since I have taken money from Speshnev . . . and now I am *with him* and *his*. I shall never be in a position to repay this sum, and anyway he would not take it back, that's the sort of man he is. . . . Don't you understand; from now on I have my own Mephistopheles."[7]

III   *Exile and Return*

Dostoevsky's presentiments of disaster proved all too accurate: on the night of April 23, 1849—a few days after a meeting at which Dostoevsky had read aloud Belinsky's famous letter to Gogol, a savage indictment of the social conditions of Nicholaevan Russia—the members of the Petrashevsky group were rounded up by the police and charged with subversion.

Dostoevsky was imprisoned in the dreaded Peter and Paul Fortress on the Neva River until his trial began later that month. It lasted until November, when the "ringleaders" of the conspiracy, including Dostoevsky, were found guilty and sentenced to death. The execution was to take place on the morning of December 22. The condemned were driven to the appointed site and the death sentence was read to them. At the very last moment, as the first three prisoners faced the firing squad, a messenger arrived with the announcement that the sentences had been commuted by imperial decree. Dostoevsky described his feelings on that terrible morning in *Idiot* [The Idiot, 1868], and it seems clear that the event did much to accelerate his incipient epilepsy. Another of the condemned lost his sanity completely. The most wicked irony of the whole charade was that the decision to commute the sentences had been taken much earlier, but the Tsar had felt that the young men would learn a salutary lesson if the announcement were delayed until the last moment. Perhaps he was right: Dostoevsky was never again to flirt with the politics of the left, and he returned from his period of imprisonment an arch-reactionary and sworn opponent of radicalism.

Dostoevsky was sentenced to four years at hard labor, to be followed by a further period of four years of exile as a common soldier. On the night of December 24, 1849, he set off on the long and arduous journey to the Omsk penal settlement. He later described his life as a prisoner in detail in the fictional guise of *Zapiski iz mertvogo doma* [The House of the Dead, 1860]. Clearly he suffered severe hardship and deprivation, but the effects of his long absence from European Russia were not wholly negative. In the penal colony Dostoevsky discovered the Russian people, as he was later to acknowledge, and developed a sympathy with and respect for the common people upon which he based the russophile populism of his later journalistic and fictional writings. The experience of prison life also provided him an unusual insight into the criminal mind, which—if we remember that each of his subsequent great novels was centered upon a crime—was of evident value to the developing writer. Close and daily contact with criminals, some of them guilty of the most appalling crimes, also disabused Dostoevsky of his earlier utopianism and faith in the essential goodness of man, although, as we shall later see, there is evidence to suggest that this process was underway even before his arrest. The Bible was the only book prisoners were permitted to read, and his renewed acquaintance with it convinced Dostoevsky that only religious, and not merely social transfiguration, could overcome man's appalling sinfulness. This was the central theme to which he addressed his great novels upon his return to life and literary activity.

In 1854 Dostoevsky was released from prison and posted to Semipalatinsk as a private in the army. He did not immediately return to writing, and in any case the works of a convicted criminal and political exile would not have been passed by the censorship board. He did, however, resume his reading, demanding from his brother such diverse matter as the works of Kant and Hegel, the Koran, economic tracts, as well as the newest works of Russian literature. The tragedies of his past had done nothing to diminish Dostoevsky's conviction that his future lay in literature. His career as a writer had been cruelly interrupted, but he was determined to begin again.

In Semipalatinsk Dostoevsky met and fell in love with Maria Dmitrievna Isaeva, a married woman who was shortly to be widowed. Maria Dmitrievna was a consumptive, one of those dauntingly complex women who live in a state of permanent anxiety and high emotional intensity. She was the perfect complement to Dostoevsky's nervous and excitable nature, and they tormented each other magnificently. A probably apochryphal tale has it that on the night before her marriage to Dostoevsky on February 6, 1857, Maria Dmitrievna slept with Nikolay Vergunov, an old flame and Dostoevsky's rival for her affections. Much of the mutual laceration, jealousy, and passion of Dostoevsky's courtship and marriage was recreated in the Rogozhin-Nastasya Filippovna affair in *The Idiot*.

During his enforced stay in Semipalatinsk Dostoevsky had become friendly with Alexander Wrangel, a young man who had taken up a post of public prosecutor there in late 1854. Wrangel interceded with the authorities on Dostoevsky's behalf, and in 1856 won permission for him to engage once again in literature with the right to publish. The writer took advantage of this, corresponding with the editors of the leading periodicals and beginning work on two short novels, *Dyadushkin son* [Uncle's Dream] and *Selo Stepanchikovo i ego obitateli* [The Village of Stepanchikovo], which both appeared in 1859. Before this, in August 1857, the journal *Otechestvennye zapiski* [Notes of the Fatherland] had published under a pseudonym the tale "Malenky geroy" [A Little Hero], which Dostoevsky had written in 1849 in the Peter and Paul Fortress. By March 1859 Dostoevsky's rehabilitation was almost complete: in that month he resigned from the army, and shortly afterwards left Semipalatinsk for Tver. He obtained permission to return to St. Petersburg toward the end of the year, and on December 16 Dostoevsky again took up residence in the capital after an absence of ten years almost to the day.

The intellectual and political climate of the Russia Dostoevsky found on his return was very different from the one he had left a decade earlier. Nicholas I had died in 1855 and Russia had lost the Crimean War disastrously, exposing in the process her backwardness and need for modernization. Nicholas's successor, Alexander II, was a reformer who recognized the stultifying nature of his father's regime and had embarked on a campaign of reform and modernization which culminated in the emancipation of the peasants in 1861. The intelligentsia too had changed: gone were the impractical, idealistic dreamers among whom Dostoevsky had passed his youth; the emphasis now was on practical activity, and the intellectuals of the new generation were far more radical and businesslike in their demands for sweeping social reform. Dostoevsky found them and the materialist ethic they preached uncongenial. The profound spiritual change wrought in him by his years of imprisonment and exile had erased all belief in the efficacy of political change while the soul of man remained sinful and unredeemed. Yet his conviction of the need for religious faith and Christ was out of consonance with the new age of practicality and materialism. Dostoevsky's prison experiences had, moreover, left him with a tendency to idealize the Russian common people, in whom, he thought, the purest springs of Christian faith remained unpolluted by the growing materialism and westernism manifested among the higher social classes. His distaste for the new intellectuals and his Russian populism formed the basic strands of his social outlook in the years following his return to the capital, and in January 1861 he and his brother founded the journal *Vremya* [Time] as a means of communicating these ideas. *Time* published three significant works by Dostoevsky: *The House of the Dead* and the novel *Unizhennye i oskorblennye* [The Insulted and Injured], both in 1861, and Dostoevsky's account of his first journey abroad, *Zimnie zametki o letnikh vpechatleniyakh* [Winter Notes on Summer Impressions], in 1863. Dostoevsky had undertaken this journey—to Germany, France, Italy, Switzerland, and England—in 1862 in the company of Appolinaria Suslova, a proud and headstrong girl with whom Dostoevsky fell passionately in love and with whom he made several trips before their intense affair ended painfully in 1865. Dostoevsky's passion for Suslova was the strongest of his life, his love for Maria Dmitrievna having long since cooled. He wrote of the mixture of pain and ecstasy the affair brought him in *Igrok* [The Gambler, 1866], whose heroine, Polina, is an evident portrait of Suslova.

In May 1863 *Time* was suppressed by imperial decree, as the result of an article it had published by Nikolay Strakhov, a literary critic, philosopher, and friend of Dostoevsky, on the Polish insurrection of that January. The article was considered unpatriotic, and although Dostoevsky stoutly maintained his journal's devotion to the Russian cause, the publication of Strakhov's piece displays the naiveté with which the Dostoevsky brothers approached the dangerous world of journalism. In January 1864 permission was, however, obtained to start another magazine, *Epokha* [Epoch]. This enjoyed none of the success of its predecessor, although it did publish some notable writers including Ivan Turgenev, and Dostoevsky's own *Zapiski iz podpolya* [Notes from Underground], which, when it appeared in 1864, was his most startling work to date. Partly as a reflection of Dostoevsky's own increasing antiradicalism, and partly as a response to the reemergence of conservative official opinion following the reforms, the *Epoch* quickly earned the reputation of a bastion of reaction and political conformity. This more than anything else led to its natural demise, and it ceased publication early in 1865.

The years 1864 and 1865 were bad ones in Dostoevsky's life. His journalistic disappointments were compounded by the end of his relationship with Suslova and two personal tragedies. Maria Dmitrievna had finally succumbed to her wasting illness on April 15, 1864. The marriage had been an unhappy one, and for the sake of Maria Dmitrievna's health the couple had lived apart in the final months, with Maria being looked after by Dostoevsky's brother-in-law in Moscow, where the climate was better. Despite this, Dostoevsky was much distressed by her death, and his grief deepened shortly afterwards when Mikhail died suddenly from a liver complaint, leaving his already impoverished brother to care for his family. These additional

in debt

responsibilities put tremendous pressure upon Dostoevsky to make money by his writing, and from this time onward the creative process was accompanied always by the specters of impatient editors, clamoring creditors, pressing deadlines, and imminent financial ruin. These circumstances were in no way alleviated by the passion for gambling which Dostoevsky had contracted during his second trip abroad with Suslova in 1863. When the *Epoch* closed, Dostoevsky fled abroad to escape his debts and set to work on a large novel which he hoped would discharge his financial obligations. This was to become *Prestuplenie i nakazanie* [Crime and Punishment], and its central themes of poverty, illness, and mental anguish reflect only too clearly the hazards Dostoevsky endured in these troubled years. Life abroad was no better: what little money he had he lost at the roulette tables of Wiesbaden, and when he took to his hotel room the proprietors refused him food and candles until he had paid for his board. In September 1865 he wrote to offer his novel to M.N. Katkov, the editor of the conservative journal *Russky vestnik* [Russian Herald], against an advance of three hundred rubles. He returned to Russia in October, but the composition of this novel took longer than anticipated, and he already owed another novel to the publisher F.T. Stellovsky, who would acquire the rights to Dostoevsky's published works if he failed to deliver the manuscript on time. Accordingly, Dostoevsky suspended work on *Crime and Punishment* and dashed off *The Gambler* in twenty-six days between writing the fifth and sixth parts of *Crime and Punishment*. In order to achieve this remarkable feat he employed a young stenographer, Anna Grigorevna Snitkina, who found him an exacting, irritable, and strangely pathetic employer. The harassed author and the quiet, businesslike girl were drawn to each other, and they were married on February 15, 1867. Dostoevsky had hoped to marry again after the death of Maria Dmitrievna, but his stormy affair with Suslova had ended in disaster, and a friendship with Anna Korvin-Krukovskaya, the beautiful elder sister of the future woman mathematician Sofia Kovalevskaya, also came to nothing. Anna Korvin-Krukovskaya was a remarkably vivacious and strong-willed eighteen-year-old at the time Dostoevsky made her family's acquaintance in the spring of 1865. She was talented and intelligent, and had already submitted stories to the *Epoch*. Dostoevsky lost his head to her, failing to notice that he himself had become an object of adoration for the younger sister, Sofia. Anna was sensible enough to recognize that marriage to the highly strung, middle-aged novelist would be disastrous for them both, and they parted. But the intensity of Dostoevsky's devotion to Anna and the whole Korvin-Krukovskaya family is suggested in *The Idiot* in the depiction of Aglaya Epanchina and her family.

Dostoevsky's relationship with Anna Grigorevna Snitkina lacked the painfully passionate intensity of his earlier loves, but it brought him an emotional stability which fostered the sustained creative activity of his later years. The serialization of *Crime and Punishment* had evoked widespread popular acclaim and gained him recognition as a major literary talent, but it yielded little in the way of financial reward, and shortly after their marriage the Dostoevskys were obliged once again to escape abroad in order to avoid impatient creditors. They were not to return to Russia until July 1871. This long period of travel, marked by poverty, compulsive gambling, illness, and personal grief (an infant daughter, Sonia, died in Geneva in May 1868), was a time of creative ferment during which the ideas for the great novels of the 1870s took definite shape. From Dresden, their first port of call, the Dostoevskys went on to Baden-Baden, where Dostoevsky quarreled with Turgenev. Relations between the two writers had soured since the days when Turgenev had contributed to the *Epoch*. While working on *Crime and Punishment* and trying to support his late brother's family, Dostoevsky had borrowed from Turgenev the sum of fifty thalers but had been unable to repay it. Now when they met again Dostoevsky's financial embarrassment was complicated by an ideological rift between the two men. Turgenev's novel *Smoke* had appeared in the *Russian Herald* in March 1867, provoking a storm of controversy by its anti-Russian attitudes. Dostoevsky was offended by Turgenev's westernism and denigration of the national ideals he himself held dear, and was unable to conceal his disgust. The two writers parted enemies and were not reconciled until they both attended the Pushkin celebrations of 1880. The most remarkable outcome of their split was the spiteful portrait of Turgenev as the effete, written-out egoist Karmazinov in Dostoevsky's novel *Besy* [The Devils, 1872].

From Baden-Baden, where Dostoevsky had succumbed disastrously to the gambling tables, he and Anna Grigorevna moved on to Geneva, stopping on the way at Basle to see Hans Holbein's painting *Christ Taken from the Cross*, which unnerved Dostoevsky by its gruesome depiction of the decomposing Savior. In Geneva, in September 1867, Dostoevsky observed the congress of the League for Peace and Freedom, a pacifist gathering of leading Russian and European radicals who opposed the imminent Franco-Prussian war.

The outspoken expression of radical and atheist opinion at this gathering outraged the conservative and deeply Christian Dostoevsky, and no doubt did much to impart a strongly antiradical flavor to the novel upon which he was working at this time, *The Idiot*. Holbein's painting also found its way into this work, and Dostoevsky must have been struck by the contrast between Holbein's implicit recognition of the sinfulness of the mankind Christ had come to save and the mythological landscapes of Claude Lorrain, which he had seen in Dresden and which proclaimed the innocence of man among glorious natural settings. Dostoevsky was subsequently to refer often to Lorrain's landscapes as images of that golden age which man had enjoyed in Genesis. *The Idiot*, depicting its hero's loss of innocence and experience of sin, surely owes much to Dostoevsky's viewing of the work of both Lorrain and Holbein. It was serialized in the *Russian Herald* throughout 1868.

In July 1869, after wintering in Florence, Dostoevsky returned with his wife to Dresden, where he began to draft plans for two ambitious works, *The Life of a Great Sinner* and *Atheism*. Neither of these was completed, but each provided much material for the novels Dostoevsky was to write in the last decade of his life. Dramatic political events distracted him from his work on these projects: in November 1869 he received news from Russia of the murder of a student named Ivanov by a group of radical conspirators led by a young intriguer, Sergey Nechaev. The event provided a dramatic focus for Dostoevsky's vehement antiradicalism. In addition, the Franco-Prussian war, which had long threatened, erupted in July 1870 and confirmed Dostoevsky's misgivings about the future of western Europe. Together these events provided the stimulus for the composition of Dostoevsky's great political novel, *The Devils*. They also persuaded Dostoevsky that it was time to renew his contact with his native Russian roots, and in July 1871 he and Anna Grigorevna returned to St. Petersburg.

IV   *The Final Decade*

Dostoevsky's return to Russia marked the start of the last decade of his life, a decade of furious literary and journalistic activity. The publication of *The Idiot* had evoked a largely lukewarm critical response, but the appearance of *The Devils* in the *Russian Herald* during 1871 and 1872, when the trial of Nechaev was arousing widespread interest, polarized the attitudes of the critics. The liberals were outraged by Dostoevsky's merciless satire against revolutionary activity, and accused him of being an enemy of progress, while the conservatives were delighted by this outspoken addition to their ranks. At the beginning of 1873 Dostoevsky was invited by the arch-reactionary Prince V.P. Meshchersky to take over the editorship of his magazine *Grazhdanin* [Citizen], a militantly conservative publication. At first Dostoevsky found his duties pleasant, and he was able to contribute to the magazine his own *Diary of a Writer*, in which he voiced his opinions on a wide variety of literary, historical, and political topics, and which remains a remarkably valuable record of Dostoevsky's views in the later years of his life. Soon, however, he began to find the pressure of the work and the vociferous condemnation of the radical press distressing. Moreover, in March 1874 he had to spend two days in prison for violating the censorship laws. Dostoevsky's association with the circle of shabby reactionaries gathered around the *Citizen* and his willing acceptance of the patronage of such influential apologists of autocratic conservatism as K.P. Pobedonostsev do not show him in a favorable light. His political reliability and orthodoxy were recognized in 1877, when he was made a corresponding member of the Academy of Sciences. In 1874, however, he made a surprising move to appease liberal opinion by writing the novel *A Raw Youth* for the progressive journal *Notes of the Fatherland*, edited by the same Nekrasov who had taken the manuscript of *Poor Folk* to Belinsky back in 1845. *A Raw Youth* was disliked by both liberals and conservatives, but the renewed contact between Dostoevsky and Nekrasov cemented a friendship and mutual respect which had survived all ideological differences between them. When Nekrasov died in December 1877 Dostoevsky attended his funeral, and, surrounded by his political enemies, read a speech in the poet's honor. Shortly afterwards, in *The Diary of a Writer*, he wrote touchingly of the early years he and Nekrasov had shared and proclaimed that "this man has remained in our heart."[8]

Dostoevsky had resigned his position on the *Citizen* in 1874, but in 1876 he began *The Diary of a Writer* again as a separate publication. This work and the plans for his final novel, *The Brothers Karamazov*, were to occupy most of his attention before his death. He still took an interest in political affairs, following avidly the trial of the terrorist Vera Zasulich in 1878, but his health was failing and he had to make several trips abroad for treatment of emphysema. In 1873 he had met the brilliant young philosopher Vladimir Solovev, and they became close friends in the later years of the decade. Dostoevsky found

confirmation of many of his own deepest beliefs in the theology of
Solovev, and in June 1878 they visited the Optina Monastery together, which provided Dostoevsky with material for the monastery
scenes in *The Brothers Karamazov*. The death of his favorite son,
Alexey, in May of that year, as a result of epilepsy inherited from his
father, also became a creative springboard for the novel. Alesha
Karamazov is an affectionate memorial to the dead son, and Dostoevsky's unjustified sense of responsibility for Alexey's death is also
reflected in the themes of paternal and filial guilt which unify the
work.

Just as his marriage to Anna Grigorevna had brought emotional
stability and a settled family routine to Dostoevsky in the last decade
and a half of his life, so did the latter part of the 1870s see him achieve
something approaching artistic and financial equilibrium. Work on
The Brothers Karamazov proceeded apace, and the novel appeared in
the *Russian Herald* in 1879–80, drawing a very favorable response.
The industry of Anna Grigorevna, who had undertaken the republi-
cation of Dostoevsky's works, brought financial solvency, and by the
end of his life Dostoevsky had managed to discharge the debts he had
incurred in the 1860s and early 1870s, although this came too late to
bring the writer much peace of mind.

Moreover, widespread adulation of Dostoevsky's genius was to
come in 1880, as an unexpected consequence of the speech he read in
praise of Pushkin at the Moscow celebrations marking the erection of
a statue to that poet. The event—which took place on June 8—was
attended by leading writers and journalists of differing political per-
suasions, including Dostoevsky's old enemy Turgenev. The emotion
and rhetoric of Dostoevsky's statement, in which he praised Pushkin's
Russianness and held out the hope that the qualities embodied in the
Russian people might lead the world to true brotherhood, temporarily eclipsed political differences. He was hailed as a prophet and
embraced by Turgenev. He died only a few months after this great
success, on January 28, 1881, as the result of a lung hemorrhage, after
winning a unique position in the heart of the Russian public. The
funeral, held two days later in the cemetery of the Alexander Nevsky
Monastery, was an event of national importance, attended by over
thirty thousand people. Ivan Popov, later a revolutionary but at the
time of Dostoevsky's death a student at the St. Petersburg Teachers'
College, recalled the occasion in his memoirs (1924):

The College was at the funeral in strength—teachers and pupils. Classes were postponed. The procession stretched over a great distance, four or five times longer than at Nekrasov's funeral. About twenty choirs sang—students, artists, pupils from the conservatory, singers, etc. Dense crowds of people lined the pavements. The common people watched the procession in amazement. I heard of an old woman who asked Grigorovich: "Which general are they burying?" And he replied: "It's not a general, but a teacher, a writer."

"I see, there are many schoolchildren here, and students. He must have been a great and good teacher. God rest his soul."[9]

CHAPTER 2

The Spring and the Balance: Works of the 1840s

THE first chapter in Dostoevsky's literary career began in 1846, when, as the author of the short novel *Poor Folk*, the young writer was championed by Vissarion Belinsky, Russia's foremost literary critic, and was immediately greeted by other leading *literati* as an heir to Nikolay Gogol, Russia's leading prose writer. It ended no less abruptly and dramatically in April 1849, when Dostoevsky was arrested for belonging to a revolutionary conspiracy. The death sentence originally passed upon him was commuted at the very last moment to hard labor followed by exile, and in December 1849 Dostoevsky left for penal servitude in Siberia. He would not return to European Russia until December 1859.

In the period between his triumphant literary debut and his arrest, Dostoevsky's immense arrogance and the inability of his proud, dreamy, and volatile character to handle sudden fame gradually alienated his early admirers. Moreover, Belinsky, who had welcomed *Poor Folk* as a work of real sociopolitical importance, a defense of society's underdog, could not understand Dostoevsky's preoccupation with the abnormal and grotesque in his subsequent works. The critic died of consumption in 1848, convinced that he had erred grievously in his enthusiasm for his young protégé, and by the time of Dostoevsky's arrest his literary reputation was at a low ebb. Only with his return from exile and the publication of his fictional prison memoirs *Notes from the House of the Dead* in 1860 did Dostoevsky reassert his literary significance.

Dostoevsky's works of the 1840s quite naturally came from the pen of a young man whose values had not yet settled down. They are uneven, and their quality in no way approaches that of the mature novels for which Dostoevsky is rightly renowned. But with the benefit of hindsight we can see that Belinsky and his contemporaries were unjust in dismissing them as unsuccessful attempts to build on the success of *Poor Folk*. The preexile works have a monolithic quality, an integrity in both thematic purpose and stylistic design, which allows the modern reader to overlook their individual shortcomings and view them as a coherent preface to the great novels which were to follow. It would, of course, require a gigantic act of faith to look for the seeds of the *greatness* of Dostoevsky's mature fiction in the works to be discussed in this chapter, but it is surely possible to discern in them the embryos of many of the thematic and stylistic characteristics which works such as *Crime and Punishment* (1866) so successfully exploit. This is not to argue that the preexile works do not deserve detailed individual analysis. They do; and many outstanding Soviet and Western scholars have served Dostoevsky well in this respect.[1] A study such as the present one, however, must restrict itself to a more distant view and emphasize those features of Dostoevsky's early work which facilitate discussion of the mature novels.

The thematic feature of Dostoevsky's preexile works which most encourages the reader to view them as a whole rather than individual entities is an insistent and unsettling preoccupation with the nature of man and the individual's relationship both to society and to his own social identity. This preoccupation is both dramatically presented and of intrinsic philosophical interest, for Dostoevsky's conclusions contradict those widely drawn by thinkers of the European Enlightenment and their heirs among social philosophers of the nineteenth century. If nothing more, Dostoevsky's early works show just how markedly thinking in the post-Romantic age had retreated from the comforting optimism which had characterized so much eighteenth-century speculation about the perfectibility of man and the possibility of overcoming the conflict between the individual's personal aspirations and the part he is obliged to play in the wider framework of society.

Historians conventionally describe the eighteenth century as the Age of Reason, and indeed it was a period when rapid advances in man's understanding of the natural world and human nature nurtured the belief that increasing enlightenment and the judicious application of rational principles to both scientific method and social development would lead to human control over Nature and ultimately to the establishment of an ideal, stable, and rational social equilibrium, one which would ensure both social order and individual freedom. The Enlightenment thus represented a dramatic reevaluation of the more pessimistic view of man's role on earth, which had formed the basis of European thinking in the past and which was derived from Genesis. As the historian Norman Hampson argues: "The first chapter of Genesis bolted the door against any optimistic interpretation of human nature or man's prospect of creating a satisfactory society on earth."[2] The Fall as described in Genesis, the acquisition of knowledge and self-consciousness, had seen man's relationship with the natural and divine order deteriorate from one of harmony to one of discord, a discord which could be healed only through his suffering and moral transfiguration, and in the next world rather than in this. Life on earth was a passage through a vale of tears, where man was at the mercy of forces over which he had no control. The preoccupation with superstition, witchcraft, and omens, so characteristic of the sixteenth and seventeenth centuries, confirms this picture of man denied happiness in this world and awaiting with apprehension the passage of the chosen to felicity in the next.

The growth of confidence in rational analysis which heralded the Enlightenment contributed to the reassessment of this view. Newtonian physics, although by no means providing a comprehensive mathematical explanation of the natural universe, nevertheless encouraged the belief that the universe was constructed upon rational principles and would yield up all its secrets as man's mastery of reason increased. The movements of the planets were no longer the consequence of forces beyond comprehension, but the ordered illustration of understood laws; God's ways were no longer so mysterious—he was a divine mathematician, infinitely more gifted than man, but working within the same parameters as human logic. The natural world, so long regarded as a prison in which man was condemned to languish in solitude, became instead, in Voltaire's famous adaptation of Liebnitz, "the best of all possible worlds," ready to surrender its blessings as man's increasing enlightenment disclosed them.

As well as holding out the promise that man could recover the control over Nature he had lost with the Fall, the Age of Reason also suggested that he could reclaim another lost ideal—that of heaven on earth. Man's alienation from Nature had been matched by his estrangement from his fellow men. War, crime, and enmity were all manifestations of the egoism man had acquired with the Fall and which effectively denied him harmony on earth. Self-will clashed with social order, and personal advantage offset all considerations of general well-being. The eighteenth century saw the beginning of a new appraisal of man's relationship to society at large and the analysis of man as a social animal. John Locke's *Essay Concerning Human Understanding*, published in 1690, anticipated the new climate of opinion in its rejection of the Cartesian principle that ideas and attitudes were innate, and that consequently man's nature was determined at birth and resisted subsequent external influence. Locke instead stressed the interaction of intellect and environment, and thus allowed for the benign influence of the latter upon the former. Enlightment would make man more rational and consequently more able to construct a stable, harmonious society where dark, "uncivilized" passions were kept in check by the moderating effects of reason. Later Rousseau was to go much further in reversing the traditional biblical view of man by asserting that, far from being born in sin, he is in his natural state noble and good, only subsequently corrupted by the malign influences of ill-ordered societies. Later again, the English Utilitarians Jeremy Bentham and J.S. Mill were to carry the ideals of the Enlightenment into the nineteenth century with their analyses of those social principles which might reconcile the aspirations of the individual with the greater good of society at large.

This faith in the perfectibility of man and the possibility of a rational society where the passions of the individual are reconciled with the demands of social order lies at the heart of Alexander Pope's *Essay on Man*, perhaps the most widely read work of the Enlightenment. Passion, or self-love, is the spring of human actions, but reason is the balance in which are weighed the social consequences of individual will.

> Two principles in human nature reign;
> Self-love to urge, and Reason, to restrain . . .
> Self-love, the spring of motion, acts the soul;
> Reason's comparing balance rules the whole.

Impulse and reason thus unite in a view of man which stresses the essential unity or complementariness of his two identities, the individual and the social. Just such an optimistic assessment of the integrity of human nature is affirmed in the lines which conclude Epistle III of *Essay on Man*:

So two consistent motions act the soul;
And one regards itself, and one the whole.
Thus God and Nature link'd the general frame,
And bade self-love and social be the same.

Dostoevsky's tales of the 1840s—indeed, his works as a whole—effectively demonstrate just how radically the Enlightenment view of man had been challenged by the period of turmoil in European social, intellectual, and artistic life which had followed upon the Enlightenment, and which is conventionally termed the age of Romanticism. In this area generalizations are particularly hazardous, but it is, I think, possible to argue that the various European Romanticisms—often chronologically distinct and varying in their individual national preoccupations—cast a uniform doubt on the moderating role of reason in human behavior and presented a more complex and unpredictable picture of man's relationship to Nature and society. The themes of the alienated individual and man in opposition to the social order were a particularly common feature in later Romanticism, and form the core of the work of Mikhail Lermontov, Russia's greatest Romantic.

Dostoevsky seems to have inherited Romantic skepticism about the civilizing influence of reason upon human nature. The heroes of his early works are individuals unable to strike a satisfactory balance between self and society. They are victims of a profound dualism, a discordant, irreconcilable clash of two identities, and this contrasts starkly with Pope's view of human behavior as the outcome of complementary, not contradictory, impulses. In Dostoevsky's heroes reason and an awareness of the needs of the social whole are manifestly unable to contain the individual's impulse toward self-assertion. The resulting conflict threatens both the happiness of the individual and all dreams of harmony on earth. Man in Dostoevsky's work, as in Genesis, is a tragic, split creature, excluded from paradise but longing for reconciliation. The impossibility of achieving such reconciliation through the exercise of reason alone was to become a dominant theme in Dostoevsky's literary works, implicitly in those before his arrest, more overtly in the novels of his maturity.

I Poor Folk

Belinsky's admiration for *Poor Folk* was consistent with his view that literature should carry a clear social message. First and foremost a social philosopher dedicated to the emancipation of the individual from the shackles of political reality, Belinsky viewed art as a powerful weapon of exposure and reform, and his emphasis on the civic role of literature was to color Russian criticism for the remainder of the nineteenth century. Through his critical articles and the enormous authority he exercised in the literary world, Belinsky hoped to foster a "Natural School" *(Naturalnaya shkola)* of literature, which, following what he regarded as the example of Gogol's work, would devote itself to the naturalistic examination of Russian reality and the exposure of social problems.[3] The Natural School attracted few writers of merit, and Belinsky's regard for Gogol as its supreme representative was a result of the critic's unwillingness to appreciate the importance of the grotesque in that writer's work. The appearance of *Poor Folk*, however, suggested that in Dostoevsky the Natural School had found a major and sympathetic talent. Dostoevsky's stylistic virtuosity, his delicate handling of character, his clever appropriation of the outmoded epistolary genre for the analysis of modern psychological dilemmas, and his subtle parody of sentimental literature all augured well for the future development of his gifts. Moreover, the novel's plot seemed to imply a natural social awareness and an empathy with the problems which beset the poor and the unimportant. *Poor Folk* takes the form of a correspondence between a lowly government clerk, Makar Devushkin, and the young woman he loves, Varvara Dobroselova. The exchange is sentimental and naive—both Devushkin and Varvara are simple souls—but their mutual affection is doomed. Devushkin struggles vainly against poverty and his own lack of influence—sometimes suffering severe degradation—in order to rescue Varvara from the clutches of her rich "protector," Mr. Bykov. Finally, however, Bykov's social superiority prevails. The first of Dostoevsky's strong-willed men, he exploits both Varvara's dependent position and Devushkin's poverty to abduct the young girl, apparently for his own sexual gratification. Poor Devushkin's dreams of personal happiness are dashed, and he is left once again to contemplate his own insignificance.

Poor Folk shows the influence of Dostoevsky's admiration for the great European social romantics Honoré de Balzac and Charles Dickens, and it does indeed have great potential as social criticism. Dostoevsky, however, appears to be more interested in the psychological effects of poverty and anonymity upon the individual than in condemning the social origins of these conditions, and it is in this apparently fine distinction that the root of his subsequent break with Belinsky lies. Devushkin, in his love for Varvara, finds himself in conflict not only with the established social hierarchies, but also with his own sense of social identity, and it is this *inner* confrontation upon which *Poor Folk* turns. A part of Devushkin's being both accepts and needs the security of belonging to a greater social whole, even though this condemns him to unimportance. He recognizes in his own naive way that the stability of society depends upon strict adherence to the established social order, and even acknowledges that such order might well reflect the will of God: "One man is ordained to wear the epaulettes of a general, another to serve as a titular councilor. One to give orders, the other to obey in fear and with resignation. This is all in accordance with a man's capabilities . . . and these capabilities are ordained by God himself" (I, 61). Yet even as he submits to the logic of this reasoning, another part of Devushkin is probing beyond the limitations of his social status: his pride is offended when he reads Gogol's depiction of a lowly clerk in his story "The Overcoat" (1842); he dreams of becoming a great poet and making a name for himself; and he endures privations, sometimes even neglecting essentials such as clothing, in order to drink tea, because "it is somehow shameful, as it were, not to drink tea" (I, 17). Alongside an awareness of his own unimportance, Devushkin nurtures unrealistic ambitions and acute self-consciousness. He lives in two worlds, in two identities, but one is mere ambition, the other is reality. His dreams of independence and the sweet aromas of spring are carried away by the smell of garbage accumulating under the window of his garret.

In a detail which anticipates Raskolnikov's position *vis-à-vis* Svidrigailov and Sonya Marmeladova in *Crime and Punishment*, Devushkin's dualism is confirmed in his relationship to two external figures, the powerful and assertive Bykov and the downtrodden and totally self-effacing clerk, Gorshkov. Poised psychologically between the two, Devushkin recognizes himself in Gorshkov (the name suggests "flowerpot"), but his pride is aroused by the independence and willfulness of Bykov (a name which suggests "bull"). His dilemma is contained in the contradiction of reason and pride. He knows that his circumscribed social identity means he can never be a Bykov, but this knowledge does not suffice to contain his proud and essentially irrational urge to assert himself. Yet all attempts to assert his will in a meaningful way inevitably fail: his hopes of personal happiness are destroyed when Bykov carries off Varvara, just as earlier his dreams of spring had been carried off by the smell of garbage. In despair Devushkin releases his frustrated ambition in inverted pride and willful acts of self-abasement, such as drinking and courting society's scorn. Such ultimately self-destructive acts are, in Dostoevsky's world, the gestures of proud and rebellious spirits, whose ambitions cannot be defused by reason or contained within a social identity which they paradoxically accept. In his illustration of this principle, Devushkin anticipates and helps to explain the behavior of Dostoevsky's later and greater masochists, such as the hero of *Notes from Underground* (1864) and Marmeladov in *Crime and Punishment*.

The Dostoevsky scholar Rudolf Neuhäuser has argued that the clear conflict between individual passions and social order in Dostoevsky's early works betrays the young writer's awareness of Charles Fourier's psychological thought.[4] This conclusion is by no means improbable when we remember that in the late 1840s Dostoevsky belonged to several circles which discussed the works of Fourier.[5] As Neuhäuser explains, "Fourier's psychological system rested on a specific understanding of human emotions which he called passions. Fourier considered them God-given means which were intended to ensure individual and social happiness and the establishment of a golden age on earth. If in actual life passions often appeared as negative features, then this was entirely due to the wrong organization of society and social institutions. He, therefore, demanded a thorough reorganization of society based on a proper understanding of the nature of human passions."[6] Devushkin's inability to assert his personality satisfactorily in the rigidly structured society he inhabits would seem to suggest Dostoevsky's sympathy with Fourier's conclusions. But it is essential to establish the emphasis of Dostoevsky's thought as early as possible: nowhere in his fiction does he allow the idea of the political transfiguration of society as a way of reclaiming the unintegrated individual to go unchallenged. Indeed, in later works such as *Notes from Underground* and *The Devils* (1872) the behavior of his characters suggests that not even the most humane, well-ordered, and rational society could heal the discordant soul of man, or contain his infinite capacity for self-willed rebellion. Fourier's secular utopia is as unrealistic a dream as that of the civilizing influence of reason. This idea emerges clearly from Dostoevsky's mature fiction, and there is little evidence to suggest that his early works would support any other interpretation.

II The Double

When *The Double* appeared shortly after *Poor Folk* in 1846, Belinsky's reaction was lukewarm. He conceded the work's talent, but felt that it was long-winded, that the central character's behavior lacked motivation, and that the narrative took a decidedly grotesque turn which sacrificed the "naturalism" of *Poor Folk* and robbed the tale of its potential value as social criticism. The charge of long-windedness is fair, even when we take into account the considerable deletions and changes made by Dostoevsky in 1865. *The Double* describes in detail the descent into madness of another lowly civil servant, Yakov Golyadkin, who, although somewhat better off than Devushkin, experiences the same conflict between his inhibiting social identity and his personal ambitions. Golyadkin's behavior oscillates between self-assertion and self-effacement, between aggression and timidity, to such a degree that his condition becomes pathological. He suspects plots and intrigues everywhere and seeks advice from his doctor, Rutenshpitz. In time, Golyadkin succumbs completely to his conflicting psychological stimuli and acts like a marionette manipulated by alternating puppeteers, a characteristic skillfully suggested in his jerky physical movements and staccato speech. His consciousness is eventually torn apart by dualism, and his aggressive tendencies are embodied in an exact double who suddenly appears and threatens to usurp his position. The double directs all his malice against the original Golyadkin, who finally goes insane and is driven away to an asylum by the sinister Rutenshpitz as the double skips gleefully alongside the carriage.

Belinsky's criticisms of the unrealism of *The Double* and the lack of explanation for Golyadkin's decline are quite unfounded. The work, in its psychological insights, its sophisticated use of point of view, and its emphasis upon human behavior *in extremis* is far more ambitious, more characteristically Dostoevskian, and ultimately more satisfying than *Poor Folk*, but Belinsky, by stressing the social naturalism of art, was understandably unable to perceive the direction in which the young Dostoevsky was moving. As Edward Wasiolek remarks, Dostoevsky was groping toward "a new causality, a new logic and psychology of motivation that was already running against the grain of contemporary taste."[7] He was, in fact, emphasizing even more obviously than in *Poor Folk* the psychological, rather than social, springs of human behavior.

As Victor Terras has observed, the question that invites Golyadkin's madness is: "How can an insignificant member of a highly organized society assert his individuality . . . without becoming a non-conformist, i.e. ceasing to be a member of that society?"[8] Like Devushkin, Golyadkin needs the security of social integration; indeed, he is horrified at the thought of the ostracism and rejection which would follow any attempt to overstep the limits of his social identity. Yet that identity cannot contain his own will and individuality. An episode early in the work illustrates this: Golyadkin has come uninvited to a party given by his superiors in honor of Klara Olsufevna, a girl for whom he nurtures a socially unacceptable passion. He is thrown out for his audacity, but in an explanation to his departmental chief, Andrey Filippovich, Golyadkin pathetically defends his rights as an individual and tries to keep his social and personal identities apart: "'This is more to do with my domestic circumstances and my private life, Andrey Filippovich,' the half-dead Mr. Golyadkin articulated in a hardly audible voice. 'This is not an official incident . . .'" (I, 134). In his timid pursuit of Klara, Golyadkin engages in a form of rebellion against both social convention and his own accepted social position which is psychologically similar to Raskolnikov's revolt in *Crime and Punishment*. Raskolnikov is a stronger and more conscious character than Golyadkin, and his revolt breaks society's laws; Golyadkin's rebellion succeeds only in shattering his sanity—something he himself recognizes on the numerous occasions when he refers to himself as a "suicide."

Golyadkin's inner rebellion and disintegrating personality are suggested from the very start of the work. He dreams of conquering the unattainable Klara, yet is afraid of his superiors; he orders suites of furniture and valuable antiques, but knows he cannot afford them; he drives around in a hired carriage and livery which are entirely out of harmony with his lowly position, yet shrinks in a confusion of shame, inverted pride, and frustration when he is seen by Andrey Filippovich; and his interview with his doctor is remarkable for its pathological mixture of aggression and humility. The extent of Golyadkin's inner conflict is suggested most dramatically in a scene where he hides unnoticed on the stairs instead of going in to Klara's party. He cannot decide whether to assert himself and enter, or humbly return home. Eventually reason tells him that his ambitions are inappropriate to his position, and he decides to withdraw: "'If I were at home now I could have a cup of tea. . . . That would be quite pleasant, to have a cup of tea. . . . Why not go home? The devil can take all this! I'll go and that'll be an end to it!'" But then he appears to rebel against this rational conclusion: "Having decided his position in this way, Mr. Golyadkin quickly dashed forward, as if some sort of spring had been touched off in him; in two strides he found himself in the refreshment room" (I, 132–33). This image of a spring overriding reason's balanced deductions is an appropriate, though undoubtedly unintentional, reminder of Pope's own analogy in *Essay on Man*. Here, however, the spring and the balance contradict rather than complement each other, and psychological chaos is the inevitable result.

At this point, in a fine passage, *The Double* takes the fantastic turn to which Belinsky objected. Returning home from his disgrace at Klara's party, through a wild Petersburg night as dark and disordered as his own soul, Golyadkin meets his double. The critics have attached many different meanings to Golyadkin Junior (Dostoevsky's name for the double). Wasiolek and Temira Pachmuss see his appearance as an attempt by Golyadkin subconsciously to purge himself of distasteful traits by transferring them to another, imaginary person.[9] Konstantin Mochulsky interprets him as an embodiment of "all the baseness and meanness" in Golyadkin's soul, a symbol of all that the timid Golyadkin would possibly like to be.[10] Roger Anderson has suggested that with the appearance of the double Golyadkin creates "two distinct images of himself, one assertive against authority [Junior], the other submissive [Senior]," and by thus externalizing his dilemma seeks to resolve it.[11] There is an important flaw, however, in Anderson's otherwise tidy argument. The double is not assertive *against authority*. His aggression is directed only against Golyadkin Senior, for his appearance merely externalizes a psychological conflict; it does not resolve it or alter it. Too puny to take up arms against society, Golyadkin becomes the sole victim of his psychological revolt, and this is well dramatized in the ensuing duel and *mutual* destruction of the two Golyadkins. The exact relationship of this duel to Golyadkin's earlier internal dilemma is confirmed by a scene late in the work where Senior hides behind a woodpile, uncertain whether to pursue his assertive, unrealistic dream of eloping with Klara or to return home instead. He has just decided on the latter course when Junior, now no longer the hidden spring of Golyadkin's self-will, drags him out of hiding and exposes him to the ridicule of Klara and his superiors (I, 224), This scene clearly repeats the inner struggle before Klara's party.

The source of the double in Golyadkin's own divided nature counters Belinsky's charge of unrealism. There is nothing intrinsically fantastic in the work, nothing that cannot be traced back to Golyadkin's weakening hold on reality. On awaking at the start of the novel he displays a premonitory inability to distinguish between dream and reality, and indeed his mind seems prepared for the eventual appearance of his alter-ego. He warns two of his colleagues: "You all know me, gentlemen, but hitherto you've known only one aspect of me" (I, 124). When his carriage and fine livery are noticed by Andrey Filippovich, Golyadkin's reaction indicates just how receptive his thoughts are to the idea of a double: "Should I bow to him or not? Should I declare myself or not? . . . Or should I pretend that I'm not really me, that I'm somebody else *strikingly like me* . . ." (I, 113: my italics). Such suggestions that the double originates in Golyadkin's imagination are subsequently confirmed when on two occasions Junior appears through glass doors which Senior has initially taken for mirrors (I, 174, 216). *The Double* is thus the first of Dostoevsky's studies in hallucination, and it makes skillful use of narrative uncertainty by not relying on a fixed, objective, and omniscient narrator but by instead allowing the point of view to move imperceptibly between the objective and the subjective. In this way the complex texture of Golyadkin's disintegrating consciousness is recreated in the narrative. This technique will be examined in greater detail later in this chapter, for in its developed form in the mature novels it represents one of Dostoevsky's most startling contributions to the techniques of the Realistic novel. It is ironic that it should first have been employed in a work which Dostoevsky's contemporaries considered a travesty of the Realistic mode.

III   *Other Works of the 1840s*

Dostoevsky's intense exploration of man's divided nature and tragic relationship to social reality continues in the more substantial of the works which appeared between *The Double* and his arrest. With very few exceptions he persists in concentrating his analysis on the same kind of lowly civil servant whose individuality is threatened by a vast, impersonal bureaucratic machine. In a sense this is a weakness, for Dostoevsky's psychological investigations are inhibited by the limited consciousness of this type of hero. Devushkin, Golyadkin, and the rest are all victims of psychopathological dilemmas of which they have no real understanding. Moreover, the narrative techniques, which often locate the point of view within the hero's own subjective perception, mean that the reader, in addition to experiencing the texture of the hero's inner world, also shares his limited understanding. Dostoevsky himself apparently sensed this technical disadvantage, for in a letter to his brother of October 1846 he announced that he had abandoned work on "The Shaved Whiskers," a similar project with a comparable hero: "This is nothing more than a repetition of old ideas which I have long ago expressed. Now I am compelled to put more original, lively and lucid ideas on paper."[12] Although he continued to be fascinated by the civil-servant type, he did go on, in "The Landlady" (1847) and "White Nights" (1848), to introduce a new hero, the "gentleman-dreamer" *(barin-mechtatel)*, remarkable for his greater imaginative capacity. But even in these works Dostoevsky was merely feeling his way, and it was not until the hero of *Notes from Underground* that he was to discover the limitless possibilities of combining his old psychological motifs with a lucid, analytical consciousness. With this barrier down, the way to the great novel-tragedies was clear.

Throughout *The Double* Golyadkin is consumed by an ill-defined sense of persecution, by a growing anxiety that the stability of his social position is somehow under threat and that his identity is about to be usurped by pretenders. Subsequent events amply justify his fears, although they remain unsatisfactorily explained. Dostoevsky was to make fear and existential unease the very basis of the tale "Mister Prokharchin," (1846). By then his estrangement from Belinsky was more or less complete, and it is hardly surprising that the critic dismissed "Mister Prokharchin" as even more worthless and impenetrable than its predecessor. Yet the work, confusing and uneven as it is, adds a further important dimension to Dostoevsky's examination of the dislocated individual in modern society, lost in the uncertainty of conflicting identities. Prokharchin is another small clerk, but he is a grotesque whose personality has been almost entirely eroded by his trivial social function. A small cog in an administrative machine, the overall structure of which he cannot even begin to understand, Prokharchin has no life outside the office. Barely articulate, he lives alone in poverty and shuns the company of his fellow lodgers. He is apparently unworried by personal desire and ambition, but in his dehumanization he has paid a high price for this total absorption into his social persona. Cracks appear in Prokharchin's life when he hears rumors that his department is to be closed. With this threat to his confidence and security his being falls apart. He has no private identity into which to retreat, and in an uneasy dream he recognizes too late his estrangement and loss of humanity. He surrenders to pathological anxiety and dies. On his death, however, it is discovered that over the years he has secreted a considerable fortune in his mattress.

It would clearly be extravagant to assert that Dostoevsky intended this slight tale to represent modern man's failure to embody the eighteenth-century ideal of the integrated individual moving easily between his public and private identities. But it does suggest a dilemma which has become increasingly acute in modern societies. Prokharchin's relationship to his work, his public life, is unsatisfactory, for, rather than providing a framework for self-development, it consumes him and leaves him pathetically adrift. The steady accumulation of capital, irrational in the light of his dire poverty, represents a rear-guard action, a final attempt to shore up his collapsing identity through possessions. Like many of Dostoevsky's later heroes, to be examined in due time, Prokharchin defines himself in what he owns and thus prefigures the accumulative instinct of modern man struggling to assert his being in a materialist world.

Variations on the theme of the alienated, dualistic individual occur in several of Dostoevsky's other preexile works. The fate of Vasya Shumkov, the hero of "Slaboe serdtse" [A Faint Heart, 1848], repeats the warning of *The Double* that madness awaits those who fail to reconcile their dreams of personal happiness with the constraints imposed by civic obligation and social insignificance. In the words of his friend Arkady, Vasya fails "to reconcile himself with himself" (I, 40), and his physical disability (he is slightly crippled) suggests this more radical disfigurement. The eponymous hero of "Polzunkov" (1848) does in fact effect some kind of equilibrium between his pride and his insignificance, but it is grotesque in the extreme. The plot of this work is trivial, but the introductory characterization of Polzunkov sheds interesting light on the kind of socially constrained individual who seeks to satisfy his aggressive instincts through deliberate self-abasement. This psychological characteristic has already been pictured in the self-destructive courses pursued by Devushkin and Golyadkin, and it is to be thoroughly examined in Marmeladov (*Crime and Punishment*), but Polzunkov is the first real example of a thoroughly Dostoevskian type, willfully delighting in the confusion of pain and satisfaction which his position affords.

Dostoevsky's adoption in "The Landlady" and "White Nights" of a new literary hero, the dreamer, is not the radical departure it first appears to be, for the new type embodies familiar psychological features. The Dostoevskian civil servant and the romantic dreamer are both creatures of two worlds, living in the grim reality of St. Petersburg but seeking self-realization elsewhere. The difference is that, whereas the private lives of Devushkin and Golyadkin conflict with social reality, the dreamer's private life avoids reality altogether. The world of the imagination offers a complete retreat from reality and its constraints, and thus polarizes the dreamer's existence: "His life is a mixture of something purely fantastic, ardently idealistic and at the same time dingily prosaic and commonplace . . ." (II, 112). The young Dostoevsky knew only too well the seductive power of the romantic imagination. As a student at the St. Petersburg Academy of Engineers, he had conceived a consuming passion for German Romanticism and the works of Friedrich Schiller. This and a sentimental friendship with an unworldly Romantic poet, Ivan Shidlovsky, had facilitated his withdrawal from life into a gossamer world of Romantic archetypes. The social realism of *Poor Folk* and its author's growing admiration for Balzac, Dickens, and George Sand had marked a turn in Dostoevsky's intellectual development: his retreat from bootless romanticism and a dawning awareness of the problems of the real world. Dostoevsky recognized that the idealist absorbed in his dreams has "blunted his talent for real life"[13] and embarked on a path leading to illusion, solipsism, and spiritual disintegration. In 1847 he wrote of man's need "to realize, fulfill and justify his Self in real life."[14] Comments such as these testify to Dostoevsky's own reconciliation with reality, as does an article he published in the newspaper *Sanktpeterburgskie vedomosti* [St. Petersburg Gazette] in June 1847 in which he presents a thoughtfully ironic account of the dreamer type.[15]

The tragedy of the dreamer lies in his inability to establish a balanced relationship between the external world of reality and the inner world of fantasy, as Dostoevsky put it in a letter to his brother written at the beginning of 1847: "The *exterior* must keep in steady balance with the *interior*. Otherwise, in the absence of exterior phenomena, the interior will assume too dangerous an upper hand. Nerves and fantasy will occupy a very large place in one's being."[16] Such an imbalance is the central psychological feature of Ordynov, the hero of "The Landlady." A lonely romantic who has lost all capacity for real life, Ordynov lives an entirely imaginary life, assimilating into his isolated dream world all his limited contact with objective life. He can no longer distinguish between the intellectual comprehension of life and its imaginative recreation. His scholarly pursuits never materialize, aptly illustrating his inability to realize his creative aspirations in real life. When he is obliged to change lodgings, his brief contact with the outside world depresses him. In a church he meets the dazzlingly beautiful Katerina and her mysterious old companion, Ilya Murin, from which point the plot becomes confused as Ordynov's imaginative embellishment of events alternates with their reality. Terras suggests that there are two plots—the objective and the subjective.[17] In the objective plot Katerina is Murin's flighty young wife. Both come from the Volga region, and their speech and dress are exotic. Murin cannot control his wife's amorous inclinations, of which the new lodger, Ordynov, becomes the object. Finally Murin complains to the authorities and Ordynov seeks new lodgings. The subjective plot, however, is much richer and is fired by Ordynov's dreamy disposition and longing for romance. His imaginative rearrangement of the facts is encouraged further by his incipient illness and delirium, so that Katerina in his mind becomes a legendary folk-princess, held in supernatural bondage by the sorcerer Murin. The exoticism of the two characters sustains Ordynov's fancy, and he becomes the young prince pledged to Katerina's liberation. There is even a hint that Katerina is Murin's daughter and that their relationship is incestuous. The subjective plot clearly owes much to folk legend, from which the theme of incest also derives. The "sorcerer's" name, moreover, suggests Ilya Muromets, the most famous Russian folk hero. What is more, specific details of Ordynov's delirium are reminiscent of Gogol's Romantic tale "A Terrible Vengeance" (1832) and Alexander Pushkin's folk-poem "Ruslan and Lyudmila" (1820), with both of which we might expect an intellectual such as Ordynov to be familiar. Dostoevsky had certainly read and admired them.

The eclecticism of "The Landlady"—its daring juxtaposition of realistic and folk motifs and its playful references to Pushkin and Gogol—was considered by Belinsky and many subsequent critics to be the work's most serious weakness; but it is in fact its most important achievement.[18] The tale presents "the dramatization of delirium"[19] and, like *The Double*, makes skillful use of narrative techniques to establish a correspondence between the hero's psychological state and the stylistic nature of the work. The confused eclecticism of the narrative in fact originates in the confusion of Ordynov's imagination. Belinsky's dismissal of "The Landlady" as "terrible rubbish"[20] seems, however, to have worried Dostoevsky, for "White Nights" appears to be an attempt to restructure the dreamer motif in the light of Belinsky's criticisms. For a start, there are many plot similarities with "The Landlady." The hero is a similarly estranged dreamer, drawn into contact with the real world after an amorous encounter. This dreamer also allows his imagination to color his view of the girl, Nastenka, who becomes for him something she is not in reality. When she abandons the dreamer in favor of another man, he recognizes the evanescence of his ideals and their incompatibility with reality, and retreats again into loneliness. There are also several specific points of detail which suggest that "The Landlady" and "White Nights" are two variants on the same idea, but space does not allow discussion of these here.[21]

In "White Nights" the grotesque, confused, and threatening atmosphere of "The Landlady" yields to a much more lucid, serene, and springlike mood, but it would be a mistake to attribute this just to the effect of Belinsky's opinions. The stylistic differences between the two works also reflect an important difference in the personalities of the two dreamers. For just as Ordynov's confused, uninhibited fantasies contributed to the narrative excesses of "The Landlady," so does the psychology of his successor affect the form of "White Nights." The new dreamer is not just a restatement of Ordynov; he represents a development, and an important one at that. He has a lucidity and analytical perception which Ordynov lacks. He clearly distinguishes between dream and reality, and is even able to describe himself in the third person. Such objectivity in the central character allows a more lucid and detached narrative style, but the same lucidity which distances this dreamer from Ordynov also aligns him with some of Dostoevsky's later characters. It is not a large step from the self-understanding and philosophic detachment of this hero to the self-analytical inertia of that grotesquely disillusioned dreamer, the Underground Man. Mochulsky is surely wrong when he asserts that "there is nothing of the underground" in the apparent serenity of "White Nights."[22] The tragedy of the Underground Man lies partly in the conflict between a Romantic, imaginative nature and an acute analytical consciousness which exposes the futility of dreaming but which is unable to deny its esthetic superiority and reconcile the dreamer with reality. In the final scene of "White Nights," where the dreamer anticipates the drabness of his future, we already discern suppressed despair and the specter of the Underground.

IV Stylistic Considerations

The arguments of this chapter, which so far have been concerned primarily with thematic features, have already suggested the stylistic richness of Dostoevsky's work of the 1840s. He moves confidently through many genres, exploring the parodistic and the epistolary, juxtaposing folk material with the techniques of psychological Realism, and breathing new life into Romantic stereotypes such as the double and the dreamer. A voracious reader, Dostoevsky was constantly conscious of absorbing diverse material in his own search for a suitable narrative technique, and many of his early works are remarkable for an overt literariness which often approaches parody. Much critical effort has been devoted to Dostoevsky's early literary methods and the influence of others on his work, but it would be both impossible and undesirable to survey the scholarship on the subject here (see the Bibliography). Instead attention will here be focused on two aspects of the early Dostoevsky's narrative method: his deliberate and ironic use of material from two great predecessors, Nikolay Gogol and Alexander Pushkin, and his adventurous exploitation of narrative point of view.

It has been argued that Dostoevsky's works of the 1840s represent "a step towards and a step away from Gogol,"[23] an obvious emulation of his superficial narrative and thematic devices coupled with an outright rejection of Gogol's grotesque, exaggerated, and unsympathetic depiction of character. But comparatively little has been said about the effect of Pushkin on these works, and that is surprising because the Pushkin influence, if initially less obvious than Gogol's, is ultimately more important in defining Dostoevsky's literary attitudes. Indeed the most important works of this period are like showcases in which the creative achievements of Gogol and Pushkin, at least as Dostoevsky saw them, are brought together, not for the purpose of reconciliation (such a task was beyond even a Dostoevsky), but in order that their differences might be more clearly distinguished. Moreover, Dostoevsky seems to suggest Pushkin's example as an antidote to those features of Gogol's method which he finds objectionable—Gogol's derisive attitude toward his characters, his unwillingness to probe beyond superficial appearances to the heart of his people, and the frequency with which his work dissolves into the most grotesque fantasy. With some justification Dostoevsky saw Gogol as a grimacing puppeteer manipulating his wooden puppets.[24] His characters, for all their animation, did not have life in them; they lacked psychological depth, for Gogol himself did not have the sympathetic understanding required to bring his people to life. Even the unsophisticated Devushkin perceives this when he reads "The Overcoat." He feels that the life of the little man deserves a more sympathetic and analytical treatment than Gogol provides in his account of Akaky Akakievich, and indeed he finds the model for such a treatment in Pushkin's "The Stationmaster" (1831), a work of comparable brevity to "The Overcoat" but one which provides a genuine insight into the complex psychology of the socially unimportant figure. As Mochulsky writes: "Dostoevsky was to learn the art of words from Gogol, but . . . he mastered the art of the psychological short story through the mentorship of Pushkin."[25]

Pushkin's works are also invoked in Dostoevsky's early tales as an answer to Gogol's indiscriminate absorption of the fantastic into his work. The psychological, social, and moral implications of Gogol's works often vanish in waves of syntactic and thematic nonsense which invariably engulf his world and transform his writings into breathless masterpieces of the comic-grotesque. Dostoevsky, who was to set himself the task of depicting "all the depths of the human soul," could admire Gogol's manner, but not emulate it. His works, even those which employ the techniques of the grotesque, are always rooted firmly and deliberately in the social reality of his day. Pushkin, however, had shown in works such as "Ruslan and Lyudmila" and "The Queen of Spades" (1834) that the fantastic could be used in art to further other ends. "Ruslan and Lyudmila" is "a sophisticated sport with the fantastic,"[26] a beautifully judged literary game, and "The Queen of Spades" a fine, ironic synthesis of the supernatural and the psychological. The clear allusions to both these works in "The Landlady" provide a counterpoint to that tale's thematic debt to Gogol's "A Terrible Vengeance," and suggest that there is more to Dostoevsky's use of the apparently fantastic than meets the eye.[27]

Similar echoes of Gogol and Pushkin occur in most of Dostoevsky's works of the 1840s, and invariably the author finds Pushkin's approach more congenial to his own analytical method. Yet Dostoevsky's professed affinity with Pushkin—he claimed in 1861 to have found in the poet "a corroboration of all my thought"[28]—barely disguises the huge temperamental distance between the two. Pushkin, in his lightness, estheticism, and detachment, belongs to the past in a way that Dostoevsky does not. There is an urgency and immediacy about Dostoevsky's work which defines him firmly as a novelist of a newer, more uncertain age, the ripples of which only occasionally disturb the timeless stability brought to Pushkin's work by his temperament and attitudes. By 1859, when Gogol's hold on Dostoevsky's imagination had slipped sufficiently to allow Dostoevsky to create a bitingly ironic caricature of the genius of the comic-grotesque in *The Village of Stepanchikovo*, Dostoevsky's works no longer displayed evidence of any methodological debt to Pushkin. The demon Gogol had been exorcised and, although Dostoevsky throughout his life professed his sincere admiration for Pushkin, the great novels of his postexile period affirm the irreconcilability of his moral and esthetic outlook with that of the poet.

It was suggested earlier that Dostoevsky's greatest contribution to the technique of the novel was his use of point of view. His works of the 1840s anticipate this in their consistent emphasis on the primacy of the subjective consciousness. Dostoevsky seems anxious to avoid the synthesizing, objectivizing function of the conventional third-person narrator, and instead allows his reader direct access to the unsynthesized, unmodified consciousness of his protagonist. In this, of course, he anticipates the stream-of-consciousness, inner-monologue technique used in James Joyce's *Ulysses*. Yet, unaccountably, Mochulsky writes critically of "the opposition of form and content" in Dostoevsky's early works.[29] Surely the opposite is true: Dostoevsky matches his narrative techniques directly with his thematic preoccupations. He presents the theme of the isolated, unreconciled individual at odds with objective social reality through a method emphasizing the dislocation of consciousness, which is not reconciled or objectified by being filtered through an omniscient narrator, who would be able to incorporate the single voice of his hero into his broader and more objective perception. An analogy with painting is perhaps appropriate here. Early art lacked perspective, and its widespread adoption by Renaissance artists marked a revolution that was not merely technical but also perceptual and philosophical. The painter who does not use perspective, who paints a distant tower the same size as an identical tower nearer by, is in fact recording reality not as it looks, but as he knows it to be. Reason and experience tell him the towers are identical and that their apparent difference in size is only an effect of perception. He is thus painting from an omniscient or, in Jacob Bronowski's phrase, "God's eye" point of view.[30] Such a viewpoint is not accessible to any single human being, and consequently perspective affords a more human view. Yet it also stresses inevitably the singularity and relativity of individual perception. Things appear differently to different observers, and only God sees from an omniscient, synthesizing, objectifying, and aperspectival point of view. Perspective urges us to acknowledge the subjectivity of experience, and the multiplicity and discordance of empirical truth. Is any one point of view necessarily truer than another? In a sense Einstein's discoveries and the consequent increasing uncertainty of modern scientific thought are the effects of introducing perspective into the synthesized, objectified, "God's eye" point of view in Newtonian cosmology. The relativistic point of view is clearly more appropriate to the depiction of our modern age, when the individual finds himself alone, confused, and at odds with "objective reality." The confidence of the eighteenth century in the unifying and synthesizing power of reason lies far behind us, and our age of uncertainty and of the unreconciled individual demands new artistic forms to capture its texture. This century's unprecedented interest in art forms which stress the subjectivity and singularity of perception—Expressionism, Surrealism, and Symbolism, for example—surely represents an attempt to acknowledge and respond to the texture of the age.

In 1929 the Soviet critic Mikhail Bakhtin coined the term *polyphonic* to describe the narrative method of Dostoevsky's novels. Bakhtin's work is perhaps the single most important contribution to the study of Dostoevsky's stylistics, and no subsequent scholar has been able safely to ignore his findings.[31] He argues that the novels of, say, Tolstoy are not truly polyphonic because, although each of their characters possesses a unique consciousness, viewpoint, and voice, these are reconciled and merged by the "monologizing" function of the narrator, who utilizes his omniscience to objectify them. Dostoevsky's novels, however, stress not the reconciliation of separate consciousnesses but their discord: "*The plurality of independent and unmerged voices and consciousnesses and the genuine polyphony of full-valued voices are in fact characteristics of Dostoevsky's novels*. It is not a multitude of characters and fates within a unified objective world, illuminated by the author's unified consciousness, that unfolds in his works, but precisely the *plurality of equal consciousnesses and their worlds*, which are combined here into the unity of a given event, while at the same time retaining their unmergedness."[32]

As Bakhtin concedes, true polyphony emerges only in Dostoevsky's mature novels, but the early works do represent a real step in that direction. *Poor Folk* employs the clumsy device of the letter form to allow direct access to Devushkin's unmerged voice; and the plurality of his style—ranging from the subjectively poetic to the tediously official—permits an insight into his conflicting aspirations which might well have been lost had his voice been filtered through an objective narrative consciousness. The subjective third-person narrative of *The Double* and "The Landlady" is a more sophisticated attempt to penetrate the unreconciled consciousness of the hero. Any attempt to report objectively the delirium of Golyadkin and Ordynov would exclude the uncertainty which is the very essence of their perception, and resolve the tension between reality and fantasy on which the works pivot. Indeed, no objective narrator could convey the hallucinatory nature of the worlds experienced by Golyadkin and Ordynov as eloquently as does Dostoevsky's use of unmerged voices. When Golyadkin's double speaks in Golyadkin's voice, using the same speech patterns and imagery, we cannot fail to recognize his subjectivity. Likewise, when in Ordynov's delirium he, Katerina, and Murin all abandon their individual voices in favor of a single folk idiom, we realize that we are sharing Ordynov's dream, fed by Romantic expectations and folk motifs.

The potentially revolutionary narrative technique of Dostoevsky's early works conforms perfectly to their view of man as an isolated consciousness unreconciled with social reality. Both the techniques and the view are entirely consonant with the modern age, and these features compel in the modern reader an admiration which offsets the many weaknesses of the tales of the 1840s. The failure of Belinsky and his contemporaries to respond sympathetically to Dostoevsky's fiction after *Poor Folk* is an indicator of the comparative swiftness of the young Dostoevsky's artistic response to the changing pressures of the time.

CHAPTER 3

Enlightened Malevolence

I N a revealing letter written from exile in 1854, Dostoevsky confessed to being "a child of the age, a child of uncertainty and doubt."[1] This view of the nineteenth century as an age which had lost the cultural confidence of eighteenth-century Europe and discovered no new governing principle of its own is already clear in Dostoevsky's preexile works. They depict a society built not upon harmony and optimism, but upon discord and existential uncertainty. The increasing complexity of Russian and European life became particularly evident to Dostoevsky after his ten-year absence. The accelerating tempo of the times was evinced in radical changes in the social and cultural order: the intellectual and artistic upheaval of Romanticism had been matched by sometimes violent convulsions in the social and political fabric of the Continent. The revolutions in France and Germany and the emergence of the bourgeoisie gave new impetus to the rise of capitalism and the institutionalization of bourgeois morality. Dostoevsky's impressions of these changes were sharpened by his first journey abroad in 1862, when he visited Germany, France, Italy, Switzerland, and England. He recorded his responses to what he saw in his polemically journalistic piece *Winter Notes on Summer Impressions*, published in 1863. In this work he drew particular attention to social unrest, the alienation of the individual, the rise of revolutionary socialism, and the growth of a pecuniary morality, all of which he considered symptomatic of developing capitalism. Above all he was struck by the penetration of egoism into all aspects of European life, and this endowed the horrors he witnessed with a genuinely apocalyptic coloring. In *Winter Notes* Dostoevsky makes much of the apocalyptic note struck by Western societies, and prepares the ground for the artistic treatment of this theme in his later novels. Dostoevsky considered egoism to be the root of social discord, encouraging as it did the morality of self-interest, promoting the alienation of man from man, and leading to "self-definition in one's personal Ego, and the opposition of this Ego to the whole of

54

nature and all other people" (V, 79). Dostoevsky's recognition of the ethics of self-interest and material well-being as the springs of Western capitalism jaded his palate to Western tastes, and he came to regard Europe as a decaying culture. His journalistic endeavors, beginning with his direction of the journal *Time* in 1861 and ending with his remarkable speech on Pushkin in 1880, allowed him to express fairly consistently the hope that Russia might, through her historical isolation, have escaped the egoism of the West, and that the Russian people might not have lost the ability to live together on the basis of love and brotherhood. Dostoevsky's journalism, however, never did justice to the intricacy of his thought. In it còmplex problems become simple polemics, and we must turn to his polyphonic artistic works for a true insight into the uncertainty of his soul. These too preach rejection of the ethics of Western capitalism, but they rarely persuade us of the greater historical destiny of the Russian people, although this is always present as an alluring dream.

Dostoevsky's works of the early 1860s record the author's sensitivity to the climate of uncertainty which was already penetrating his native land. They reflect the growing political and social confusion of post-Emancipation Russia, the first tentative steps of Russian capitalism, the spread of materialist morality, and the attempts of the younger generation of Russian thinkers to erect social philosophies on the basis of human egoism. They also constitute a sustained warning that the eighteenth-century dream of rational social order and the nineteenth century's faith in utopian socialism based on humanist idealism are inadequate to regulate morality in the new and uncertain age. Dostoevsky's critique of pure reason, that "unfounded fiction of the eighteenth century" (V, 78), was, as we have seen, already well formulated in his preexile work, but *Winter Notes* and the novels which accompanied it are newly ferocious in their rejection of socialist brotherhood and the kind of romantic Rousseauism which fired revolutionary socialism with its assertion of man's natural goodness and the possibility of social harmony based on this virtue. Dostoevsky had, of course, been drawn before his arrest to idealism and abstract humanism, and had found in Schiller a sympathetic soul. Moreover, he had participated directly in revolutionary socialist circles and familiarized himself with the utopian socialist thought of Charles Fourier, Claude Henri Saint-Simon, and Pierre Leroux. These facts have led the majority of Dostoevsky's biographers to seek the origins of an apparent volte-face in his intellectual development in the period of Siberian exile. Certainly he was arrested for socialist

conspiracy, and equally certainly he returned from exile a vociferous
opponent of abstract humanism and socialism. What is more, his
prison memoirs, *The House of the Dead*, clearly show that Dostoevsky's experience of the dark and unpredictable souls of criminals, such
as the child-murderers Gazin and Orlov, did much to disabuse him of
his naive faith in natural virtue. Such men were a dark blot on the
dream of social happiness, for, as Dostoevsky wrote in *Winter Notes*,
"you only need the finest filament to fall into the machine, and
everything at once cracks and falls to pieces . . . . In order to make
hare stew, you must first have a hare. But we don't have the hare; that
is, we don't have a nature capable of brotherhood" (V, 79–81). Neither
reason nor idealism can resurrect a depraved soul. In Dostoevsky's
postexile works he spurns humanist utopias, becoming a novelist with
a religious mission. There is to be no harmony without redemption,
no salvation without God, and no paradise on earth.

I   *Idealism and Socialism in the Works of the 1840s*

Dostoevsky's retreat from idealistic humanism and socialism became quite clear in the works which followed his return from exile,
but even in the works of the 1840s, written while Dostoevsky was
associated with socialist groups, there are interesting indications of
what was to come. The unfinished novel *Netochka Nezvanova* (1849)
describes the experiences of a young girl struggling against a family
background of poverty and emotional chaos. Her mother is a meek
creature, and her father, Efimov, a gifted, but arrogant musician.
When her parents die, Netochka eventually finds herself adopted by
the gentle dreamer Alexandra Mikhaylovna, who is punished for an
innocent sexual indiscretion by her pompously self-righteous husband, Petr Alexandrovich. The novel suggests the moral inadequacy
of sentimental idealism. The "virtue" of Netochka and Alexandra
affords no answer to the romantic egoism of Efimov or the cold moral
hypocrisy of Petr. Netochka's growing rebelliousness in the closing
pages of the fragment seems to disclose an awareness of the need for
something more than passive virtue.

In "Mister Prokharchin" too we discern the signs of disillusionment with abstract humanism. The spiritual isolation of Prokharchin
is emphasized by the fraternity of his fellow lodgers. Under the
direction of a certain Mark Ivanovich they meet each month for cards
and discussion, but there is more to these gatherings than meets the
eye. We learn that Mark is "a clever and well-read man" who speaks

in "a fine, flowery style." His group is quite cabalistic: its members meet "like brothers," in order to enjoy "the bubbling moments of life." They like to argue and "talk of the exalted." "But since prejudices were excluded from the whole company, the general harmony was in no way impaired" (I, 241). These details point, quite inescapably in the context of the late 1840s, to the sort of socialist discussion circle which Dostoevsky had attended at Petrashevsky's, one devoted to abstract discussion with a distinctly idealistic bent.

Mark and his companions try to overcome Prokharchin's isolation, which they misconstrue as willful individualism, with arguments redolent of the kind of abstract humanism Dostoevsky must have heard from Belinsky during their period of intimacy in the mid-1840s. Mark tries to shame Prokharchin back into human communality by stressing the apparent egoism of his withdrawal: "What are you? You're a sheep! You're neither here nor there! Are you the only one in the world, is that it! Was the world made just for you! Are you some sort of Napoleon! Is that it!" (I, 257). "You're neither here nor there!" With these words Mark establishes his credentials. Any love he possesses for humanity is the impersonal, universal, abstract variety Dostoevsky came to despise. His outlook ignores the individual atoms in the universal scheme. Alongside the universal the individual has no rights, and Mark would deprive Prokharchin of the right even to be afraid: "Who thinks of you, my dear sir? Have you the right to fear? Who are you? What are you? You're a zero, sir; a round pancake, that's what!" (I, 255). Mark's comments here expose a fundamental flaw of abstract love: its mathematical philanthropy, which through ignorance of, and scorn for, individual human nature sacrifices man for the sake of mankind. This critique of abstract humanism was to culminate in *The Brothers Karamazov* (1880), where Dostoevsky counters it with Christian love. But even in "Mister Prokharchin" the hero's unsettling dream of man's duty to love his fellow men affords an alternative to Mark's abstract philanthropy and anticipates the message of Dostoevsky's mature fiction that true brotherhood must be founded upon moral, rather than social, transfiguration.

"A Faint Heart" matches the critique of abstract humanism in "Mister Prokharchin" with its benignly ironic debunking of that other pillar of utopian socialism—naive idealism, with its faith in man's ability to live in harmony on the basis of natural virtue and fraternal love. The story is clear but tender in its exposure of the bankruptcy of romantic "Schillerism," for such an outlook had been the emotional mainstay of Dostoevsky's youth, and he discarded it with evident regret. Vasya Shumkov opposes the emptiness of his public life as a clerk with the rich emotional idealism of his private existence. He dreams of personal happiness constructed on the basis of his sentimental friendship with Arkady and his romantic love for Liza Artemeva; it is an ideal, Schilleresque triangular relationship, with love and friendship existing in harmonious equilibrium. But Vasya's idealism cannot withstand the withering touch of reality. His official commitments assume monstrous proportions in his imagination and dwarf his pursuit of personal happiness. Vasya has, in the love of Liza, the friendship of Arkady, and the benevolent concern of his superior, Yulian Mastakovich, all the natural virtue and fraternal love he can handle; yet these are not enough to heal his tragic dual identity and guarantee his happiness. Naive idealism, virtue, and fraternity are all very well, but they do not work in the real world.

The philosophical significance of "A Faint Heart" as a stage in Dostoevsky's withdrawal from utopianism is disclosed through a clever network of literary and political references. For example, both the specific details and the sentimental tone of Vasya's relationship with Liza recall Nikolay Karamzin's tale "Poor Liza" (1792), the most widely read literary example of the idealistic cult of sensibility in the early nineteenth century. Dostoevsky uses the phrase "poor Liza" to address his heroine, and we are told that she once had a fiancé whom she loved dearly but who abandoned her when posted elsewhere by the army. It goes without saying that the same fate befalls the lovers Liza and Erast in Karamzin's tale. The mawkish naiveté of "Poor Liza" was inappropriate to Russian literature of the 1840s, and Dostoevsky's transcription of it emphasizes the redundancy of the idealistic sensibility.[2]

There is also a literary source of the sentimental friendship between Vasya and Arkady: it recalls that between the Chevalier des Grieux and the faithful Tiberge in l'Abbé Prévost's novel *Manon Lescaut* (1731). Prévost's work is also about the impotence of idealism, and in the preface to his novel he draws attention to the gulf between lofty emotion and reality.[3] Dostoevsky actually refers to *Manon Lescaut* in "A Faint Heart": in a scene shortly preceding the destruction of his idealism Vasya buys for Liza a "Manon Lescaut" bonnet, which he clearly feels will express his feelings for her. She, however, is singularly unimpressed by the hat, despite Dostoevsky's vigorous if ironic prompting (II, 27). The fate of the "Manon Lescaut" bonnet is an eloquent symbol of the inappropriateness of Vasya's idealism. Equally eloquent is the ironic fact that he buys the hat at the shop of a certain Madame Leroux, where he is overawed by "all that is great and beautiful" (*vse prekrasnoe i velikoe*) on her shelves. Such ecstatic vocabulary hardly befits a row of hats, no matter how charming, but it does remind us of the dreams of the exalted and beautiful (*vse prekrasnoe i vozvyshennoe*) over which the young Dostoevsky enthused during his early infatuation with Schiller. Moreover, Madame Leroux's namesake is, of course, Pierre Leroux, the most highly regarded utopian socialist thinker of the day, well known in Russia through his journal *La Revue independante*.

So in "A Faint Heart," in Madame Leroux's hatshop, abstract idealism and utopian socialism—two vital stages in the young Dostoevsky's intellectual development—are brought together and gently but firmly discarded. Yet how do we reconcile this apparent retreat from utopianism and abstract humanism with the documented fact of Dostoevsky's participation in socialist intrigues? The whole question deserves, and has received, detailed examination,[4] and it is possible to conclude that Dostoevsky's disillusionment with the dream of humanism was well advanced before his arrest, and that his association with the Petrashevsky and Durov circles was attributable more to the charismatic influence of Belinsky and personalities such as the mysterious Nikolay Speshnev, a leading figure in the Durov group, than to any real intellectual sympathy.

II   The Insulted and Injured

In 1861 Dostoevsky published *The Insulted and Injured*, which in length, atmosphere, and design is a transition between the works of the 1840s and the major novels which were to come. It is a patchwork mixing ideas later developed in *Winter Notes* with thematic and stylistic devices drawn from the European social melodramas of Eugène Sue, Victor Hugo, and Dickens. The figure of Nelly, in particular, owes much to Dickens's Little Nell (*The Old Curiosity Shop*).

The novel is narrated by Ivan Petrovich, a young novelist, whose love for Natasha Ikhmeneva is thwarted when she falls in love with Alesha, the son of Prince Petr Valkovsky, a willful and enigmatic figure. Valkovsky and Natasha's father are bitter enemies, and both oppose the liaison between their children. Ihkmenev disowns Natasha, and Valkovsky does all he can to entice his weak-willed son to marry a rich princess, Katya. Eventually Alesha abandons Natasha and she returns to her father, who forgives her. But all this is too late for Ivan Petrovich, who is dying.

A subplot of the novel tells of the young girl Nelly, the unacknowl-
edged daughter of Valkovsky, who is protected by Ivan Petrovich.
Nelly's mother has been cursed by her own father, Smith, for her
affair with Valkovsky, and here the lines of the subplot run parallel to
the main intrigue. The Nelly plot, however, ends tragically. Her
mother is not forgiven by Smith, and Nelly dies with her hatred of
Valkovsky unappeased.

Behind this melodrama there is much that is autobiographical in
The Insulted and Injured. The initial literary success of Ivan Petrovich and his good relations with the critic B. are a lightly disguised
account of the start of Dostoevsky's own career. Indeed, Ivan's first
novel has a plot drawn directly from *Poor Folk*. Moreover, Ivan's
personality is very similar to that of the young Dostoevsky: he suffers
bouts of existential anxiety (III, 208);[5] he complains bitterly of having
to write under a deadline; and his love for a woman who is involved in
an affair with another man recalls Dostoevsky's painful courtship of
his first wife.[6] But above all Ivan shares the naive romantic
utopianism of the young Dostoevsky and his tragic powerlessness
before the pressures of reality. These autobiographical elements
serve a serious purpose: they show that *The Insulted and Injured* is
not merely an abstract and impersonal settling of accounts with
idealism. Through the figure of Ivan Petrovich, Dostoevsky breaks
finally with his own idealistic past.

In *The Insulted and Injured*, as later in *Winter Notes*, it seems to be
Dostoevsky's distaste for the capitalist ethic and bourgeois morality
that motivates his exposure of the naiveté of idealism. The shifting
social order of the age is symbolized in the moral decline of the
nobility, represented by the Valkovskys. The Prince has abandoned
all pretense of aristocratic honor in the pursuit of his own advantage,
for he recognizes that honor is an outmoded concept in the age of the
financial ethic. Even his simpleminded son understands this, and
complains to Natasha: "What sort of princes are we? Only by birth—
in all other respects what is there that is aristocratic about us? For a
start we have no particular wealth, and wealth is the most important
thing. Today the leading prince is Rothschild" (III, 238). The full
implications of Alesha's remarks are exposed in *The Idiot* (1868) and *A
Raw Youth* (1875), where the pecuniary ethic receives detailed treatment. The competitiveness and discord which under capitalism
dictate human relationships are in *The Insulted and Injured*—for the
first time clearly in Dostoevsky's fiction—symbolized in the image of
the city. In this passage the narrator is introducing the story of Nelly:

"This was a gloomy story, one of those gloomy and poignant stories which so often occur, imperceptibly and almost mysteriously, under the leaden St. Petersburg sky, in the dark and obscure backstreets of a large city, amongst the extravagant seething of life, the dull egoism, the conflicting interests, the sullen depravity, the secret crimes— amongst all this hell of a senseless and abnormal existence . . ." (III, 300). For Dostoevsky the nineteenth century could have found no more appropriate embodiment than the modern city for the divisive morality of capitalism.

The malevolent Valkovsky is the unacceptable face of capitalism: he has none of its industry, but all of its egoism and acquisitiveness. In a scene central to the novel's philosophical design, one which foreshadows Svidrigailov's tavern conversation with Raskolnikov in *Crime and Punishment*, he describes to Ivan his philosophy of egoism. He considers self-interest natural to human nature and al-truism as weakness or hypocrisy. He is the first to proclaim in Dos-toevsky's novels the view that "Everything is for me. The whole world was created for me" (III, 365), which in one guise or another disfigures the moral outlook of so many Dostoevskian heroes. His rejection of natural virtue is aggressively uncompromising: "I know for certain that at the basis of all human virtues lies the most profound egoism. The more virtuous a deed, the more egoism there is in it. Love oneself—that is the only law I acknowledge." Moreover, he takes perverse delight in confronting moral idealism with his own moral ugliness: "I have a characteristic which you have not yet seen—a hatred of all that banal and worthless naiveté and pas-toralism; and for me one of the most piquant pleasures has always been firstly to feign that manner, enter into the spirit, encourage and reassure some eternally young Schiller, and then suddenly discon-cert him, lift my mask before him, transform my enraptured face into a grimace, and stick out my tongue" (III, 360). Against this kind of rational malice, the four idealistic souls—Ivan, Natasha, Alesha, and Katya—are helpless; and Valkovsky manipulates them like puppets. In their helplessness they suggest the impotence of idealism in the face of evil, but they go further than this: in their behavior they confirm Valkovsky's assertion that egoism, and not idealism, is the mainspring of human nature. The apparently ideal and romantic love which unites Ivan, Natasha, and Alesha is in fact rooted in mutual torment and perverse self-hurt. Natasha illustrates this when she explains her love for Alesha to Ivan: "There is something bad about my love for him. Even in our happiest moments I foresaw that he would bring me only torment. But what can I do when from him even torment is now happiness?" (III, 199). Natasha seems to revel in this self-flagellation, as does Ivan himself by continually exposing himself to the distress caused by Natasha's infatuation with Alesha. Dostoevsky describes this subtle perversion of romantic love and Christian self-sacrifice as "the egoism of suffering" (*egoizm stradaniia*, III, 386), and it is to become a driving force behind several of his later women characters, such as Natasya Filippovna (*The Idiot*) and Liza Tushina (*The Devils*). The novel's other insulted and injured characters—Ikhmenev, Nelly, and Nelly's mother—display a similar egoism of suffering, although Alesha Valkovsky manifests a variation of it in the "naive egoism" (*naivnyi egoizm*, III, 390), concealed beneath his apparently innocent love for Natasha.

The Insulted and Injured thus presents a highly complex view of human nature, and suggests that its imperfections are beyond the healing capacities of idealism and naive utopianism. The dream of natural virtue and socialist brotherhood is once again discredited in the ironic account of the socialist discussion group to which Alesha belongs. We learn that the circle is run by Levenka and Borenka, two young men whose names derive from Levon and Borinka, the loquacious but empty-headed friends of the repulsive Repetilov in Alexander Griboedov's classic comedy, *Woe from Wit* (1825).[7] This circle and the kind of discussion it conducts have much in common with the Petrashevsky group, and the introduction of this further autobiographical detail stresses once again the origins of Dostoevsky's reappraisal of utopianism in his own spiritual development. In *The Insulted and Injured*, for the first time in Dostoevsky's novels, the idea of the spiritually healing power of suffering is opposed to the dream of heaven on earth. Natasha, always more perceptive than her partners in idealism, recognizes that it offers perhaps the only salvation for the insulted and injured human soul: "Somehow or another we have to gain our future happiness through suffering; purchase it by some new torments. Suffering will cleanse all" (III, 230). The introduction of this Christian motif marks the start of a new phase in Dostoevsky's literary career. As Mochulsky remarks: "To the humanist lie regarding man's natural sinlessness there is opposed the religious truth of original sin. The utopian idyll ended in *The House of the Dead*. The religious tragedy has begun."[8] We might dispute Mochulsky's timing of this change, but not his diagnosis.

III Notes from Underground

Dostoevsky's two-pronged attack on the ethics of reason and the insubstantial "solutions" of romantic idealism reaches its polemical climax in *Notes from Underground*, published in 1864 and written under appalling personal circumstances. Dostoevsky's first wife, Maria Dmitrievna, was dying, yet the author was obliged to continue work in order to provide material for the journal *Epoch*, which he ran with his brother as a successor to *Time*, but which was equally ill-starred. In *Notes from Underground* we stand on the threshold of Dostoevsky's maturity. The work crowns the achievements of his earlier period by synthesizing and deepening many former themes; it marks "an abrupt change in Dostoevsky's approach to characterization"[9] through its introduction of an acutely self-analytical hero, and stands as a prelude to the later novels. It is also remarkable for its new philosophical tenacity and toughness. The first of Dostoevsky's great novels of ideas, it gives philosophical respectability to many of its author's earlier preoccupations by its sharply analytical manner. In form it is highly experimental, for although ostensibly a monologue, the narrator's restless peregrination between different narrative voices and personae gives the work paradoxically greater polyphony and philosophical conflict than Dostoevsky's earlier works possessed.

In Part I of *Notes from Underground* the hero engages an imaginary interlocutor in a discussion of the nature of man which stresses the role of caprice and free will in human nature. This part, which has occasionally been published separately, is a bitter attack on scientific determinism and all philosophies which assert the primacy of necessity in human behavior. In stressing the importance of conscious free choice and diminishing the role of reason, self-interest, and contingency in human motivation, it is truly "the best overture for existentialism ever written."[10] Part II is a fictional pendant to Part I, both in its illustration of the hero's philosophical and psychological credo and in its subtle undercutting of his assumptions about himself. He relates an event which occurred many years earlier, when he indulged his love of capricious self-laceration by attending a dinner for a colleague whom he despised. The incident brings anguish to both the hero and his colleagues, but he perversely prolongs his offense against seemliness and at the same time he secretly smolders with the desire for reconciliation with those he despises. He follows

them to a bordello, where he channels all his accumulated spite into
the ruthless emotional blackmail of a naive young prostitute, Liza.
When he has won Liza's trust and unsettled her with dreams of
reform and idyllic family life, he reasserts his emotional and moral
independence by paying for her services and thus confirming her
inferiority to him.

By all standards *Notes from Underground* is one of the strangest
and most urgent works of modern fiction. "Easily assimilated only by
a profoundly diseased spiritual organism,"[11] it has found in modern
urban man the ideally sympathetic reader, and in twentieth-century
Existentialism a fuller discussion of its speculation about the nature of
man. It is perhaps the greatest critique of narrow intellectualism and
overrefined consciousness ever written, as well as a disturbing rejection of the ideals of the Enlightenment. Yet, as was always the case
with Dostoevsky's mature work, the universal philosophical significance of *Notes from Underground* required the impetus of immediate
polemic to give it form. It was intended as a refutation of the ideas of
Nikolay Chernyshevsky (1828–89), a leading materialist philosopher,
whose works—including the essay *The Anthropological Principle in
Philosophy* (1860) and the novel *What Is to Be Done?* (1863)—had
generated considerable interest by their assertion that the apparent
complexity of human behavior could be explained on the basis of
scientifically determinable principles. A disciple of Bentham and
Mill, Chernyshevsky held that self-interest was a primary impulse in
human nature, but that through the exercise of reason it could be
made to coincide with the interests of society as a whole. He used the
image of the Crystal Palace, built in London to house the 1851 World
Exhibition, as a symbol of the future rational, technological utopia.
Chernyshevsky's faith in rational self-interest, so clearly derived from
Enlightenment ideals, offended Dostoevsky by stripping man of his
mystery, by defining his behavior as the inevitable outcome of scientific law, and by depriving him of a soul and moral freedom, the two
aspects of his being which, according to Christianity, could alone
bring him to salvation.[12] The hero of *Notes from Underground* was
conceived as the rotten apple in Chernyshevsky's barrel, an exaggerated incarnation of the perversity which is in all men, and which
dissolves the foundations of all rational utopianism. He shrieks his
revolt against determinism with hysterical insistence, but his voice is
not Dostoevsky's. In this work, as elsewhere, we must acknowledge
the primary law of Dostoevsky's artistic world: his characters speak
for themselves and not necessarily for their author. Dostoevsky's

dislike of scientific determinism was as keen as the Underground Man's, but that does not imply that he sympathized with the alternatives offered by his hero.

The Underground Man considers his condition representative, albeit extreme: "I have merely taken to its limits that which you are afraid to take half-way" (V, 178), he rebukes his reader. Moreover, he emphasizes that he and his behavior are very symptomatic of the nineteenth century, which he describes as "the age of negation" (V, 110), in clear contrast to the affirmative spirit of the Enlightenment. Negation is the essence of his revolt, as he zealously defends his freedom from the encroachment of anything that would limit it. A finely tuned consciousness is his key tactical weapon in this struggle: he constantly analyzes his behavior, ever alert—*en marge,* in the currency of Existentialism—to the dangers of consequentiality, contingency, and necessity, which in ordinary life prevent man from acting freely, consciously, and capriciously. He argues that man, in order to live authentically as a self-creating being, must resist all self-definition and refuse to submit to anything which would impair his freedom, even if this means acting against his own self-interest, flying in the face of reason, and rebelling against the very laws of nature. Here we see him for what he is: the antithesis spawned by the theses of the Enlightenment pushed to their logical limits, where they yield to absurdity. The Underground Man tries to get himself thrown from a billiard-room window, for he knows that such an act, although against his immediate self-interest, serves "a more advantageous advantage" (V, 111): the right to assert "his own willful, free volition, his own caprice, however wild, his own fantasy, inflamed sometimes to the point of madness" (V, 113). He acknowledges the logic of mathematics, but reserves for himself the right to make two and two add up to five if he wishes, for "twice two is four is no longer life, gentlemen, but the beginning of death" (V, 118–19). He submits to no scientific or natural law, for although he might accept its validity, he will not be imprisoned by that acceptance: "What are all these laws of nature and arithmetic to me if I don't happen to like them?" (V, 105). Suffering and pain are the usual outcome of such revolt, but even here the Underground Man derives an advantage, for suffering further refines consciousness and closes the circle of revolt.

The normal man of limited consciousness, bred in the lap of nature and not in the retort of self-analysis, lacks the Underground Man's existential freedom, but he does retain the ability to act. The conscious man acts when he has found grounds for action, but the heightened consciousness of the Underground Man dissolves every impulse to action in a sea of analysis, doubt, and contradiction. Like Hamlet, the Underground Man discovers that "the direct, immediate and legitimate fruit of consciousness is inertia" (V, 108):

> And thus the native hue of resolution
> Is sicklied o'er with the pale cast of thought.
>
> (*Hamlet*, Act III, Scene 1)

Here is the paradox in the Underground Man's stance: "all consciousness is an illness" (V, 102), and he envies the natural man's capacity for action, but at the same time he despises him for his stupidity. His own "freedom" is constraining, for he cannot move without compromising it. His self-denial at the end of Part I, when he insists that he has been lying "like a cobbler" (V, 121), shows us how demanding his freedom is: he must reject all he has said in order to avoid self-definition as a man who avoids self-definition! Such freedom is a denial of freedom; it is entirely negative, and saps the will it is supposed to liberate. As A.D. Nuttall observes,[13] the Underground Man is on the run, forever obliged to confirm his frail and sterile freedom in ever more' outrageous outbursts of irrationality. In the words of Michael Holquist, "he is constantly making experiments in ontology, a mad scientist in the cluttered laboratory of his own identity."[14]

In his flight from the constraints of reason and necessity the hero of *Notes from Underground* incarnates the spirit of Romantic Man, and his Romanticism is particularly evident in his love of paradox and the exotic, as well as—equally importantly—in his literariness and responsiveness to the "noble and the beautiful" (V, 132). He is a romantic dreamer like Ordynov. Dreams provide an alternative retreat from the trials of reality and create an evanescent illusion of freedom. Throughout his confession the hero's constant rationalization of circumstances is matched by an equally constant tendency to refashion the reality of his existence into "beautiful forms of being" (V, 133). He dreams of reconciliation he cannot attain, of love, friendship, and acceptance, and his dreams ennoble his squalid existence. He is, as Holquist carefully demonstrates, engaged in the Existential task of writing his own libretto of life, but he has "no rules to guide him except those which derive from his reading."[15] He is acutely aware of his own bookishness, in both the episode with his colleagues and his attempts to "save" Liza. Tragically, however, his razor-sharp consciousness also penetrates the illusions of romantic idealism. He cannot believe in his dreams, but the contrast between the impossible freedom and beauty of his fiction and the unseemly constraints of the real world inflames his spite still further. "They won't let me . . . . I can't . . . be good!" he sobs to Liza (V, 175), but this is because his concept of good is impossibly romantic, and he will not accept second best. He will be "either a hero or filth" (V, 133), and retreats to the Underground, his personal limbo located between fact and fiction, to feed on his wounded pride and take perverse pleasure in the piquant contrast of ideal and reality.

But the Underground affords no real retreat, and in the two concluding chapters of Part I the hero sees through its sham. "To hell with the Underground!" he cries, and goes on to put into the mouth of his imaginary interlocutor his most telling reservations. He recognizes that he is trying to escape the prison of reason through *rationalization* of his fears. He uses reason to expose both its own inadequacy and the insubstantiality of dreaming, but he never transcends it. His unreason is always reasoned, bred in the retort of his intellect. He complains that reason suppresses life, yet he knows nothing of life outside his Underground, which is itself a trap sprung by consciousness. His revolt is intellectual only—he lives vicariously within the confines of his own consciousness, effectively defusing his enthusiasm for "living life" (*zhivaia zhizn'*, V, 176). The affair with Liza confirms the life-denying qualities of the Underground Man. This deformed product of reason's retort, this captive of consciousness, defiles the simple, innocent life of the young prostitute. Life, in the guise of Liza, becomes the sacrificial victim of his rational spite. He might assert his independence and intellectual courage, but he is afraid of life. "You thirst for life, but resolve life's questions with logical confusion . . . and how afraid you are!" he reasons with himself. "There is some justice in your stance, but no moral purity" (V, 121). He prides himself on his consciousness, but this leads him only to sophistry. His heart remains uneducated, and "without a pure heart, full, correct consciousness is impossible" (V, 122). This idea that rational consciousness deforms "living life" will become an important motif in Dostoevsky's great novels, particularly in *Crime and Punishment* and *The Brothers Karamazov*.

Dostoevsky intended at the end of Part I to advocate Christian faith as a means of attaining moral freedom without falling into the trap of consciousness, but his design was frustrated by the intervention of

the censor, who balked at the thought of Gospel passages emanating
from this hero's profaned lips. His cuts outraged Dostoevsky: "That
swine of a censor. The passages where I jeered at everything and
sometimes blasphemed *for form's sake* he let through, but he suppressed the place where from all this I deduced the need for faith and
Christ."[16]

So the Underground Man remains unredeemed, all his rhetorical
flourish merely an attempt to dignify the fact that he is a squalid,
pathetic, and impotent egoist. His unreconciled contradictions,
which always threaten to disperse his being in a chain reaction of
denial, are conveyed in the chorus of dissonant "voices" which constantly strain against the "monologic" form of the confession.[17] On
the unstable interface where two worlds touch—the real, with its
intractable and inhibiting laws of nature, and the ideal, with its
deceptive liberation through the fiction of "the noble and
beautiful"—the Underground Man carves out a third, the Underground itself. But his world is founded only upon perversity and
denial, as he confronts the rational world with its absurdities and
rebukes the romantic, ideal world for its groundless utopianism. He
never really escapes the currency of either reason or romanticism, as
his flair for intellectual paradox and romantic literariness confirms,
and in rejecting the ethics of reason and romance he fails to generate
an alternative. In his Underground he prides himself on his
privileged vantage point, lacerates himself with his own estrangement, and delights in the intoxicating vertigo, which he believes
derives from his being above morality, but which his ignorance of life
suggests is the consequence of his being beneath it.

The test-tube man, infected with the very reason he despises, must
discover other perceptual avenues into the world of "living life," must
learn how to love life without necessarily understanding its rationale,
and thereby regain the harmony with life which reason itself destroyed at the time of the Fall, and which reason tried unsuccessfully
to rebuild in the aspirations of the Enlightenment. Partly through his
own spiritual poverty, and partly through the monumental stupidity
of Dostoevsky's censor, the hero of *Notes from Underground* fails to
achieve all this. Raskolnikov, his successor in *Crime and Punishment*,
is much more successful in his step toward salvation.

CHAPTER 4

The Principle of Uncertainty: Crime and Punishment

It is the psychological account of a crime. The action is contemporary, taking place in the present year. A young man, sent down from university, from a middle-class family and living in dire poverty, through thoughtlessness and some shaky notions, having fallen under the spell of some of these strange, "half-baked" ideas that are floating about in the air, has decided to break out of his appalling situation in one go. He decides to murder an old woman, the wife of a titular councillor, who lends money at interest. The old woman is stupid, deaf, ill and greedy. She demands a Jew's percentage. She is evil and oppresses another person in that she torments her younger sister who keeps house for her. "She's not fit for anything." "Why does she live?" "Is she of any use to anyone at all?" etc.—such questions confuse the young man. He decides to kill her and steal her money in order to help his mother, who is living in the district, and to save his sister, who lives as a paid companion in a landowning family, from the lascivious demands of the head of that family— demands that threaten her with ruin. Also to finish his studies, to go abroad and then for the rest of his days to be honest, steadfast and unflinching in fulfilling his "humane debt to mankind," which will of course "expiate his crime," if, indeed, the word crime can be applied to such an act against a deaf, stupid, wicked and sick old woman, who does not herself know why she lives, and who might die anyway in a month's time. . . .

He passes almost a month after the crime before the final catastrophe. Nobody suspects him, nor could they. And here the whole psychological process of the crime unfolds. Insoluble questions confront the murderer, unsuspected and unanticipated feelings torment his heart. Divine justice and the earthly law claim their rights, and in the end he is *compelled* to give himself up, compelled so that even if he is to perish in penal servitude he might once again be united with people; the feeling of separation and isolation from mankind, which he has experienced since the crime was committed, torments him. The law of justice and human nature take their course and destroy his convictions with little difficulty. The criminal himself decides to accept suffering in order to expiate his deed. But here I find it hard to elaborate my thought fully.

Apart from this there is in my tale a suggestion that the criminal fears the prescribed judicial punishment for a crime less than the lawyers think, partly because *he himself experiences a moral need for it.* (VII, 310–11)

The above is taken from a letter Dostoevsky wrote in September 1865 to M. N. Katkov, the editor of the journal *Russian Herald,* asking for an advance against a proposed novel. It provides a useful plot summary of the work which was to become *Crime and Punishment* and which appeared in Katkov's journal in 1866. Already in this draft we can recognize the student Raskolnikov, his poverty, his intoxication with currently fashionable utilitarian ideas, and his fierce pride which will not allow him to let his mother and his sister, Dunya, fall into the clutches of the wealthy landowners Svidrigailov and Luzhin. We also recognize the old moneylender, Alena Ivanovna, and her sister Lizaveta, who become the victims of Raskolnikov's "utilitarian" crime. Finally, Dostoevsky stresses to Katkov another striking feature which survives into the finished novel: the criminal's own search for punishment which leads him to suffering and salvation.

For the final version of the novel Dostoevsky combined these motifs with ideas from another work he had planned in the early 1860s. This was to have been called "Pyanenkie" [The Drunkards] and was to have dealt with the current wave of drunkenness in Russia by concentrating upon its effects on the family. This theme, continued in the novel as a subplot, allows Dostoevsky to introduce two important characters: Marmeladov, the self-destructive drunkard, and his daughter Sonya, a sentimental prostitute who makes a significant contribution to Raskolnikov's salvation.

I   *The Search for a Motive*

One feature mentioned in the letter to Katkov that did not, however, survive is the sureness with which the central character and his motivations are delineated. As the novel grew under Dostoevsky's pen, his notebooks and drafts show that he went from uncertainty to uncertainty in depicting Raskolnikov and his crime, even jotting down reminders to himself to elucidate the murderer's motives more clearly.[1] It would be easy enough to conclude from this that Dostoevsky at the time of writing to Katkov had simply not suspected the full richness and potential of his character and his theme, but this would be too simple a conclusion. Uncertainty is an important artistic principle in much of Dostoevsky's work, and it is at the very heart of *Crime and Punishment*. As Philip Rahv has written: "The indeterminacy is the point. Dostoevsky is the first novelist to have fully accepted and dramatized the principle of uncertainty or indeterminacy in the presentation of character."[2]

In *Crime and Punishment* Dostoevsky sacrifices to the principle of uncertainty many of the conventional prerogatives of the novelist: his most far-reaching sacrifice was that of omniscience. In this work the novelist looks at the world through the eyes of an Einstein, not of a Newton. He deliberately eschews the omniscient or "God's eye" point of view; he rejects the possibility of a narrator who has an absolute vantage point which allows him to see events in a perspective not accessible to the characters in the work. In *Crime and Punishment* the narrator enjoys no consistent perceptual advantage over the participants: he sees the world through the same haze of subjective uncertainty as Raskolnikov does. It is this above all else that gives the novel its permanently nightmarish quality.

The most obvious manifestation of this kind of uncertainty is in the presentation of motive. Raskolnikov becomes a "criminal in search of his own motive;"[3] he does not in the end know why he committed his crime, and neither does the reader. The narrator offers us no definite explanation, only a share in Raskolnikov's confusion. The Katkov letter shows that Dostoevsky originally conceived Raskolnikov's crime as a means of exposing the absurdity of the moral utilitarianism characteristic of many leading intellectuals in the 1860s, most notably Chernyshevsky. *Crime and Punishment* was to be a polemical novel continuing the campaign against Chernyshevsky and his followers begun in *Notes from Underground*. The philosophic materialists of the 1860s, who exercised enormous influence particularly over the younger generation, attempted to bring to the solution of moral questions the same confidence and certainty that modern scientific analysis had brought to the solution of empirical questions. Reason, they argued, had yielded great insights into the workings of the natural world; could it not also yield a more scientific approach to the traditionally difficult yet no less pressing problems of the moral world? Man's capacity for rational analysis and understanding grew with each generation, yet still he based his moral behavior upon inherited and ill-defined notions of right and wrong. In attempting to apply scientific principles to ethical and moral questions, Chernyshevsky and his contemporaries fell into a crude moral utilitarianism that was roughly based on the notions of self-interest and the greatest good for the greatest number. Philosophical utilitarianism in the hands of Chernyshevsky degenerated into a vulgar materialism and narrow rationalism which Dostoevsky came to abhor. In *Notes from Underground* he had strikingly demonstrated that all human behavior could not be reduced to rational self-interest and considerations of strict utility. In *Crime and Punishment* he wanted to show that the application of these principles was less likely to lead to morally enlightened behavior than to barbarism. Raskolnikov's thought processes, as outlined in the Katkov letter, illustrate this point: for the greater good of humanity at large and his worthy family in particular, Raskolnikov is prepared to murder a fellow human being.

The utilitarian principle undoubtedly remains a major aspect of Raskolnikov's crime in the finished novel. Indeed, he does not finally renounce it until his conversion in the Epilogue. In a conversation with Dunya late in the novel he vigorously defends the morality of his crime in utilitarian terms: "'Crime? What crime!' he cried in a sort of sudden frenzy. 'That I killed a vile, harmful louse, an old hag of a moneylender of no use to anybody, for whose murder one should be forgiven forty sins, and who bled poor people dry. Can that be called a crime? I don't think about it, and I have no desire to wipe it out'" (VI, 400). But the utilitarian ethic alone can satisfy the demands of neither the reader nor Raskolnikov himself for a comprehensive explanation of his act. In a sense, this affirms Dostoevsky's point that the complex and often contradictory impulses behind human action cannot in the end be reduced to simple causal chains or primary motives. But Raskolnikov, as a "man of the sixties," cannot countenance the possibility that he has committed an irrational or irreducible act. He craves a comprehensive motive to restore his belief in the lucidity of human values and behavior. Yet rational utilitarianism is not adequate to the task, and he loses himself in the maze of his own personality. He embarks upon his crime ostensibly with the aim of robbery to further the fortunes of himself and other socially worthy people at the expense of a worthless parasite—a simple and logical adjustment of society's faulty arithmetic. Yet he fails to ascertain in advance the extent and whereabouts of his victim's wealth; he leaves with only a few cheap trinkets which he soon abandons under a stone and never reclaims. At no stage does he consider the possibility of appropriating the old woman's wealth without resorting to murder. It quickly becomes obvious that Raskolnikov has not murdered in order to steal; he has fabricated a shabby robbery in order to murder. He has only murder on his mind, not the appropriation and redistribution of wealth.

After the murder the utilitarian motive slips farther and farther into the background as Raskolnikov's probing intellect discerns the shapes of other and more disturbing implications of his act. It is worth remembering that he is rarely troubled by the murder of Lizaveta, the innocent victim of an unanticipated turn of events. This second killing does not engage his concern, for it was an unpremeditated, simple, even "innocent" slaying with a clear motive: Raskolnikov killed Lizaveta in order to escape. It is the "rationally justified" murder of the old hag that gnaws at his soul and that in the end he cannot account for.

Porfiry Petrovich, the examining magistrate, is the first to associate the murder with the ideas expounded in an article of Raskolnikov's on crime, and thus to open the way to an explanation of the crime, not in terms of Raskolnikov's professed utilitarian altruism, but in the light of his insane pride, egoism, and craving for power. Raskolnikov's article, published without his knowledge, is a product of the narrow, cloistered intellectualism which characterizes the young ex-student and makes it so difficult for him to enter the mainstream of life. It is composed of the cramped and arid thoughts engendered by the coffinlike room in which he leads only the ghost of a life. The article divides humanity into two distinct categories: the *Supermen*, such as Newton and Napoleon, who by virtue of their originality, strength of will, or daring, write their names boldly in the history of human achievement; and the *Lice*, the ordinary men and women who are the bricks and not the architects of history and who contribute nothing new. The former, according to Raskolnikov, have an inherent right to moral and intellectual freedom; they create their own laws and may overstep the bounds of conventional law and morality. The latter are condemned by their ordinariness to a life of submission to common law and common morality; their sole function is to breed in the hope of one day giving birth to a Superman.

Clearly belief in any such division of humanity must tempt the man of pride into a harrowing dilemma of self-definition; and Raskolnikov is a man of immense pride. Does he therefore murder in the conviction that, as a superior man, he has the right to brush aside conventional morality in order to expedite the contribution he must make to history? This is unlikely, for, although Raskolnikov is seduced by his pride into longing for the status of Superman, his persistent doubts as he plans and rehearses the murder reveal all too clearly his uncertainty and fear of the Superman's freedom. Is the crime therefore conceived as a grotesque act of self-definition, whereby by assessing his reaction to moral transgression Raskolnikov seeks to choose his true self from the differing options offered by his pride and his uncertainty? This affords a tantalizingly plausible explanation of the murder; after all, we would expect the abstract Raskolnikov to respond most readily to abstract motives. Somehow it is impossible to imagine this unphysical intellectual murdering in response to such physical needs as hunger or want; but we can imagine him chasing the specter of self-knowledge. Moreover, Raskolnikov's need of self-definition is acute; in the novel's early chapters he oscillates wildly between satanic pride and abject humility, between unbounded admiration for the strong and limitless pity for the weak. For example, soon after returning from a dress rehearsal for the killing which will set him beyond morality into a realm of godlike ethical freedom, he falls into paroxysms of despair and commits himself into God's hands: "Lord! Show me my way, and I'll tear myself away from this accursed . . . dream of mine!" (VI, 50). Shortly before this, an episode in which Raskolnikov witnesses the attempts of a predatory male to take advantage of a frightened and abused girl clearly highlights his divided loyalties. The purposeful man and the humiliated girl represent the two categories of humanity described in Raskolnikov's article, for the man is prepared to sacrifice both conventional morality and the girl to satisfy his own will. Raskolnikov's initial response is one of compassion for the suffering girl; he intervenes, calls a policeman, and offers the girl money. But "at that moment it was as if something had stung Raskolnikov; in an instant he seemed to become a different man" (VI, 42). Suddenly his pity for the girl becomes scorn, and he yields her to the libertine. The duality of Raskolnikov's response is underlined later by his friend Razumikhin's comment that "it is as if there are two opposing personalities in him, each taking turns for supremacy" (VI, 165).

But the crime could be an authentic attempt at the resolution of this duality only if Raskolnikov were genuinely uncertain to which category of humanity he belonged, and this is not the case. In his pride he might long to be a Napoleon, but he knows that he is a louse, knows it *even before he commits the crime*, as he later acknowledges: "and the reason why I am finally a louse is because I am perhaps even nastier and viler than the louse I killed, and I felt *beforehand* that I would say that to myself *after* I had killed her" (VI, 211). The implications of this admission are startling: Raskolnikov embarked upon the murder of the old woman knowing in advance that he had no right to kill and no clear motive, and, moreover, clearly anticipating the destructive effect such an act would have upon the rest of his life. Perhaps it is this he has in mind when he later asserts: "Did I really kill the old hag? I killed myself, not the old hag! At that moment in one blow I did away with myself for good!" (VI, 322). This feature of Raskolnikov's behavior illustrates the incompatibility of knowledge and pride. Raskolnikov's knowledge that he is ordinary and has no special right to overstep conventional moral limits cannot contain his proud and essentially irrational need to assert himself. In the end his crime is an act of terrifying inconsequence: a proud, petulant, and meaningless protest against the certain knowledge that he is not superior; a moment when the demands of frustrated pride are so insistent that he is prepared to sacrifice the whole of his future to them. "I simply killed; I killed for myself, for myself alone, and at that moment it was all the same to me whether I became some sort of benefactor of humanity or spent the rest of my life catching people in my web and sucking the life forces out of them like a spider" (VI, 322).[4]

This view of Raskolnikov's crime as an act of defiant, directionless, self-damaging aggression is clarified by the character of Marmeladov, the ex–civil servant whom Raskolnikov meets in a tavern and with whose family he later becomes involved. Dostoevsky's novels frequently explore aspects of the central hero by investing secondary characters with these same features in an exaggerated form. In this way the demonic Svidrigailov helps our understanding of Raskolnikov's will to power, and the meek Sonya clarifies his opposing streak of humility.[5] Likewise, Marmeladov helps us comprehend the importance of thwarted ambition in the execution of Raskolnikov's crime. Like Raskolnikov, Marmeladov willfully embarks upon acts which he knows will merely expose his mediocrity. He regularly abases himself before his fellow drinkers in the tavern; he takes great pains to demonstrate his worthlessness; he freely proclaims that his wife pulls his hair and that through his own fault his daughter Sonya has become a prostitute. He confesses that he sells his wife's stockings for drink—"her stockings, mark you, not her shoes, for that at least might somehow approximate to the normal order of things, but her stockings! I drank away her stockings, sir!" (VI, 15). Like Raskolnikov, Marmeladov hurts himself out of petulant, inverted pride. He keenly feels his inferiority—particularly by comparison to his wife's previous, though mostly imaginary, social grandeur—but knows that he cannot overcome it. His pride consequently seeks a perverse satisfaction in behavior that confirms and exaggerates his humble status. It is a common paradox of Dostoevsky's world that an act of self-hurt and self-abasement can be the expression of unlimited pride denied a more direct outlet. So in the end Raskolnikov's crime is revealed as neither the conscious outcome of a rationally defined ethic nor the deliberate transgression of a free man pursuing a moral course of his own making. The young student's attempts to invoke such motives are mocked by the terrifying emptiness of his act, which he comes to recognize as a Marmeladov-like gesture of aimless defiance, undignified by motive, uninhibited by considerations of reason and self-interest, and obstinately unyielding to analysis.

II   Time and Space

In *Crime and Punishment* the principle of uncertainty encompasses more than the question of motivation. Even the spatial and temporal coordinates of the novel are blurred and at times distorted by a narrator whose precise nature and point of view are neither clearly defined nor absolutely fixed. The notebooks reveal that the adoption of a narrative point of view presented Dostoevsky with his greatest difficulty in writing the novel. He originally planned to use the first-person confession form, which would have allowed direct and easy access to the thought processes of the hero, but which would have created real difficulties when it came to filling in the objective details of the world in which the murderer moves. Dostoevsky wrestled with this form until the third and final draft, when a new approach occurred to him: "Narration from point of view of author, a sort of invisible but omniscient being who doesn't leave his hero for a moment" (VII, 146). The third-person narrator anticipated in this comment is retained for the novel itself, but his omniscience is open to doubt. Complete omniscience would have robbed the novel of its haunting uncertainty and provided the reader too clear an insight into Raskolnikov's behavior and motivation. As Gary Rosenshield has argued, the success of the narrator in the final version derives from his "selective omniscience."[6] This is achieved by a mobile point of view, whereby at certain times the narrator describes the objective world, at other times the world as refracted through Raskolnikov's consciousness. The result is a confusion of dream and reality and a warping of the reader's sense of duration and location. The first chapter illustrates this particularly well, as the alleys of St.

Petersburg, with their stifling heat, dust, stuffiness, and smells, are conveyed to the reader in terms of the impression they make upon Raskolnikov. These details of the physical world, in passing through Raskolnikov's awareness, lose their tactile and sensual authenticity and are transformed into psychological stimuli. Thus we have no sense of the stifling July heat penetrating Raskolnikov's body as the summer sun burns Levin in the famous reaping scene in Tolstoy's *Anna Karenina*. Instead it sears his mind. Raskilnikov seems to lack all sensual awareness: sense impressions are conveyed in relation to his frame of mind. The physical world thus becomes a confirmation and externalization of the hero's inner world. The stuffy heat speaks not of physical suffocation, but of Raskolnikov's mental and moral claustrophobia. Only when the narrator breaks the subjective spell to give us a brief description of Raskolnikov's physical appearance do we experience a sense of concrete, objectively confirmed detail (VI, 6).

In much the same way our sense of real space is distorted by this subjective third-person narrative. Many years after the appearance of *Crime and Punishment* Einstein argued that we cannot experience space in the abstract, independent of the matter that fills it; and it is Raskolnikov's consciousness that fills this novel. Like a gravitational field, it warps the space around it. For example, the description of Raskolnikov's room as seen through Raskolnikov's eyes at the start of the novel is uncomfortably inconsistent with objectively narrated events which occur in this same room later. The room appears to shift its size with the narrative point of view. The early description is clearly conditioned by Raskolnikov's own sensations of claustrophobia: he is oppressed and haunted by ideas, theories, pride, poverty, and illness, and the room he describes with hatred upon waking from a restless sleep resembles a tomb. A mere six feet long, not high enough for a man to stand, littered with dusty books, its yellow wallpaper peeling from the walls, it is dominated by a huge, clumsy sofa (VI, 25). The description accords so perfectly with what we know of Raskolnikov's state of mind that we hardly distinguish where his consciousness ends and the outside world begins. Yet a few chapters later, as Raskolnikov lies in bed semidelirious after the crime and the narrative adopts a more objective course in order to permit the introduction of several new characters, our sense of the room's size is quite different. As the sick Raskolnikov is visited by his maid Nastasya, his friend Razumikhin, the doctor Zosimov, and his sister's suitor Luzhin, the "tomb" seems to open out in order to accommodate each new arrival.

Distance is equally intangible. When, in Chapter 1, Raskolnikov visits his victim's flat, we have no real sensation of his physically moving from one environment to another. Dostoevsky tells us that "exactly seven hundred and thirty" paces separate the pawnbroker's flat from Raskolnikov's hovel, but the precision of this figure is entirely numerical. Locked inside Raskolnikov's consciousness as he rehearses a multitude of doubts and hesitations, we measure the physical distance only in terms of the number of thoughts which flash through his mind.

But the most uncertain quantity of all is time. Nearly all readers of *Crime and Punishment* experience the loss of a sense of duration in the course of the novel. It seems hardly possible, but the entire action requires only two weeks, and Part I a mere three days. Directed by the narrative mode into the inner world of Raskolnikov's turbulent imagination, we lose our temporal reference points. Absolute time ceases to be; we know time only as Raskolnikov experiences it. At moments it is severely retarded—indeed, in Part I, as Raskolnikov prepares for the kill, its flow is all but arrested; later the sense of time is violently accelerated as Raskolnikov undergoes the vertiginous fall from his crime to his confession. In this way time becomes a function of consciousness: Rahv draws a significant parallel between Dostoevsky's use of time and the *durée réelle* of the French philosopher Henri Bergson.[7] We might go further and suggest an analogy with Einsteinian time, which, like Dostoevsky's, depends fundamentally upon point of view. For Einstein there could be no absolute time: the time experienced by separate observers differed according to their relative motion. Dostoevsky seems to be suggesting something very similar in a cryptic remark in the drafts for *Crime and Punishment*: "What is time? Time does not exist; time is only numbers. Time is the relation of what exists to what does not exist" (VII, 161). This remark might perhaps be interpreted as meaning that there is no abstract, absolute time. Time exists only when actualized in an event or series of events. The importance of this for *Crime and Punishment* is that events and their duration are experienced differently by different observers. Through Raskolnikov's consciousness the reader of the novel observes only the hero's experiences of intervals between events. There are no events narrated with consistent objectivity which form reference points against which to judge Raskolnikov's sense of time.

III *Point of View and the Secondary Characters*

We can express these ideas in another form: when the narrative of *Crime and Punishment* is in its subjective mode, as it is for much of the time, Raskolnikov's consciousness threatens to deprive the outside world of its *otherness*, of its objective reality. It not only devours objective space and time, it also colors the reader's view of other characters. Nearly all the characters in the novel are presented in terms of their relevance to Raskolnikov; few survive the discoloring effects of his dominant presence. The weakly presented Sonya soon loses all traces of "otherness," of independence, and becomes merely a pledge of Raskolnikov's salvation through humility and suffering. The fascinating Svidrigailov resists absorption longer, but in the end is identified with Raskolnikov's alternative fate, that of pride, will, and death. Razumikhin does escape absorption completely, and his name—deriving as it does from the word *razum* (reason, intelligence)—suggests his role as a moderating presence, a touchstone of reality. Dostoevsky's lesser characters contrast interestingly with those of Tolstoy. In *Anna Karenina* the Oblonskys and Levins stand partly inside and partly outside Anna's world, and they broaden the novel by creating and sustaining the impression of a real world of alternatives. The secondary personages in *Crime and Punishment* afford no such refuge from the commanding consciousness of the central character.

This can be illustrated in many ways. Marmeladov, for instance, seems to exist only to clarify Raskolnikov's humiliated pride. The entrance of Svidrigailov (VI, 213–14) is marked by a confusion of dream and reality; for a while we are uncertain that he exists at all. But the finest example of a character losing his "otherness" in the presence of Raskolnikov's consciousness is found in the detective, Porfiry Petrovich, who is gradually transformed from genial policeman to the very incarnation of Raskolnikov's need to be discovered. R. P. Blackmur has suggested that had Porfiry not existed Raskolnikov would have had to invent him,[8] and in a very real sense Raskolnikov does invent this subtle and all-knowing detective who finally confronts him with his own guilt. An interesting feature of *Crime and Punishment* is the way Raskolnikov, to borrow Edward Wasiolek's expression, "is not running away from the crime but *toward* it."[9] This feature is anticipated in the letter to Katkov, where Dostoevsky writes of the murderer's compulsion to give himself up. In the novel, through a combination of despair, pride, disgust, rebellion, and alienation, Raskolnikov deliberately provokes suspicion against himself. He revisits the scene of the crime and arouses the suspicion of the house painters; he deliberately toys with the police official, Zametov, almost confessing to him on one occasion (VI, 125–26); and he is drawn into three encounters with Porfiry, encounters which illustrate superbly Dostoevsky's creation of uncertainty through the use of a mobile point of view.

Raskolnikov is drawn to Porfiry like a moth to a candle, a comparison Raskolnikov himself employs on his way to their first encounter (VI, 190). The transformation and assimilation of Porfiry begin almost as soon as they meet. The affable detective suddenly winks mockingly at Raskolnikov, and this leads the young student to believe that Porfiry knows everything. For a moment he thinks that his imagination is running away with him: "What if this is a mirage and I'm wrong about everything . . . . Perhaps there is no ulterior motive here?" (VI, 195). And of course it is an illusion, created by the fact that both our and Raskolnikov's views of Porfiry are colored by the criminal's desire for arrest. Only a few pages earlier a more objectively narrated account of Porfiry's physical appearance allows a less disturbing explanation of his strange wink: "Porfiry's face would even have been good-natured, were it not for the expression in his eyes—a sort of wet, watery glint—and his eyelashes, almost white and blinking, *conveying the impression that Porfiry was winking at somebody*" (VI, 192: my italics).

By his interpretation of Porfiry's wink Raskolnikov begins to rob Porfiry of his objectivity. At times from this point onward the conversation with Porfiry seems uncannily like a monologue in which Raskolnikov rehearses and analyzes his own doubts about his crime and his right to kill. For example, Porfiry remarks: "But tell me this: how can one distinguish these extraordinary people from the ordinary ones? Are there any special signs at birth? . . . Because, you must agree, should any confusion arise and a member of one category think he really belongs to the other and start to 'eliminate all obstacles,' as you so happily put it, then—" (VI, 201). Porfiry has here restated Raskolnikov's initial uncertainty, as well as his pride and his realization that he has transgressed without a moral right to do so. In reply Raskolnikov describes how such people—and he has himself in mind—would behave after such an unjustified crime: "You won't even need to employ anyone to whip them, they will do it themselves, because they are very well-behaved. . . . Moreover, they will impose various public penances upon themselves; the result is both beautiful and edifying . . ." (VI, 202). This is precisely what Raskolnikov is doing in seeking out Porfiry and mentally transforming him: he is "whipping himself" and doing penance.

Porfiry's apparently uncanny ability to restate Raskolnikov's earlier thought processes with remarkable exactness is exhibited in the subsequent encounters between the two characters. He discusses in principle many of Raskolnikov's own specific fears, including the fear of not knowing whether one is under suspicion or not (VI, 261). At times he even poaches precise turns of phrase from Raskolnikov's mind: he repeats the image of a moth being drawn to a candle (VI, 262); he even—and this is the most uncanny coincidence of all—repeats *word for word* a rather striking piece of advice given earlier to Raskolnikov by Svidrigailov, when nobody else—least of all Porfiry—was within earshot. During the funeral service for Mrs. Marmeladova, Svidrigailov had urged Raskolnikov to come and see him with the words: "Take heart. Let's have a talk sometime. . . . Ah, Rodion Romanych, what all men need is air, air, air! That above all!" (VI, 336). In their final meeting Porfiry urges Raskolnikov to give himself up, saying: "Life will pull you through. You'll get to like it yourself afterwards. All you need now is air, air, air!" Raskolnikov is so taken aback by the repetition of so cryptic a remark that for a moment he too seems to doubt Porfiry's objectivity: "Raskilnikov shuddered. 'Who are you?' he cried. 'What sort of prophet are you?'" (VI, 351–52). Psychological insight may be invoked to explain Porfiry's profound understanding of Raskolnikov's nature, but not even the cleverest psychology can allow a man to read another's mind as clearly as this.

Occasionally, as the result of either a deliberate shift in point of view or a moment of clarity for Raskolnikov, the real Porfiry displaces the subjective one. For example, when Raskolnikov breaks down before him and invites the detective to arrest him, a totally new and strange Porfiry emerges, one who is not only genuinely concerned and upset, but who also seems to believe that Raskolnikov is innocent and the victim of a persecution complex (VI, 264–65). Reconciliation of these inconsistencies in Porfiry's behavior is possible if we acknowledge the existence of two Porfirys, the real and the imagined, whom we see alternately as the narrative point of view oscillates.

Dostoevsky's treatment of Porfiry can be profitably discussed in Bakhtin's terminology. Bakhtin argues that Dostoevsky's polyphonic novels sustain many separate points of view and many separate character "voices" which are not synthesized or "monologized" by a commanding narrative voice. Raskolnikov's oscillating perception of Porfiry—sometimes dream, sometimes reality—is betrayed by changes in Porfiry's "voice." During the hallucinatory passages Porfiry lacks a distinctive individual voice: his speech is a parodistic restatement of Raskolnikov's own thoughts and imagery. When, however, Porfiry is more objectively perceived, he acquires a distinctive voice which strikes both Raskolnikov and the reader by its strangeness or "otherness."

The final interview is handled magnificently. In it Raskolnikov's consciousness assimilates Porfiry completely, to create a phantom who satisfies all the demands of his urge to be caught. By this point Porfiry has lost all semblance of reality; like a ghost he visits Raskolnikov, who is alone in the room where the murder was conceived, and like a ghost he afterwards disappears, never to return. And, indeed, there is no need for him to reappear, for after this scene, in which he finally confronts Raskolnikov with his guilt, the latter has no further need of his fantastic, imaginary duel with the detective. The next stage in the development of his desire to be caught and punished must be real—a proper confession to the authorities. Raskolnikov's final interview with Porfiry is a rehearsal for the real confession and arrest.

Immediately prior to Porfiry's "visit" Raskolnikov has heard that the house painter Mikolka has confessed to the murders, and that Porfiry has apparently accepted his confession. Raskolnikov would appear to be no longer the object of Porfiry's pursuit. Accordingly Porfiry initially appears to denounce all his previous suspicions and insinuations as an aberration, and is as charming as possible toward the object of his past pursuit. But suddenly, with Porfiry's chase apparently ended, Raskolnikov's need for punishment reasserts itself: "Raskolnikov felt the rush of a new kind of fright. The thought that Porfiry considered him innocent suddenly began to alarm him" (VI, 345). This alarm is immediately reflected in Porfiry's "behavior." His conversation after Raskolnikov's "rush of fright" is very different from the apologetic tone he has employed before it. He reverts to a detailed examination of the murderer's behavior throughout the affair. With remarkable perception he isolates the motives behind every step, from the conception of the idea and the writing of the article on crime, through to the anguish experienced after the murder. Raskolnikov is thrown into confusion by this new turn, and realizes that only one thing stands in the way of his desired goal of exposure: Mikolka and his spurious confession. Accordingly, in the next part of Porfiry's explanation Raskolnikov *has Mikolka disappear*. More precisely, his imagination creates a Porfiry who discusses Mikolka in such a way that the description approximates more and more to that of Raskolnikov himself. As Peace remarks, Mikolka is transformed into a "shadowy double" of Raskolnikov.[10] We learn that, like Raskolnikov, Mikolka is a fantasist who lives a hermit's life; that he has been profoundly affected by St. Petersburg; that, like Raskolnikov, he has succumbed to strange ideas—"he kept reading, old, 'true' books and in the end read himself silly"; and that he longs for suffering (VI, 347). Moreover, he is a religious schismatic, a point that conveys its full significance only through the original Russian, which adds a final, playful, linguistic seal to the parallels established between the two characters: *"On iz raskol'nikov."* The original image of Mikolka is in this way blurred and replaced by an image of Raskolnikov himself—an image which, though indistinct, is recognizable. With Mikolka thus removed, Porfiry's next comment can be: "Why, *you* are the murderer, Rodion Romanych! you are the murderer, sir!"

IV Ethics and Esthetics

Despite all the uncertainties upon which *Crime and Punishment* rests, one overriding certainty is sustained throughout the novel: the conviction, shared by author, reader, and hero, that the crime is in the final analysis wrong. Raskolnikov is aware of the wrongness of his behavior even before he acquires, in the Epilogue, the moral understanding of *why* it is wrong. He is aware of the wrongness of his crime even during those moments when he vigorously defends it on intellectual and utilitarian grounds, for in the end the criteria against which he measures his actions derive not from the intellect but from those deeper regions of the human soul, the existence of which had been so fervently denied by rational philosophy. For example, all Raskolnikov's attempts to justify his crime are persistently confounded by the intangible, irrational, but nonetheless incapacitating sensations of alienation which overcome him from the moment of the murder onward. Despite his conviction that it is possible to commit a murder in a calculated, conscious manner, he is immobilized by a loss of will that immediately follows the act of violence. In a similar fashion he is subsequently attacked by totally unanticipated sensations of estrangement from his family, the officials at the police station, indeed from humanity as a whole, despite the fact that his self-imposed isolation had never previously worried him.

The most serious threats to Raskolnikov's attempts to come to terms with his crime spring, however, from an area of his being and a definite set of values which he apparently has never before considered relevant or applicable to ethical problems. These values comprise Raskolnikov's esthetic sense.

Any attempt to explain Raskolnikov's reaction to his crime in terms of his esthetic responses must be prefaced by a brief discussion of Dostoevsky's own esthetic views, particularly his belief that man's esthetic and ethical values are related. In his esthetic views Dostoevsky was essentially a Platonist, firmly adhering to the concept of ideal beauty. For Plato true beauty resulted from the combination of esthetic perfection with moral perfection, purity of form with purity of purpose. Man is attracted to beauty precisely because it represents for him an ideal combining harmony, perfect form, good, and purity toward which he—imperfect, inharmonious, and impure—can strive. It was this Platonist concept of the unity of ethical and esthetic categories which led Schiller to propose the possibility of the moral transfiguration of man through his esthetic awareness, an idea which Dostoevsky inherited from his lifetime devotion to the German writer. As Robert L. Jackson remarks: "The notion of beauty and the ideal . . . migrated from Plato through medieval Christian esthetics down to the romantic esthetics of Schiller and Chateaubriand, Schelling and Hegel."[11] But it had not migrated without opposition. Many writers of the late Romantic temperament—Byron and Lermontov, for instance—had attempted to make the case against Platonist ideal beauty by depicting an esthetically attractive evil. The figure of the Romantic hero in European literature had often presented the qualities of revolt, cynicism, and moral indifference in a positive and attractive light, combining formal elegance and style, not with a moral ideal but with moral bankruptcy. We remember in Lermontov's *Geroy nashego vremeni* [A Hero of Our Time] Vera's comment about her lover Pechorin, that "in nobody else was evil so attractive."[12]

The idea that immoral or amoral qualities could combine with formal attractiveness to produce a satisfying esthetic experience was an idea which Dostoevsky opposed throughout his life. In the figure of the Romantic hero morally neutral qualities had acquired formal elegance, but this elegance was for Dostoevsky essentially sterile. It was purely formal and could not be confused with true beauty since it lacked the ideal moral dimension. Dostoevsky elaborated his views on many occasions, in both his critical writings and his *belles-lettres*. In his essay of 1861 "Mr.——bov and the Question of Art," he dismisses the Romantic quest for beauty in evil as an esthetic aberration, a result of the self-indulgence and moral indifference current among the Byronic Romantics:

We have seen examples where man, having achieved the ideal of his desires and not knowing what else to aim for, being totally satiated, has fallen into a kind of anguish, has even exacerbated this anguish within himself, has sought out another ideal in life and out of extreme surfeit has not only ceased to value that which he enjoys but has even consciously turned away from the straight path, and has fomented in himself strange, unhealthy, sharp, inharmonious, sometimes even monstrous tastes, losing measure and esthetic feeling for healthy beauty and demanding instead of it exceptions.[13]

We see this esthetic confusion in *The Devils* in the figure of Stavrogin, himself a Byronic figure gone to seed who deliberately marries a cripple in order to excite his perverted but flagging esthetic sense. It is significant that, as Peace points out,[14] Stavrogin's wife is an ugly echo of that ideal of classical beauty, the Madonna. The same confusion leads Dmitry Karamazov to the conclusion that there must be two kinds of beauty—ideal beauty (the beauty of the Madonna) and unhealthy beauty (the beauty of Sodom). For Dostoevsky there was no such ambiguity: beauty and the ideal went hand-in-glove. Strakhov cites Dostoevsky as saying: "Only that is moral which coincides with your feeling of beauty."[15] And in a well-known letter to N.D. Fonvizina Dostoevsky gives Christ as an example of perfect beauty precisely because in the Classical manner Christ embodies an ethical ideal in perfect physical form. In the same letter he echoes Schiller by suggesting that the esthetic sense, as manifested in love for the beauty of Christ, provides an ethical guide which is superior to reason's conception of truth: "Moreover, if it were proved to me by somebody that Christ lay outside the truth and that the truth actually lay outside Christ, then I would rather remain with Christ than with the truth."[16] For Dostoevsky esthetic standards are absolute and immutable: only that which is good can be beautiful. But in defending this point of view Dostoevsky had to contend not only with the esthetic confusion characteristic of the late Romantic temperament, but also with a contemporary crisis in esthetics caused by the rise of philosophic materialism in Russia in the 1860s and represented by the esthetic views of a whole new generation of social and literary critics, most notably Chernyshevsky and Nikolay Dobrolyubov. It was against the background of this new esthetic revolution that *Crime and Punishment* was written, and it is small wonder that Dostoevsky devotes a considerable amount of space in his novel to a discussion of esthetics and an ultimate affirmation of ideal beauty.

The literary critics of the 1860s denied the unity of esthetic and moral categories; but whereas the Romantics had merely inverted Platonist esthetics, the Utilitarians rejected the value of beauty, or at least relegated it to a secondary role. Its place was taken by utility. The moral value of a work of art was to be measured by its usefulness, not its beauty. Thus writers and artists were urged by the Utilitarian critics to communicate moral truths and appeal to their audience's ethical sense without feeling obliged, in Dobrolyubov's words, to "cultivate the esthetic taste of the public."[17] Moreover, Chernyshevsky's apparent disregard for form in his prolix novel *What Is to Be Done?* (1863) stemmed from his belief that the ethical content of a work or deed could be realized in unesthetic form. Dostoevsky's greatest journalistic polemic against the utilitarian "esthetic" is contained in "Mr.——bov and the Question of Art," where he reaffirms his faith in the unity of content and form by criticizing the tales of the Ukrainian writer Marko Vovchok, tales which Dobrolyubov had welcomed despite their lack of artistry.

Raskolnikov's crime in *Crime and Punishment* is conceived with the total disregard for form in the face of moral content characteristic of the men of the sixties. Rationally, and in the terms of the new Utilitarian ethic to which he thinks he subscribes, Raskolnikov can justify his crime. He plans to murder a *useless* old woman moneylender and appropriate her wealth in order to further his own career, a career which is potentially *useful* to society. By the same act he will both liberate his mother and sister from the financial burden of supporting him, and also free other potentially valuable students from the financial clutches of the old woman. Having in this way justified his crime morally, Raskolnikov shows no overtly *moral* remorse for the rest of the novel, at least if we exclude his religious conversion in the Epilogue, a conversion which Mochulsky dismisses, with good reason, as a "pious lie" on Dostoevsky's part.[18] Indeed, we have seen that in an interview with his sister Dunya shortly before his confession he defends the ethics of his act in no uncertain terms. In view of his conviction that his crime is morally acceptable, Raskolnikov initially feels no need to justify it esthetically. But his subsequent esthetic disgust at his "ugly" crime points back to a

Platonist concept of the unity of ethics and esthetics. Throughout much of the novel Raskolnikov's crime, so justified by reason and the new Utilitarian ethic, is censured by his esthetic sense. Why does his crime strike him as ugly; why does he rebel against it when he can defend it ethically? Raskolnikov is forced to realize that although his Utilitarian age may pretend to have created a new ethic, it has not discovered a new esthetic. Beauty is absolute and ideal; a new age cannot create a new beauty.

Raskolnikov is a rationalist, but one whose rationalism is flawed by a developed esthetic sensibility. The conflict between his rational response to a situation and his esthetic response accounts for much of his confusion in *Crime and Punishment*. This confusion exists even before the crime is committed, and is apparent on the occasions when Raskolnikov voices doubts about his own intentions. An important feature of Raskolnikov's precrime doubts is the fact that they are of an esthetic, not a moral, nature. The thought of the murder troubles him by its lack of esthetic form, by its ugliness:

Raskolnikov went out in a decidedly confused state. This confusion became stronger and stronger. As he went down the staircase he even stopped once or twice as if suddenly struck by something. Finally when he was already in the street, he exclaimed: "Oh God! How *repulsive* this all is! And will I, will I really . . . . No, it's *nonsense*, preposterous!" he added decisively. "And really, how could such a *horror* enter my head? Is my heart really capable of such *filth*? The main thing is it's *filthy, foul and disgusting, disgusting!*" (VI, 10: my italics)

On another occasion Raskolnikov dreams of a mare's being beaten to death by a peasant, an incident which he compares to his own proposed crime. His response to this dream demonstrates again that his revulsion from an act of violence is esthetic rather than moral, and his first reaction is to describe the dream as *bezobraznyi*—"ugly," but more literally "without form." He then continues:

"God! Will I really take an ax, hit her over the head with it, smash her skull . . . slip about in the sticky warm blood, force the lock, steal and tremble; hide myself, all covered in blood . . . with the ax . . . . Will I really? . . .

No, I cannot bear it, I cannot bear it! Let there be no doubt about all these rational deductions, let everything that has been decided in this last month be as clear as day and arithmetically just, Lord I shall still not be able to decide on this action!" (VI, 50)

Here esthetics confront reason and rational ethics as surely as they do in Dostoevsky's letter to Fonvizina quoted above, and at this stage in the novel Raskolnikov has reached an impasse. Moral and intellectual justification is not enough: he must overcome his esthetic revulsion before he can murder. He must invest his proposed crime with *form*, with an esthetic dimension, in order to make it more than merely intellectually attractive. This he does by invoking the Romantic myth of Napoleon. In the wake of the Romantic movement Napoleon had developed almost into a cult figure, a man who had realized in deeds many of the ideals of Romanticism. In the name of freedom he had changed the very course of history, and the face of Europe. He had torn a hole in the fabric of accepted historical thought and elevated man to unprecedented heights. For Raskolnikov Napoleon is the epitome of the superior superman he describes in his essay on crime. But Raskolnikov is attracted to Napoleon not only intellectually, as a model for the act of transgression against established laws, but also esthetically. Raskolnikov seizes upon the Romantic image of Napoleon as the esthetic formula which will allow him to commit his crime: in his eyes, as in the eyes of history, Napoleon has given form, style, elegance, and grandeur to the act of violence. As Valery Kirpotin remarks in a stimulating discussion of the Napoleonic myth in *Crime and Punishment*: "Raskolnikov is attracted not by the historical Napoleon, but by the myth of Napoleon . . . . Myth has estheticized Napoleon and surrounded his name with an iridescent halo."[19] Napoleon is Raskolnikov's demon, taunting him with the idea that willful cruelty, violence, and evil can be noble and beautiful. Late in the novel—too late as far as Raskolnikov is concerned—Napoleon's demonic qualities are revealed to the despairing murderer. In an interview with Sonya he insists: "I myself know that the devil has led me on . . . . The devil killed that old hag, not I!" (VI, 321–22).

The esthetic appeal of Napoleon's example—his "beautiful and monumental deeds" (*krasivye i monumental'nye veshchi*, VI, 319)—permits Raskolnikov to kill, but is it enough to sustain him after the crime, when he has had time to reflect upon what he has done? It would appear not. The real Napoleon has found refuge from his violence in myth; Raskolnikov cannot do so. He is a creature of reality, and in his coffinlike room he must face the full horror of his crime. Moreover, esthetics, not ethics, return to torment him. He is shocked at the way he has been deceived by a myth, and despairs at the esthetic gulf which separates the style of Napoleon from his own squalid crime:

"No, those people are not made in the same way; a real *ruler of men*, to whom all is permitted, takes Toulon by storm, causes wholesale carnage in Paris, *forgets* an army in Egypt, *throws away* half a million lives in his Moscow campaign and gets away with a witticism at Vilna. After his death monuments are erected to him—for him it would appear *all* is permissible. No, such men are not of flesh and blood, but of bronze!"

A sudden, not quite relevant thought almost made him laugh:

"Napoleon, the pyramids, Waterloo—and a scraggy, vile old hag, a moneylender with a red box under her bed; what could Porfiry Petrovich make of it! Could he make anything of it? No, his esthetic sense would not let him. A Napoleon crawl under an old woman's bed? Nonsense!" (VI, 211)

Even Napoleon's witticism at Vilna must haunt Raskolnikov, for it is not without relevance to his own predicament: "From the sublime to the ridiculous there is only one step, and posterity must judge."

Raskolnikov demonstrates the esthetic nature of his despair even more clearly in a discussion with Dunya late in the novel. Here, as we have seen, he vigorously defends the morality of his crime but criticizes its form: "Ah. It did not have the form; it lacked the esthetically right form! Well I just cannot understand why dropping bombs on people or killing them by regular siege is a more respectable form" (VI, 400). The answer is that only myth can invest the act of violence with form; posterity has judged Napoleon very kindly indeed. But Raskolnikov's crime is not only, as Kirpotin points out, the debunking of the Napoleonic myth: in its ugliness it also serves to reaffirm Dostoevsky's belief that the morally repulsive cannot be realized in beautiful form except in myth.

V *Svidrigailov*

If the myth of Napoleon serves in the novel to promote, at least for Raskolnikov, the illusion of esthetic evil, of "beauty in Sodom," then the reality of Arkady Svidrigailov serves to dispel this same illusion. Svidrigailov is Napoleon's counterbalance, a debasement of the Romantic superman. Furthermore, with this character as surely as with Prince Valkovsky in *The Insulted and Injured* (1861), Dostoevsky also seems to be squaring accounts with the Byronic Romantic hero, be he demon or human. Svidrigailov strips not only Napoleon of his myth and esthetic aureole, he does the same for Byron's heroes and Lermontov's Pechorin. He exhibits the world-weariness, unorthodoxy, and moral indifference of the Romantic hero, but in repulsive form.

Svidrigailov's entrance into the novel is preceded by mysterious rumors of his sensualism, cruelty, and callousness. There are suggestions that he is responsible for the deaths of his wife, a servant, and a young girl whom he had seduced. His first actual appearance comes at a very significant moment for Raskolnikov, who has just recognized the full horror and hideousness of his crime. The entrance of Svidrigailov intrudes into a dream in which Raskolnikov has unsuccessfully attempted to kill the old woman again, a dream which offends his esthetic sense and reveals to him the difference between himself and the Napoleonic myth. Raskolnikov's attitude to Svidrigailov is ambiguous from the start: he finds him repulsive and addresses him with disgust, but at the same time he is attracted and strangely fascinated by the man. The ambiguity of Raskolnikov's attitude finds a parallel in the combination of beauty and repulsiveness in Svidrigailov's physical appearance:

Raskolnikov rested his right elbow on the table, propped up his chin on the fingers of his right hand and gazed intently at Svidrigailov. He examined his face for about a minute, for he had always previously been struck by it. It was a strange sort of face, rather like a mask: white, but with red cheeks and crimson lips, with a light blond beard and blond hair that was still fairly thick. The eyes were somehow too blue and their expression too heavy and still. There was something terribly unpleasant in that handsome and extraordinarily young-looking face. (VI, 357)

This combination of beauty and repulsiveness recurs in the physical appearance of Stavrogin, who, like Svidrigailov, is a moral bankrupt, a parody of the Romantic hero and, if rumor is to be believed, a criminal responsible among other things for the seduction and death of a child.

The fascination which Svidrigailov exerts is due above all else to Raskolnikov's unwilling recognition that he has much in common with Svidrigailov. The rumors which preceded Svidrigailov persuade Raskolnikov that here is a man who, like himself, has transgressed traditional laws and morality by a willful act of violence. Moreover, like Raskolnikov, Svidrigailov appears to suffer from no *moral* doubts about his behavior, although—as we shall see later—there are strong indications that he too is the victim of an esthetic sensibility disturbed by the violence he has committed.

Svidrigailov, too, is quick to recognize the kinship between Raskolnikov and himself, whom he compares to "berries from the same tree" (VI, 221). Both are drawn together and seem to expect some kind of lead or example from each other. Indeed, Raskolnikov confesses as much late in the novel, when he has become esthetically estranged from Svidrigailov: "'How indeed could I even for a moment have expected anything from the filthy villain, that voluptuary and rogue!'" (VI, 374) "He hurried to Svidrigailov. He himself did not know what he expected from him, but the man exerted some sort of power over him" (VI, 353). Dostoevsky emphasizes the moral identity of Svidrigailov and Raskolnikov by means of symbolic suggestion in the interview between them which follows Svidrigailov's first appearance. In his opening remarks on his attempted seduction of Dunya, Svidrigailov confronts Raskolnikov with a gross adaptation of his own theories on the moral justification for his crime: "What was there in all this that was particularly criminal on my part, if we discard prejudice and look at the matter objectively?" (VI, 215). Svidrigailov does not acknowledge his own moral responsibility, just as Raskolnikov defends the morality of his crime to Dunya in the passage cited earlier. Nor is Svidrigailov troubled morally by his responsibility for the death of his wife: "My conscience is perfectly clear on that account" (VI, 215).

Despite his insistence that his conscience is completely clear, Svidrigailov does confess that he is visited by his wife's ghost, an admission which disturbs Raskolnikov profoundly, for in his recent dream he has encountered the victim of his own crime and has been unable to get rid of her: "'How was it that I knew something like that must be happening to you!' muttered Raskolnikov, and was at once amazed that he had said such a thing. He was violently agitated" (VI, 219). Raskolnikov has once more recognized himself in Svidrigailov, a point the latter acknowledges immediately: "'Wha-at? Did you really think that?' Svidrigailov asked with surprise. 'Really? Well, didn't I say that there was a great deal in common between us?'" (VI, 219). Finally, the moral identification between them is completed when Svidrigailov informs Raskolnikov that in the course of his married life he has used violence against his wife, his later victim, on only three occasions: "In the whole seven years of our life together I used the whip only twice (that is if you don't count a third occasion which was in any case rather ambiguous)" (VI, 216). This is perhaps an unimportant point, but it seems worth remarking that Raskolnikov, too, has used his instrument of violence—the ax—only twice, against Alena and Lizaveta, if we do not count the third, rather ambiguous occasion—his recent dream.

In the moral independence of Svidrigailov, in his contempt for accepted laws, Raskolnikov recognizes both himself and his Superman; but he cannot reconcile this recognition with the esthetic disgust which Svidrigailov arouses in him. On almost every occasion when Raskolnikov addresses Svidrigailov the words "with revulsion" (*s otvrashcheniem*) occur, for Svidrigailov's actions are esthetically a far cry from the "beautiful and monumental deeds" of Napoleon, and they bring home to Raskolnikov just how base his own behavior has been.

Raskolnikov is affected initially by the ugliness of Svidrigailov's mind—he shudders to see his own idea on the right of the strong individual to transgress common law presented without form or elegance, just as in *The Devils* Stepan Verkhovensky sees an unesthetic distortion of the noble ideas of his generation in the Nihilists of the 1860s. "I am terribly afraid of that man," says Raskolnikov of Svidrigailov (VI, 225), and so he should be, for Svidrigailov debases the myth of the Superman as surely as did Raskolnikov's own crime. The following passage, in which Svidrigailov sets forth his ideas on eternity, demonstrates the ugliness of his mind as well as the combination of fear and revulsion with which Raskolnikov contemplates it:

Svidrigailov sat lost in thought.
"What if there are only spiders there or something like that," he said suddenly.
"He's mad!" thought Raskolnikov.
"We always imagine eternity as a concept impossible to understand, as something huge. But why must it be huge? What if instead we imagine one tiny room, something like a village bathhouse, very dirty and with spiders in every corner. And that's all eternity is. Sometimes, you know, I imagine it is just like that."
"Can you really not imagine anything more comforting and more just than that!" exclaimed Raskolnikov with a sick feeling.
"More just? But perhaps that is just, and you know, I would certainly make it like that deliberately!" replied Svidrigailov with a vague smile. This horrible [*bezobraznyi*] answer suddenly made Raskolnikov's blood run cold. (VI, 221)

In his conduct, too, Svidrigailov debases the Napoleonic ideal by stripping it of its formal elegance. He revels in the dirt and squalor of the St. Petersburg backstreets; he is most at home in seedy restaurants and bars. Indeed, it is in such a restaurant that Svidrigailov confesses to Raskolnikov his predilection for vice. Whereas Napoleon exercised his moral independence in great historical deeds, Svidrigailov exercises his moral indifference in the brothels and taverns of St. Petersburg; Napoleon takes Toulon by storm, Svidrigailov seduces young children. It is, as Napoleon reminds us, only a small step from the sublime to the ridiculous, or indeed to the squalid, but this is a step Raskolnikov cannot accept. He can accept his Superman only when he is cloaked in the grandeur and nobility which myth bestows; he cannot accept the gross distortion of his rational ideal which Svidrigailov represents. In this respect he is, as Svidrigailov insists, a Schiller and an idealist, whose esthetic sense prevents him from accepting the horrors invented by, and carried out in the name of, reason.

VI   *The Esthetic Louse*

"The fear of esthetics is the first sign of weakness!" exclaims Raskolnikov to Dunya (VI, 400), and in so doing he reveals the acuity of his insight into his own predicament. His dislike of ugliness prevents him from coming to terms with his own crime as surely as it prevents him from accepting Svidrigailov. Even though intellectually he can accept crime, he will never be a Superman as long as he is esthetically disgusted by the act of violence. His esthetic sense prevents him from completing the act of transgression which his crime represents. He has the intellectual and ethical freedom of the Superman, but the esthetic inhibitions of a louse, if we may employ the terminology by which he divides mankind into two camps. "I am an esthetic louse!" (*esteticheskaia ia vosh'*) he cries in a critical moment of self-doubt: "I was in too much of a hurry to step across [from being ordinary to being a Superman] . . . . I didn't kill a person, I killed a principle! I killed a principle, but I did not step across, I remained on this side . . ." (VI, 211). The principle which Raskolnikov has destroyed is his conviction that ethical standards are created and judged by reason alone, that a crime condoned by reason may be committed with impunity. In his attitude to both his crime and his double Svidrigailov, Raskolnikov demonstrates that the true judge of the ethical quality of an act or a person is the esthetic sense. For this reason a man becomes a Superman, and possesses true moral independence, only if he can renounce his esthetic sense. But Raskolnikov's respect for esthetics is too great to allow him to do this. Esthetic indifference transforms a man into a monster, as Stavrogin (*The Devils*) amply demonstrates in his assertion that he can see no distinction in beauty between some voluptuous and brutish act and an heroic exploit (X, 201).

Esthetic disgust at an immoral act also contributes to Svidrigailov's downfall. He does not possess the esthetic indifference he would like: he demonstrates his scorn for ideal beauty by intending to seduce an innocent child who, significantly, reminds him of the Sistine Madonna, but he recoils in horror from every mention of a young girl whose corruption and death he has occasioned. A dream in which he is confronted with the transformation of an innocent girl into a seductive whore is largely responsible for his eventual suicide. As he himself remarks, he is the victim of his own monstrosities.

A man's intellectual decisions will always be subject to reconfirmation by his esthetic sense, and this is a theme to which Dostoevsky returns in his later novels. In *The Brothers Karamazov*, for instance, Ivan Karamazov's intellectual revolt against God's creation runs counter to his esthetic sense. The devil, the very incarnation of metaphysical revolt, appears to Ivan in a dream, offending against his esthetic sense just as Svidrigailov offends Raskolnikov: "Moderate your demands," says the devil. "Don't demand from me 'everything great and beautiful' and you'll see how well we'll get on together. You are really angry at me because I did not appear to you in a red glow, in 'thunder and lightning' and with scorched wings, but introduced myself in so modest a form. You are offended first of all in your esthetic feelings and secondly in your pride. How could such a vulgar devil appear to such a great man! I'm afraid you have that romantic strain so derided by Belinsky" (XV, 81).

In a similar way Raskolnikov cannot "get on" with either Svidrigailov or his own crime as long as he demands from them "everything great and beautiful." He too must moderate his demands: he must not expect evil to provide a satisfying esthetic experience, for evil cannot do so. The esthetic sense for both Ivan and Raskolnikov is a disadvantage in their attempts at rebellion, it is indeed the first sign of weakness, but it also contains the germ of their salvation. Esthetics reveal to Raskolnikov the deceit of rational, Utilitarian ethics; they prevent him from coming to terms with his crime and open the way for moral regeneration, as Schiller promised. For Ivan esthetics offer the key to reconciliation with God's creation and an escape from the cul-de-sac of reason. Man's esthetic sense, his feeling for true beauty, is the best antidote he has to the monstrous morality which reason on its own can create, and his best guide to true ethical standards. For true beauty is, in Dostoevsky's world, always associated with moral perfection. Put as simply as possible, beauty—and man's unerring feeling for ideal beauty—will save the world. It is appropriate that this sole certainty among all the uncertainties of *Crime and Punishment* should be formulated unequivocally in *The Idiot* by Dostoevsky's favorite hero, the saintly Prince Myshkin.

CHAPTER 5

The Failure of an Ideal: The Idiot

THE Idiot was written between 1867 and 1869, while Dostoevsky and his wife were drifting from city to city in Europe. The family's personal circumstances were appalling: Dostoevsky suffered severe and frequent epileptic fits; money was in chronically short supply, although that did not deter the writer from wasting what little he had to satisfy his consuming passion for gambling. The short novel *The Gambler* is an interesting product of Dostoevsky's unhealthy preoccupation with roulette. In 1868 the youngest member of Dostoevsky's family, Sonya, died in infancy. In the light of all this it is hardly surprising that the plot of *The Idiot* is erratic and confusing. Yet the basic idea of the novel is very simple: Prince Myshkin, a meek and frail young man, returns to Russia after an absence of several years, during which he has received treatment for epilepsy at a Swiss clinic. As a result of his illness and long absence, he has remained a child, naive and idealistic. He hopes to influence the people he meets in Russia by his simplicity, meekness, and honesty. But his positive moral qualities prove an embarrassment in nineteenth-century Russia. He inadvertently offends all he meets: the Epanchin family, who take him under their wing, and in particular the youngest daughter, Aglaya, whose love he is unable to return; a group of grasping radicals gathered around the young Burdovsky, who feels he has a right to a sum of money Myshkin has inherited; a dying young egoist, Ippolit; and the proud and touchy Ganya Ivolgin. But, most disastrously, Myshkin's naiveté destroys the lives of Rogozhin, a passionate sensualist, and Nastasya Filippovna, a proud and willful beauty who cannot forgive her seduction by a prominent businessman, Totsky. Myshkin's compassionate admiration for Nastasya Filippovna provokes the jealous Rogozhin first to an assault on the Prince himself, and then, at the climax of the novel, to the murder of Nastasya Filippovna. Faced with the awareness of his own complicity in the tragedy, Myshkin lapses again into idiocy.

I The Idiot *as Allegory*

Of all Dostoevsky's novels *The Idiot* is the most obviously contrived. It is a complex allegory which, as it pursues its capricious and sinuous course, elaborates two of Dostoevsky's greatest ideas: his apocalyptic vision of modern Europe poised over the abyss of moral disintegration, and his resistance to the belief held by many of his contemporaries that man's social and moral chaos may be overcome in this world. One resorts to the interpretation of a novel as allegory with some misgivings, for the category is too often reserved by critics as a final resting place for recalcitrant works of art which do not respond to a more delicate and direct analysis. Yet in Dostoevsky's case the allegorical approach is more justified than in most others, for his works consistently reveal such devices of allegory as significant proper names, obtrusive symbolism, literary or biblical echoes, and conventional physical descriptions that suggest the inner state of his characters. The overtly contemporary trappings of the novels—their urban settings, their characters drawn from newspapers and afflicted with modern neuroses, their alertness to current polemic—all of these disguise a core of myth, both pagan and Christian, which when it surfaces often threatens the credibility of the contemporary veneer. In the light of this it is difficult to agree with one critic's view that *The Idiot* "is not anchored in the realm of the allegorical, but in the realm of social and psychological reality."[1] Certainly it contains finely wrought characters and scenes of clear contemporary relevance: the complex yet comprehensible psychology of Nastasya Filippovna and the wry social polemic contained in the Burdovsky subplot spring immediately to mind as examples. Yet in the end there is too much in this novel that remains unclear; too much in both plot and character depiction that cannot be explained within even the most extended limits of social and psychological probability. Such a view can, of course, be only an opinion; the difficulty of establishing criteria for Realism in art must be acknowledged. But it is an opinion that gains support from Dostoevsky's own obvious concern in the course of *The Idiot* for how the artist represents reality. In a digression at the beginning of Part IV, as well as earlier in the words of the minor character Lebedev, Dostoevsky describes art as a process of distillation rather than depiction, concerned with revealing the essence of reality rather than recreating its texture. The artist creates "types very rarely encountered as such in real life, but who nonetheless are almost more real than reality itself" (VIII, 383).

Dostoevsky's method of distilling the essential significance of reality is best illustrated by the nature of the relationships he establishes between his characters. Very often these bonds are forged in order to satisfy the requirements of symbolism rather than those of psychology or probability. How otherwise may we account, for example, for the immediate rapport and mutual recognition established between the worldly and experienced Nastasya Filippovna and the newly arrived, innocent Myshkin at the Ivolgin home (VIII, 89)? Since the two characters have never met before, their mutual recognition must be traced back to the relationship between the allegorical counterparts they are supposed to suggest, Christ and the fallen woman, Mary Magdalene. Likewise the initial encounter of Myshkin and his alter-ego, Rogozhin, on the train from Warsaw makes up in symbolic importance for what it lacks in authenticity, as does the scene toward the end of the novel when Myshkin and Rogozhin walk to their vigil over Nastasya Filippovna's body in step, but on opposite sides of the street. This polarization defies both psychological explanation and probability, but it has a compelling symbolic appropriateness. Seen literally, it is little more than clumsy melodrama, but as a symbolic recapitulation of the uneasy contrapuntual relationship that has existed between the dark and passionate Rogozhin and the fair and quiet Prince, both of whom are responsible in their way for the death of Nastasya Filippovna, the scene is highly satisfying.

Professor Peace suggests that allegory is the skeleton beneath the "living flesh" of *The Idiot*.[2] His remark is quite apt, for, in addition to implying that there is more to the novel than the bare bones of allegory, it also stresses the latter's primary role. Without the supporting framework of allegory the rest of the novel—the incisive psychological insights, the revealing pictures of the Russian leisured and mercantile classes and the vitriolic social polemics—simply could not stand.

II   The Idiot *and the Apocalypse*

At the heart of *The Idiot*, uniting its contemporary facade and its undercurrent of allegory, lies its apocalyptic mood, its sense of the imminent disintegration of the society it describes. Throughout the book there is an almost hysterical urgency, a feeling that the Russia of the Totskys, Rogozhins, and Ivolgins is in its final death agony. Of Dostoevsky's four great novels, only *The Devils* matches the hysterical quality of *The Idiot*. In *Crime and Punishment* one feels that the spiritual disease afflicting Raskolnikov has not yet spread to everyone in the novel, and the work ends with a promise of reconciliation, not the threat of Armageddon. *The Brothers Karamazov*, too, ends with a promise, as Alesha and the children meet over little Ilyusha's grave and pledge loyalty to his memory. But *The Idiot* and *The Devils* end with the eruption of that death and violence which has threatened throughout both novels. In *The Idiot* the murder of Nastasya Filippovna precipitates Myshkin's return to darkness, and the hope contained in Stepan Trofimovich's last pilgrimage, which concludes *The Devils*, is not enough to offset the orgy of murder and suicide that accompanies it.

Interestingly, these two most apocalyptic of Dostoevsky's novels were written during that protracted period which the author spent abroad. He had fled Russia in early 1867 to escape debts and improve his health, and he did not return until July 1871. Perhaps we can trace the hysteria of these two novels partly to the fact that Dostoevsky was separated from the Russia he was trying to describe and kept in touch through newspapers, hardly the source of a balanced picture of life's texture. Moreover, Dostoevsky—touchy, overwrought, and profoundly nationalistic—was compelled to spend his period of separation from Russian roots in Western Europe, that bustling, over-commercial, overindustrialized seat of rationalism, socialism, and revolution, a source of plagues which since Peter the Great had been threatening to engulf his native land. For Dostoevsky Western Europe was a most eloquent symbol of modern man's spiritual decline, and it was from this vantage point that he made his observations of Russia. *The Idiot* ends on a revealingly anti-Western note as Mrs. Epanchina cries: "It's time we came to our senses. And all this, all this life abroad, all this Europe of yours, it's all just a delusion, and all of us abroad are just a delusion . . . . Mark my words, you'll see for yourself!"

As Solzhenitsyn was to do more than a century later, Dostoevsky marks his period of unwilling "exile" in the West with a bitter warning that the quest for material security without the framework of a governing moral principle will mean the fall of Western civilization, and he expands this warning to include Russia's westernized ruling classes. From its earliest conception *The Idiot* was intended to portray the decline of a Russian family through its emphasis on material, rather than spiritual, riches. This idea survives and is expressed most vividly, if somewhat ridiculously, in the character of Lebedev, that comic mouthpiece of serious ideas. At the Prince's birthday gathering

Lebedev, a self-styled interpreter of the Apocalypse, is goaded into an attack upon the spiritual vacuum of modern society: "All of this as a whole is damned, sir! The whole spirit of these last few centuries of ours, taken as a whole with its scientific and practical emphasis, is perhaps indeed damned, sir!" (VIII, 310). Modern man, in his relentless drive to satisfy the demands of reason, egoism, and material necessity, has lost the sense of spiritual well-being to be derived from an ideal which provides moral and metaphysical certainty. Modern man has no faith; there are only science, industry, commerce, and capital. Lebedev complains that it is folly to try to erect a material fortune upon a foundation of spiritual poverty, and directs this particular criticism at contemporary socialists with their "carts bringing bread to the whole of humanity, without a moral basis for this action" (a quotation that combines a well-known statement by the Russian socialist Alexander Herzen with Christ's injunction that man should not live by bread alone[3]). In a deliciously irreverent anecdote Lebedev goes on to tell of a twelfth-century monk who, after twenty years of cannibalism, confessed and went to the stake for his sins. What was it, asks Lebedev, that drove him to confession despite the tortures that awaited him?

There must have been something much stronger than the stake and the flames, stronger even than the habits of twenty years! There must have been an idea stronger than all misfortune, famine, torture, plague, leprosy and all that hell which mankind could not have endured without that binding idea which guided men's hearts and enriched the waters of life. Show me something resembling that force in our age of vice and railways . . . . Show me an idea that binds mankind today with even half the force as in those centuries . . . And don't try to intimidate me with your prosperity, your riches, the infrequency of famine today and your rapid means of communication! There is more wealth now, but less strength; the binding idea is no more; everything has grown soft; everything and everyone is overcoddled! (VIII, 315)

Lebedev's frenetic ravings reveal the polemical core of the novel. His preposterous tale of the spiritually sound cannibal-monk contains the germ of Dostoevsky's own apocalyptic vision of modern Europe, doomed by its spiritual flabbiness to wallow in material well-being without the governing force that gives life purpose. Lebedev's ideas are rescued from ridicule when they are repeated in essence by the novel's seriously conceived hero, Prince Myshkin. In a conversation with Ippolit late in the novel Myshkin characterizes nineteenth-century man as a spiritual nomad, devoid of certainty:

Men in those days (I assure you I've always been struck by this) were not at all the same people as we are now, not at all the same race. They were a different breed. People in those days were somehow motivated by a single idea, but nowadays they are more nervous, more developed, more sensitive. They seem to be motivated by two or three ideas at the same time. Modern man is broader, and I swear this prevents him from being such an integrated creature as he was in those times (VIII, 433).

Myshkin's subsequent violent outburst against socialism and catholicism at the soirée where he is introduced to the Epanchin family's friends contains a further development of this view of contemporary European man: "Why, socialism too is the child of catholicism and the essential catholic nature! It too, like its brother atheism, was born of despair, in opposition to catholicism as a moral force, in order to take the place of the lost moral force of religion, to quench the spiritual thirst of parched humanity! . . . ." (VIII, 451).

In his conclusions, however, Myshkin is more cautious than Lebedev, who sees nothing but damnation issuing from mankind's spiritual poverty. Lebedev finds a symbol of mankind's state in the vivid apocalyptic image of the four horsemen:

We are in the time of the third horse, the black one, and of the rider with the balance in his hand, for everything in our age is weighed in the balance and settled by agreement, and people are only seeking their rights: "a measure of wheat for a penny, three measures of barley for a penny," and with all this they still want to keep a free spirit, a pure heart, a healthy body and all the rest of God's gifts. But they won't keep them by demanding their rights alone, and there will follow the pale horse, and he whose name is Death, and after him comes Hell. . . . (VIII, 167–68)

This apocalyptic image dominates the novel; it is taken up and embellished by a whole network of lesser references to Revelation.[4] These echoes of the central image do not always lend themselves to precise interpretation or to close analogy with the events and characters of the novel, but they do serve to sustain in the reader's mind the apocalyptic note struck by Lebedev, and thus to color the way he looks at the events of the novel. For example, there is an unsettling resemblance between the Apocalypse's central concern with judgment and condemnation and the same themes as represented in the situations and characters of *The Idiot*. In this way Myshkin's anecdotes about the execution he witnessed in Lyons and his friend who was condemned to death only to be reprieved at the last moment, as well as Ippolit's view of himself as condemned by nature, all fit into the apocalyptic frame of the novel.

Moreover, the fallen state of nineteenth-century Europeanized Russia forms a close parallel to the fall of Babylon described in the Apocalypse. Chapter 18, verse 2 of Revelation, for instance, describes a Babylon that has become "the habitation of devils" and "a cage of every unclean and hateful bird." For Dostoevsky, peering myopically at Russia from distant Europe, his native land appeared indeed to teem with all kinds of devils—socialists, nihilists, and atheists—and he incorporated this idea in the very title of his later novel, *The Devils*. But the Russia depicted in *The Idiot* is also overrun with a multitude of "unclean and hateful birds": there is the moneylender Ptitsyn, whose name derives from the Russian word *ptitsa*, meaning "bird"; there is the mendacious Lebedev himself (*lebed'*—"swan"), as well as the avaricious Ganya Ivolgin (*ivolga*—"oriole").

Other proper names also echo Lebedev's explanation of the Apocalypse. For example, the image of the third horseman is revived in "The Scales," the name of the hotel where Myshkin arranges to meet his young friend Kolya shortly before Rogozhin's attack. Furthermore, the person who protects Mrs. Epanchina as her *protégé*, who is regarded as an arbiter of taste by the false society she inhabits and whose blessing Myshkin must receive before he can be welcomed in society, is a certain Princess Belokonskaya, whose name suggests the fourth horse, Death (*belo*—"white"; *kon'*—"horse").

Such are the perhaps rather cheap devices used by Dostoevsky to fashion the corrupt society depicted in *The Idiot* into a nineteenth-century equivalent of doomed Babylon, awaiting only the arrival of the Lamb, the Son of God, and the terrible judgment he will bring. Moreover, Dostoevsky's Babylon, like its biblical equivalent, is presided over by a "whore," the willful Nastasya Filippovna, seduced as a young woman by the businessman Totsky, and now bent upon a perverse revenge involving her own destruction. Details from the biblical account of the fall of Babylon are woven through Dostoevsky's novel. Chapter 18 of Revelation, for example, describes how "the kings of the earth, who have committed fornication and lived deliciously with her [the Whore], shall bewail her, and lament for her, when they shall see the smoke of her burning. . . . And the merchants of the earth shall weep and mourn over her . . . and shall stand afar off for the fear of her torment, weeping and wailing" (verses 9, 11, and 15). In Dostoevsky's apocalypse the kings of the earth are, as Ganya Ivolgin recognizes, the merchants themselves, the men of money; and three of them—Epanchin, Totsky, and Ptitsyn—at the end of Part I bemoan the self-destructive course pursued by Nastasya Filippovna, and yet at the same time fear her and stand to one side.

Nastasya Filippovna's deliberate self-abasement, her urge to confirm her fall from innocence publicly by scandalous scenes and by parading herself as "Rogozhin's slut," are all part of an elaborate, if perverse and indirect, scheme of revenge against those who have abused her, a vengeance which she knows will culminate in her own death at Rogozhin's hands. As Ptitsyn remarks to Totsky at the end of Part I, her behavior is similar to that of the Japanese warrior who disembowels himself before his enemy as a form of aggression. Yet, alongside her desire for vengeance, which she nurtures by deliberately sharpening her consciousness of her fallen state, Nastasya Filippovna yearns also for her own lost innocence. This is, of course, a paradoxical state, for innocence and vengeance cannot coexist. Yet Nastasya Filippovna persists in longing for both, a situation dramatized by the way she is equally drawn throughout the novel to two men: to Myshkin, who sees only her innocence; and to Rogozhin, who affirms her fallen state and her right to revenge. It is fitting that the novel's allegorical nature, the clear linking of its themes with similar ones to be found in the Apocalypse, should also include the divided nature of Nastasya Filippovna. As well as being the fallen woman at the heart of this modern Babylon, she is also—as her surname Barashkova implies—associated with the Lamb (*barashek*—"lamb"), the Bible's symbol of innocence and forgiveness. As we shall see, the Lamb or Christ-figure introduced into Dostoevsky's apocalyptic allegory is the novel's meek and saintly hero, the idiot Prince, Lev Nikolaevich Myshkin.

III *Money and Egoism*

In *The Idiot* Dostoevsky's attack upon the spiritual poverty of modern man is centered on his seduction by the power of money. In none of his other great novels does money assume such a widespread significance in both the conception of the characters and the dynamics of the plot. The arrival of the destitute Myshkin sharpens our awareness of the importance of money in the Russia he discovers: he is treated with amused contempt by society until he inherits a small fortune. The respect he acquires as a result of his inheritance, a respect that allows people to turn a blind eye to his "idiocy," demonstrates that in this society money makes the man. Indeed the characters at the top of this social pyramid are men skilled in investment: the businessman Totsky, the shrewd financier General Epanchin, and the vulgar but well-heeled moneylender Ptitsyn. Ganya Ivolgin draws the logical conclusion from this state of affairs when he announces to Myshkin his intention to suffer privation in order to amass capital. He knows very well that he is a man without talent, but he is also conscious that "having amassed a fortune I shall—mark my words— become a highly original person. The most disgusting and hateful thing about money is that it even endows people with talent" (VIII, 105). Ganya's remarks shed light on the determination of status in a society such as that of nineteenth-century Russia, where a man's personal qualities are ignored (witness the treatment of Myshkin before his inheritance) and where the rise of the middle classes has dislocated what had previously been a clearly defined social hierarchy (Myshkin belongs to one of Russia's oldest aristocratic families, but that counts for little when he lacks money). In such a society a man is judged not by what he *is*, but by what he *owns*. Moreover, the strong invariably take from the meek, who, despite what Myshkin believes, will inherit nothing. Radomsky, a friend of the Epanchin family, elaborates this point in his fiery discussion with the radicals, when he describes a society where "the right of might" prevails (VIII, 245).

Money is the prime determinant of social status to such an extent that even the socially unimportant characters in *The Idiot* are mesmerized by it. It is notable that many of the characters Myshkin meets upon his arrival in Russia introduce themselves with a remark about money. In the opening scene on the train, for example, Rogozhin and Lebedev confine their conversation with the Prince to the cost of medical treatment in Switzerland and Rogozhin's recent inheritance. Later, when Myshkin has settled as a lodger in the Ivolgin household, he is warned not to lend money to the General. Shortly afterwards the other lodger, Ferdyshchenko, peers around the Prince's door to ask whether he has any money. Moreover, the rivalry between Ganya and Rogozhin for Nastasya Filippovna's favors finally leads to an auction in which the two suitors try to outbid each other. Rogozhin's winning bid of a hundred thousand roubles is significantly wrapped in a copy of the *Stock Exchange Gazette*, and the scene where this package is thrown into a grate and Ganya refuses to pull it from the flames is one of the most dramatic of the novel (VIII, 145–46). Finally, even the old friendship between Lebedev and General Ivolgin is destroyed after a purse of money is found missing.

But acquisitiveness is not the only symptom displayed by a society that otherwise lacks any governing principle. The naive Myshkin encounters others: egoism, pride, rampant self-will. In his initial experience these take the rather innocent forms of Mrs. Epanchina's childish capriciousness and her daughter Aglaya's haughty self-centeredness. But Myshkin is compelled also to look upon the darker face of egoism: first in the hysterical insistence upon personal rights of Burdovsky and his radical henchmen; then in the murderous, selfish passion of Rogozhin and the studied rebellion against cosmic order preached by the young consumptive Ippolit; and finally—a recognition that comes to Myshkin too late—in the willful self-destruction of Nastasya Filippovna, in whose self-abasement Myshkin has seen only meekness. Lacking the sort of governing idea described by Lebedev in his tale of the cannibal monk, the society pictured in *The Idiot* splinters into separate and isolated individuals, all demanding their rights, craving money and flaunting their self-will. It is a measure of Myshkin's inexperience that he should on his arrival mistake this empty and unstable mix of individuals—egos suspended in a vacuum—for the sort of genuine communion of which he had dreamed in the isolation of his Swiss clinic.

IV *Myshkin and Christ*

But then, both literally and metaphorically, Myshkin is a man from another world. Kept apart by illness from his fellow men, he has spent several years prior to his arrival in Russia in the sterile environment of a Swiss clinic. He is a man of twenty-seven, but his emotional and intellectual development has been arrested; he has the heart and mind of a child. We can see immediately how Myshkin's period of suspended animation and his consequent ignorance of the pressures of modern life permit Dostoevsky to create a powerful dramatic conflict: what happens when a grown-up child, a complete innocent, is introduced into the maelstrom of passion, avarice, egoism, and intrigue that is modern European life? It is highly appropriate that Myshkin should arrive from Switzerland, the country that has such a long history of neutrality and only passive participation in European affairs, the sanctuary for refugees from European social, political, and intellectual activity.

But Myshkin's otherworldliness also has a metaphorical significance. He is clearly intended as a nineteenth-century restatement of the Quixotic knight errant, whose innocence allows him to preserve intact the idealistic vision of a golden age, despite the threatening encroachment of a much more prosaic reality. In a letter written to his niece, Sofia Ivanova, in 1868[5] Dostoevsky cites Cervantes's hero as a model for Myshkin, and traces of this model survive in the finished novel. When Aglaya, for example, receives a note of friendship from Myshkin, she conceals it in a copy of *Don Quixote de la Mancha*. She is also responsible for reading at a family gathering Pushkin's poem "The Poor Knight," whose theme obviously parallels Myshkin's self-denying love for Nastasya Filippovna. Moreover, it is difficult not to see in Myshkin's impassioned plea for utopia at the Epanchin soirée sentiments similar to those expressed in Quixote's speech with the acorn (*Don Quixote*, Part I, ch. 11). Both display a naive faith in the possibility of introducing a golden age, a heaven on earth, a possibility that is ironically contradicted by the behavior of people around them. Dostoevsky at this stage in his life rejected any heaven on earth. His association with utopian socialists in the 1840s had convinced him that all earthly utopias were the dreams of fools, madmen or, even worse, fanatics. The image of Christ had become for Dostoevsky a pledge that harmony and redemption will be possible for man only through suffering and resurrection.

This brings us to Myshkin's other allegorical identity. In addition to suggesting the chivalrous knight, he is also presented as a Christ-like figure, preaching the virtues of meekness, truth, and compassion. The failure of his ideals and his mission, encapsulated in the final scene of the novel, where Nastasya Filippovna lies a victim of Rogozhin's passion and Myshkin himself has returned to a state of idiocy, confirms his tragic flaw—Myshkin is only a Christ-*like* figure; he is human, not divine. His hopes of winning the trust of the characters he meets through his personal example of compassion, truthfulness, and humility betray his fatal ignorance of human nature. He is a victim of the utopianist's fundamental misconception—the belief that man is by nature good and that his goodness need only be discovered and nurtured. For Dostoevsky such a view ignored the Old Testament doctrine that man is born in sin, and that this sin has to be expiated, not obviated. Unlike Myshkin, Christ came from another world not to establish a heaven on earth, but to show the way to redemption in the next.

The image of the idiot evolved slowly during Dostoevsky's preparatory work on the novel, and Myshkin does not emerge in recognizable form until the sixth and seventh drafts,[6] but when the full image of the idiot Prince did finally come to Dostoevsky he noted it in terms which already suggested a close affinity between his hero and Christ. The Christ/Prince was evidently seen by Dostoevsky as a vital dramatic antithesis to the apocalyptic note struck by the other characters in the novel, many of whom had survived from much earlier drafts. What is more, Dostoevsky had been reading Renan's *Life of Jesus*, traces of which survive in the delineation of Myshkin's character.[7] There are distinct similarities between details of Christ's life as told in the gospels and Myshkin's personal history. Both enter the real world from another, quite different one in order to preach the virtues of humility, truth, and compassion. Indeed Myshkin confesses to the Epanchin sisters that he perhaps regards himself as a philosopher who has come to teach (VIII, 51). Moreover, throughout the novel Myshkin seems to regard Switzerland as a sort of heaven, where his innocence had remained intact and his faith unshaken, a far cry from the complexities of Russia which tempt, torment, and confuse him. It is to Switzerland that he longs to escape when the pressures of his new life in Russia become too much for him.

The anecdotes Myshkin relates about his stay in Switzerland provide some of the clearest parallels between him and Christ. For example, he tells of how he befriended a young consumptive, Marie, who had been seduced by a traveling salesman and who was consequently spurned by the whole village, including the priest and her own mother. Moved by deep compassion, Myshkin gives her money and kisses her on the cheek. Through this gesture he gradually wins over first the children of the village and then the others. The fallen Marie is resurrected, accepted back into the community, and knows great happiness in the short time left to her before her death. The whole story, even down to the girl's name, is quite obviously intended to be read as an allegorical reworking of the tale of Christ and the fallen woman, Mary Magdalene, Myshkin's subsequent friendship with the children of the village, whom he treats as adults and to whom he does not lie, reminds us of another biblical image—Christ surrounded by the children. Like Christ, Myshkin is disliked by the elders and teachers of the village because he tells the children only the truth.

But the identification of Myshkin with Christ is not confined to the Swiss episodes. It is, like the apocalyptic imagery, a strand that runs throughout the novel. A brief examination of some of the most outstanding examples should serve to show this. First, as with Christ, very little is known about Myshkin's formative years, an omission which is attributable to his fragile nervous condition, for large stretches of his life are unknown even to him. When he is taken semiconscious to Schneider's clinic, the only thing which makes an impression upon him is the sound of an ass braying as he enters Switzerland. This suggests, if somewhat dimly, Christ's triumphal entry into Jerusalem on an ass. The first thing Christ encountered on his arrival in Jerusalem were the merchants and moneylenders conducting their trade on the steps of the temple. Here too Myshkin undergoes a parallel experience: his arrival in Russia is marked by an immediate acquaintance with merchants (Rogozhin, Totsky, and so on) and moneylenders (Ptitsyn). Even the other characters in the novel appear to recognize Myshkin's Christ-like characteristics. Evgeny Radomsky, for instance, compares Myshkin's attitude to Nastasya Filippovna with Christ's defense of the fallen woman. Aglaya, too, insists that Myshkin's mission is to "resurrect" Nastasya. What is more, both General Epanchin and his wife, quite independently and for widely differing reasons, react to Myshkin's arrival with the feeling that he has been sent by God to help them in their difficulties.

Later in the novel two further episodes involving Myshkin have possible biblical counterparts: his long retreat from St. Petersburg to collect his thoughts may be compared with Christ's retreat into the wilderness; and the scene where he discusses socialism, atheism, catholicism, and the Golden Age with the much more experienced guests at the Epanchin soirée is clearly analogous to the young Christ's teaching of the elders.[8] At times Myshkin's words strike one as paraphrases of some of Christ's utterances: for example, his remark that "humility is a terrible force" (VIII, 329) and his belief that "compassion is the main and perhaps the only law of all human existence" (VIII, 192). Here one could even adduce Myshkin's comment to Lebedev shortly after his arrival in Pavlovsk to recuperate from his first epileptic fit, when he asks him not to send any of his visitors away: "Let them all come, if they wish" (VIII, 199). Such were Christ's instructions to his disciples when they sought to turn away the children brought to him to be healed.

V   The Flawed Christ

But if Myshkin is a Christ, he is a flawed one. The most striking feature of his behavior throughout the novel is the rift between his intentions and his achievements. His naive and childlike simplicity, which has had such a benign effect upon the people he knows in

Switzerland, becomes a disruptive and ultimately lethal force when transferred to the "real world" of nineteenth-century Russia. For example, his faith in compassion as "the main and perhaps the only law of all human existence" is amply justified by the results he achieves in Switzerland: his pity resurrects the fallen and despised Marie. In Russia another despised woman seduced by another wandering businessman awaits resurrection, and Myshkin sets about his task in the same way, responding with immediate compassion to the suffering he detects in Nastasya Filippovna's portrait and kissing the picture as he had kissed Marie's cheek. But the resurrection Myshkin longs to bring to Nastasya (the name *Anastasiya* means "the resurrected one") is not to be attained as easily as the new life he brought to Marie. Myshkin's compassionate and self-denying love for her is misconstrued by all: it arouses the jealousy of Aglaya, the indignation of society and, most lethally, the murderous passion of Rogozhin. Myshkin's pity brings to Nastasya Filippovna not resurrection but death. The paradox of Myshkin's benign ideals and destructive actions is suggested in his very name, Lev Myshkin (Lev—*"lion"*; *myshka*—"little mouse"). The mouse becomes a lion when unleashed in the world.

The effects of all this are not confined to Nastasya Filippovna. Within hours of his arrival Myshkin has alienated Ganya by his naive interference in the latter's pursuit of Aglaya, and embarrassed General Epanchin by ingenuously bringing up the name of Nastasya Filippovna in the most inappropriate company. Subsequently his attempts at tact wound Burdovsky's vanity, shame the unfortunate General Ivolgin, and arouse the poisonous hatred of the prickly and rebellious Ippolit. His decision to steer a moderate course between the two rivals for his love, Nastasya and Aglaya, offends both. His assurances that he is not to be considered a rival for possession of Nastasya Filippovna drive the proud and passionate Rogozhin first to attempted murder, and then to murder. The list of such incidents could be extended considerably.

It is not that Myshkin is unaware of the results of his attempts to put his ideals into practice. A minor character, Prince Shch., warns him that heaven on earth is more difficult to attain than he dreams in the simplicity of his heart (VIII, 282). Even Dostoevsky offers a veiled warning in the first chapter that what is appropriate to Switzerland is not suitable for Russia. Admittedly he has in mind Myshkin's quite eccentric apparel, but the implications are not lost on the reader. But perhaps Myshkin's awareness of the precious nature of his dreams of harmony is best conveyed in his ambiguous attitude toward his own illness, epilepsy. The aura that precedes an epileptic fit affords Myshkin his most acute insights into beauty, harmony, and reconciliation, but he knows that these insights cannot be prolonged for they are soon overwhelmed by the chaos and darkness of the fit itself. Realizing the fragility of his ideals, Myshkin is reluctant to elaborate them to others for fear of debasing them by his inability to translate ideas effectively into form. His fit at the Epanchin soirée is thus doubly appropriate in that it follows Myshkin's attempts to communicate his dreams of harmony to others, and strikes at the very moment when he reveals his ecstatic vision of a future golden age, when man's highest ideals will be embodied in the behavior of ordinary people. Myshkin's illness is a pledge of the impossibility of achieving heaven on earth. It is the flaw at the very heart of Dostoevsky's most harmonious hero.

The hallmark of Myshkin's mission is thus its failure, but it is a failure which Dostoevsky anticipated. Indeed the idea of failure seems to have been with Dostoevsky from an early stage in the conception of his "positively good" hero. This accounts for the diffident tone of the letter to his niece, in which he outlines his projected novel:

The main idea of the novel is to depict the positively good man. There is nothing more difficult than this in the world, particularly at present. All those writers who have set out to depict the *positively* good man have always shirked the job—and not just our writers, but European ones as well. For this is a boundless task. The good is an ideal, and neither we ourselves nor civilized Europe has got anywhere near working out an ideal. There has existed on earth only one positively good man—Christ; so that the appearance of this boundlessly, infinitely good figure is in itself, of course, an endless miracle. . . . Of all the good characters in Christian literature the most complete is Don Quixote. But he is good only because he is at the same time ridiculous. Dickens' Pickwick (an infinitely weaker conception than Don Quixote, but nonetheless still immense) is also ridiculous and succeeds only because of this. Compassion is aroused for the ridiculed good man who does not know his own worth, and because of this sympathy is evoked in the reader. This arousing of sympathy is the very secret of humor. . . . I have nothing of this sort in my novel, absolutely nothing, and consequently I am terribly afraid it will be a positive failure.[9]

By the final version, of course, Dostoevsky had recognized the need to invest his positively good man with a flaw to ensure him both compassion and credibility, and Myshkin becomes the victim of epilepsy. Like other creators of positive heroes, Dostoevsky draws back from the challenge of creating a flawless hero, for he knows that such a figure could not be human, but would be, like Christ, divine. Myshkin's epilepsy is Dostoevsky's acknowledgment of man's imperfect state.

Myshkin's initial innocence and his subsequent development is the dramatic device Dostoevsky chooses to convey his lack of faith in the perfectibility of man. The Myshkin who arrives as an innocent from Switzerland carries within himself, in the form of his epilepsy, a metaphor for the inevitable destruction of his idealism. Prior to his arrival he is not, in Dostoevsky's eyes, a human being at all, *for he has not known sin*. He is the product of a retort, a homunculus bred in the sterile laboratory of Schneider's clinic. He is an artificially grown replica of that which no longer exists on earth—man untainted by the Fall. The remainder of the novel, depicting Myshkin in the "real world" of Russia, a world which not only has known sin but which is suspended above Armageddon, traces Myshkin's inevitable decline as his humanity, suppressed by years of isolation, asserts itself. Myshkin, of course, resists his fall, but the process is unstoppable, the end result inescapable; for only Christ and not a merely Christlike figure is without sin. As a result Myshkin's purely Christian love for Nastasya Filippovna is compromised by a growing personal love for Aglaya; his initial refusal to judge people, based on the belief that only God has the right to judge, yields to a growing suspicion that Rogozhin is bound to destroy Nastasya; and the purity of heart suggested by his total lack of material wealth is darkened by his highly symbolic inheritance. Myshkin inherits more than money on his arrival in Russia—he acquires also his due legacy of human weaknesses.

VI *Rogozhin*

The decline of Myshkin centers upon his increasing intimacy with two of the novel's secondary characters: Rogozhin and Ippolit. These are Myshkin's alter-egos, embodiments of those qualities of which he has been artificially deprived: sexual egoism and intellectual arrogance. These are qualities that man acquired at the moment of his fall from the paradise of Eden. At that moment Adam claimed the right to know for himself the ways of God and was punished for this intellectual arrogance with isolation, sexual self-awareness, and bodily shame. *The Idiot* dramatizes these features of Original Sin in the destructive sexuality and selfishness of Rogozhin and the rampant egoism and willful rebellion of the dying Ippolit. This helps to explain, at least symbolically, why Myshkin insists on the presence of both Rogozhin and Ippolit when he decides, at his birthday party (Part III, chs. 3 and 4), to embark upon a new and less ascetic way of life.

Rogozhin's function in the novel must, one suspects, arouse mixed feelings in most readers. Undoubtedly a compellingly melodramatic figure, he is nevertheless a little too markedly contrived as a schematic complement to Myshkin, who dogs the hero's steps like a supernatural double. In Rogozhin in particular the bones of Dostoevsky's novel poke through its flesh. In the early drafts the qualities subsequently embodied in the two figures of Myshkin and Rogozhin overlapped in a single character, a fact which confirms the complementary nature of the two. Rogozhin is the dark opposed to the light of Myshkin, the passion that throws his compassion into relief, the physical strength that emphasizes his weakness. Like the concepts of good and evil, neither can be defined or understood without the other. In 1849 at the tribunal set up to investigate the Petrashevsky affair, Dostoevsky commented on the need for the artist to depict both black and white, in terms which evocatively anticipate the Myshkin-Rogozhin relationship:

Is it possible to depict something only in bright colors? How can the bright side of a picture be visible without the dark? Can there be a picture that does not have light and dark together? We are aware of the concept of light only because there is such a thing as darkness. We are told to depict only the heroic, only the virtues. But without vice we will not recognize virtue; the very concepts of *good* and *evil* derive from the fact that good and evil have always lived together, side by side.[10]

That Myshkin and Rogozhin are supposed to represent the unity of such opposing concepts is suggested at the very start of *The Idiot*. On the train from Switzerland Myshkin finds himself sitting opposite Rogozhin. Dostoevsky's purely schematic physical descriptions emphasize first a link between the two—they are of the same age—but then go on to associate Myshkin with light (*svet*) and Rogozhin with darkness (*mrak*). We learn, for example, that Myshkin is fair-haired, with a light beard and sunken cheekbones, and that "his eyes were large, blue and steady; in their look there was something tranquil . . ." (VIII, 6). Rogozhin, on the other hand, has dark hair, a swarthy appearance, and a vigorous manner that suggests passion, suffering, and a total lack of the harmony discernible in Myshkin. Moreover, Rogozhin's heavy clothing implies that he is quite accustomed to the icy winds, both literal and figurative, that blow through the Russia about to be described, whereas Myshkin's light and unsuitable dress suggests that he is totally unprepared for what awaits him in his new life. In these physical descriptions, as always in Dostoevsky's novels, the heroes wear their souls on their sleeves for all to see.

The qualities of darkness, physical robustness, passion, and lack of form become leitmotifs consistently associated with Rogozhin. The description that opens Part II, chapter 3 shows, for example, that Rogozhin's house duplicates many of the features of its occupant. Despite his lack of familiarity with the area, Myshkin recognizes the house immediately "because of its peculiar physiognomy." It is gloomy (*mrachnyi*), with very few windows to let in the light. It is very solidly constructed, but totally devoid of pleasing form, "completely without architectural merit." Myshkin is struck by its ugliness and darkness as soon as he enters: "How dark it is! You live gloomily. . . ." The house has other features which help to define the soul of its owner: it has been associated with the sect of the Castrates (religious sectarianism is often linked with murder in Dostoevsky's novels[11]), and the ground floor is leased to a moneylender. Moreover, the house reeks of death: Nastasya Filippovna is reported to have remarked that she believes there is a corpse hidden beneath the floor; pictures of Rogozhin's deceased father hang on the walls; and there is another painting depicting the most awful death of all: a copy of Holbein's *Christ in the Tomb* hanging in the gloomy chambers and depicting a dead Christ whose decomposing body holds out little hope of resurrection. Holbein's painting is central to an understanding of Rogozhin's role in the novel. He contemplates it with pained yet compulsive fascination, although it is one of the most unnerving paintings of all time, as Ippolit later concurs. It presents one of the most hopeful moments of spiritual history—Christ's death for mankind with its promise of resurrection—as one of the most hopeless. The figure of Christ, which for Dostoevsky was the very summit of ideal beauty since it was the Word made flesh, is here presented as ugly, decaying, and deformed. No trace of inner beauty can be discerned beyond the broken form. Like Myshkin, this Christ, too, is human, not divine.

Yet Rogozhin's almost religious fascination with this painting—it is a sort of anti-icon in his home—is entirely appropriate, for it is his task always to negate the primitive ideals of Myshkin. The Prince argues that "beauty will save the world"; Rogozhin surrounds himself with form-denying chaos and destroys the beauty of Nastasya Filippovna, whose portrait Myshkin had worshiped. Myshkin believes that the ideals of Christ will save this fallen world; Rogozhin displays a Christ vanquished by death. Myshkin dreams of life everlasting; Rogozhin epitomizes spiritual death.

Yet like two poles in a merciless dialectic Myshkin and Rogozhin are fated to come together, not in the reconciliation of synthesis but in the explosive, destructive violence of matter meeting antimatter. At Rogozhin's house Myshkin and his alter-ego exchange crosses in the hope of becoming spiritual brothers, but the exchange is an empty gesture—the value of Myshkin's cross is debased by its previous owner, who had sold it for drink—and the final affinity of Myshkin and Rogozhin is denied until the last scene, which demonstrates their mutual complicity in the death of Nastasya Filippovna. But this scene is only the culmination of a process of rapprochement that accelerates as the novel progresses. Complicity with Rogozhin is the dark fate that awaits the "positively good man" from the moment he leaves the artificial paradise of Schneider's clinic and enters the world of nineteenth-century Russia. Rogozhin's presence always serves to confirm Myshkin's growing human weaknesses. He appears on the stairs of Myshkin's hotel and attempts to murder him only after Myshkin's trust in Rogozhin has yielded to the suspicion that he will resort to violence (Part II, ch. 5). He appears mysteriously in the gardens near the Prince's Pavlovsk retreat, at the dead of night, immediately after the birth of Myshkin's personal love for Aglaya, which diverts him from his selfless devotion to Nastasya Filippovna (Part III, ch. 3). But mostly Rogozhin serves as a symbolic denial of the possibility of Myshkin's translating his luminous ideals into workable form. The dark figure of Rogozhin represents formless chaos itself, and Myshkin's attempts to begin his esthetic education by reading Pushkin with him (VIII, 457–58) can only fail. Rogozhin remains the criterion against which we measure Myshkin's own unsuccessful bid to give form to his ideals. By the end of the novel Myshkin's own actions point to his failure, for he too becomes the destroyer of form. He accidentally breaks the fragile formal beauty of the Chinese vase at the Epanchin soirée; he offends the delicate sensibilities of Ippolit and General Ivolgin, both of whom are tellingly compared to pieces of fine porcelain; and finally he is compelled to take his place alongside Rogozhin in that last, tragic celebration of the destruction of a beautiful ideal—the haunting vigil over the corpse of Nastasya Filippovna, who is directly the victim of Rogozhin's passion but whose death is indirectly attributable to Myshkin's compassion.

VII *Ippolit*

Ippolit Terentev is the second of Myshkin's tragic alter-egos, and a further sign of the fall that awaits him. Most readers find Ippolit an irksome and overweening character, with an irritating presence not softened by anything like the seductive melodrama that makes Rogozhin palatable. Yet certain things must be said about him. Ippolit is an example of man at his most rebellious. His existence, like that of the Underground Man, is a dark blot on the dream of universal harmony. He is alienated by that rebellious egoism which illness has concealed from Myshkin. Yet at the same time he is clearly intended as another yardstick against which we must assess Myshkin's success or failure as "the positively good man," for Ippolit is Myshkin deprived of his saintliness and given a human face and human weaknesses. As Professor Peace has demonstrated, the links between them are carefully constructed.[12]

Ippolit is, like Myshkin, a victim of God's will. He is a condemned man, obliged to bear the burden of illness and early death despite the contributions he feels he could make to mankind. "Why is it," he argues, "that Nature creates the finest creatures only in order to laugh at them?" (VIII, 247). Myshkin, too, is one of God's finest creatures, and his qualities are mocked by his illness; moreover, Myshkin talks at length in the early chapters of the novel about the plight of the condemned man. He recalls an execution he witnessed at Lyons and a friend who was condemned to death but reprieved at the last moment, a detail obviously drawn from Dostoevsky's own experience in 1849. From these instances Myshkin apparently draws the conclusion that condemnation of man by man is wrong and that legal killing is infinitely worse than the spontaneous crime for which the convict is punished. But despite his opposition to capital punishment and man's cruelty to man, Myshkin displays an attitude of resignation and acquiescence toward the sign of his own condemnation by God, his epilepsy. Myshkin the Christian does not challenge the will of God, even when this means the ruin of his own life. But Myshkin's humility is an insult to Ippolit; he responds to his death sentence with rebellious rage. He wants to know why God has seen fit to condemn him, and refuses to die with humble resignation unless he is allowed to understand the reason for his death. Like Ivan Karamazov, Ippolit demands an insight into the workings of God's will, and this of course is a legacy of man's fall from grace. In his rebellious arrogance Ippolit reveals his humanity, and he devises a petulant revolt against the God who has condemned him. He will not die humbly; he will take the only course left through which he can assert his own will—suicide. In the event Ippolit's attempt to shoot himself fails, for he loads the revolver incorrectly, but even here there is a covert link between him and Myshkin, for shortly before Ippolit's attempted suicide, Myshkin has been discussing with Aglaya the correct way to load a revolver (VIII, 294).

Myshkin and Ippolit are also united by a strange dream they both have. During his reading of an apology for his life, the "Necessary Explanation," Ippolit confesses to moments when an excruciatingly painful awareness of his own alienation from life overwhelms him. At such moments he is more aware than ever of the participation of all things living in the great feast of life, and of his own exclusion: "What is your nature to me, your Pavlovsk park, your sunrises and sunsets, your blue sky and your smug faces, when the whole of that feast which has no end has begun by excluding me and me alone from participation? What is all this beauty to me when every minute, every second . . . . I'm compelled to recognize that even that tiny little fly over there, buzzing around me in the sunlight, has a place in this feast, in this chorus; that it knows its place, loves it and is happy. And only I am an outcast . . ." (VIII, 343). Myshkin is troubled by Ippolit's remarks because, as he reveals at the end of the same chapter, he too has known equally painful moments of estrangement; and moreover, these moments have been prompted by exactly the same experience of witnessing, in the image of a fly in the sunlight, the beauty and harmony of the feast of life, from which he too is an exile. "He had suffered dumbly, in isolation, but now it seemed to him that he had said all this at the time, that he had used the very same words, and that Ippolit had taken that 'fly' from him, from his words and tears at that time . . ." (VIII, 352).

But although Myshkin and Ippolit are potential brothers in misfortune, they are held apart by the way they react to their condemnation and exclusion from life's feast. Ippolit urges the assertion of the will and Myshkin its effacement, arguing that "humility (smirenie) is a terrible force." But, as was the case with Rogozhin, opposite poles attract, and Myshkin finds himself increasingly drawn toward Ippolit's position, both on the level of psychology and that of symbol. Despite his opposition to the condemnation of man by man, he begins to judge his acquaintances. His growing suspicion of Rogozhin is an early example of this, and later he is increasingly irritated at the behavior of Lebedev, Lebedev's nephew, and Keller. It is to Keller that he confesses his growing vulnerability to base and "double" thoughts.

But it is perhaps on the level of symbol that Myshkin's affinity with Ippolit is most strongly suggested. After Ippolit's confession and Myshkin's concern over the similarity of their dreams, Myshkin falls asleep on the green bench where he has arranged an assignation with Aglaya. (It is worth remarking here that Ippolit too is increasingly attracted to Aglaya.) His fitful sleep is punctuated by disturbing and strangely revealing dreams. First he sees the face of Ippolit and remembers a warning given shortly before by Radomsky to the effect that Ippolit now has nothing further to lose and is therefore quite capable of murdering a dozen people out of spite. Myshkin immediately rejects the idea that Ippolit could become a criminal. But then the image of Ippolit is displaced in Myshkin's dream by that of Nastasya Filippovna, "but strangely she did not seem to have the same face as he had always known, and he desperately wanted not to acknowledge her as the same woman. In this face there was so much remorse and horror that it seemed to be the face of a great criminal who had just committed a terrible crime . . . . His heart froze; nothing, nothing at all would allow him to admit that she was a criminal; but he sensed that at any moment something terrible was about to happen, something he would remember for the rest of his life" (VIII, 352).

The face of a potential criminal, Ippolit, here compels Myshkin to reassess his view of Nastasya Filippovna. Throughout the work Nastasya Filippovna has been important to Myshkin as the embodiment of an ideal. He has persisted in seeing in her a symbol of suffering and humility. Her deliberate self-abasement, her courting of dishonor, represent for him her desire to be reborn through the humble acceptance of suffering. But now, wiser after his experience with Ippolit's revolt, Myshkin realizes that Nastasya Filippovna's apparent humility conceals a huge reservoir of pride. Her "humility" is indeed a terrible force, but not in the Christian sense. She humiliates and abases herself not out of any desire for reconciliation, but out of a craving for willful revenge, as a form of protest against her condemnation. And this aligns her not with Myshkin's Christian humility, but with Ippolit's willful rebellion. The moment when her image displaces Ippolit's in Myshkin's dream, and both display their capacity for criminality, represents the Prince's acknowledgment that her behavior provides the fatal link between his own humility and Ippolit's pride. In this world even the redeeming force of meekness is perverted into pride. The apparently irreconcilable figures of Myshkin and Ippolit begin to overlap; the Prince's fall from humility begins.

VIII *Conclusion*

In the decline of the "positively good" Myshkin into those weaknesses of humanity exhibited by Rogozhin and Ippolit, *The Idiot*
describes the failure of an ideal which Dostoevsky had cherished in
his youth, but which he had abandoned after his flirtation with
utopian socialism in the 1840s: the belief in the possibility of a golden
age, a paradise on earth. As Dostoevsky implied in his late story "Son
smeshnogo cheloveka" [The Dream of a Ridiculous Man, 1877],
utopia is the dream of innocents who have failed to acknowledge the
sinfulness of man. Reconciliation and harmony are attainable only in
the next world, not in this; and Myshkin's mission among the spiritual
ruins of nineteenth-century Europe ends only in chaos and darkness.
His own ideals disappear under a new attack of his illness; his fallen
woman achieves not reconciliation, but violent death; his erstwhile
fiancée, Agalya, seals her spiritual ruin by fleeing Russia and marrying a
Catholic Pole—for Dostoevsky a fate far worse than death. And
with the destruction of the Prince and his ideals, his two alter-egos
return to the void—Rogozhin goes to imprisonment and exile, Ippolit
to death.

And the fallen world that has proved too much for Myshkin re-
sumes its interrupted pursuit of money, power, and personal rights.
But for Dostoevsky the Christian a debt is still owed; the threat of
Armageddon still hangs over his native land, and it is to fall with
unprecedented ferocity and violence in the next of Dostoevsky's great
novels, *The Devils*.

CHAPTER 6

The Desert of the Will:
The Devils *and* A Raw Youth

I N late 1869 Dostoevsky was in Dresden. Public response to *The Idiot* had been less than enthusiastic, and the author himself was dissatisfied with the novel whose theme he had so cherished. Any fears that his artistic powers were declining had been dispelled by the recent completion of *The Eternal Husband*, technically perhaps the most accomplished of Dostoevsky's works. Yet this novella was a short and, by Dostoevskian standards, light piece: the novelist still longed to produce a major work which would fire the imagination of the Russian reading public as *Crime and Punishment* had done. For some time he had been drafting plans for a series of novels dealing with the loss and reacquisition of faith. The notebooks include the working titles of *Atheism* and *The Life of a Great Sinner* for this ambitious project. Upon his arrival in Dresden Dostoevsky set about his task with urgency. He was disturbed, however, by several manifestations of political instability in both Western Europe and Russia. The Franco-Prussian war, which began in July 1870, and the subsequent rise and destruction of the Paris Commune confirmed Dostoevsky's view that Western Europe had abandoned Christ and was about to collapse. Moreover, the western sickness seemed also to have afflicted his own land. Russia in the late 1860s and early 1870s teemed with all kinds of socialists, nihilists, and anarchists, all of whom preached the destruction of the present order to make way for a new secular paradise. The inspiration for many Russian radicals was Mikhail Bakunin, the exiled revolutionary, whose energetic exploits Dostoevsky followed in the European press.

In November 1869 an event had occurred which seemed to Dostoevsky to symbolize the full horror of the political sickness spreading through his native land: a young student, Ivanov, was murdered at the Moscow Agricultural Academy by a small political group led by an intriguer, Sergey Nechaev. This event, which became a *cause célèbre* in Russia, struck Dostoevsky all the more forcibly because his young brother-in-law had been a fellow student of Ivanov's at the academy. Nechaev, who already had a colorful political record, claimed to represent Bakunin and organized an underground political group which Ivanov joined.[1] When Ivanov's commitment came under suspicion Nechaev persuaded the other members that he was a risk and had to be eliminated. He was subsequently murdered on the academy grounds and his body was tossed into a pond. The murder focused all Dostoevsky's political passions and provided a dramatic event around which to construct a "pamphlet novel" attacking contemporary nihilism. Dostoevsky's own association with subversive groups in the 1840s sharpened the edge of his polemic, and he set to work with the zeal of a reformed man to expose the horrors of radicalism. His ambitious plans for *The Life of a Great Sinner* receded to make way for a political statement of real urgency. In the spring of 1870 he wrote: "I mean to utter certain thoughts, whether the artistic side of it goes to the dogs or not. . . . Even if it turns out to be a mere pamphlet, I shall say all I have in my heart.[2] Drawing on newspaper accounts and his own rich vein of antinihilism, Dostoevsky worked for over a year in Dresden on his "pamphlet-novel." He returned to Russia in July 1871, at the start of the sensational Nechaev trial.

But the novel that began as a mere political statement became more complicated as the work progressed. The role of straightforward pamphleteer ill suited Dostoevsky: he could not suppress his commitment to a major work on atheism and salvation, and almost against his will elements from *The Life of a Great Sinner* crept into his political novel. By the end of 1870 Dostoevsky had destroyed much of his original material and started again. The Ivanov murder was relegated to a secondary plane and the center of the new version was occupied by an enigmatic figure from *The Life of a Great Sinner*, a figure that was to become Nikolay Stavrogin.

The fusion of political polemic and material from Dostoevsky's great philosophical project is not as capricious as it might seem. Antiradical polemic had been the springboard for *Notes from Underground* and *Crime and Punishment*, and it had penetrated even *The Idiot*. Moreover, the political nihilism exhibited in the Nechaev affair is enriched in *The Devils* through juxtaposition with Stavrogin's outstanding feature, his *spiritual nihilism*. *The Devils* thus becomes a two-pronged analysis of nihilism in its many forms: political, philosophical, emotional, and spiritual. This marriage of politics and philosophy makes *The Devils* the supreme antinihilist novel.

The completed work relies heavily on the Nechaev affair for its plot details. It tells of a small provincial discussion group loosely gathered around Stepan Trofimovich Verkhovensky, a faded liberal-Westernizer[3] whose political heyday had been in the 1840s but who is now reduced to living off the charity of the leading local landowner, Varvara Petrovna Stavrogina. The group is harmless enough until the arrival of Verkhovensky's son Petr, who, claiming to represent a large revolutionary organization, quickly ousts his father as ringleader and imparts to it an altogether more radical flavor. Ugly incidents break out in the town: an icon is desecrated, a Bible-seller is compromised, political pamphlets are distributed, and unrest is fomented among workers at a local factory. Matters come to a head at a fete organized by the Governor's wife, Julia von Lembke, where radical speeches are made, a great writer, Karmazinov, is disgraced and incendiarism breaks out, claiming the lives of an associate of the group, Captain Lebyadkin, and his halfwitted, crippled sister, Maria.

When a member of the group, Ivan Shatov, wishes to leave as the result of a change of his convictions, Petr persuades the other members to murder him. He then flees, leaving the rest to face the consequences of their action.

Against this background is traced the story of Nikolay Stavrogin, Varvara Petrovna's son, who arrives with Petr. Stavrogin is enveloped in mystery: he shows signs of madness; he fights a duel with Gaganov, whose father he has offended, and fires into the air; it turns out he is married to Maria Lebyadkina. Yet all are drawn to him: Shatov worships him, as does another member of the group, the suicidal maniac Kirillov; women are fatally attracted to him, particularly Shatov's meek sister, Dasha, and the beautiful Liza Tushina, despite the latter's engagement to Mavriky Drozdov; Petr wants him to lead his political movement, and to this end even attempts to gain Stavrogin's complicity by engineering the murder of his embarrassing wife. Yet Stavrogin remains aloof and enigmatic, the victim of a profound, existential boredom relieved only by his eventual suicide.

The novel culminates in an epidemic of murder and suicide, which is only partially offset by the spiritual rebirth of old Stepan Trofimovich, who recognizes the mistakes of his life and embarks on a pilgrimage in search of God and the Russian people. Along the way he dies.

The Devils was serialized in Mikhail Katkov's journal *Russian Herald* in 1871 and 1872, but Katkov insisted that a chapter in which Stavrogin confesses to the violation of a young girl, who then takes her own life, be omitted. This chapter, "U Tikhona" (At Tikhon's), was to have followed chapter 8 of Part II and contains a long interview between Stavrogin and the holy elder Tikhon, in which much of Stavrogin's mysterious past is disclosed. It was not reinstated in the subsequent book edition of the novel, but since it sheds so much light on Stavrogin's personality some editors have appended it to recent editions.

I   *The Politics of* The Devils

Dostoevsky's political polemic in *The Devils* is conducted on two fronts: a series of vitriolic caricatures of political figures and types is complemented by a rejection of socialism and revolution on philosophical grounds. The novel is rich in satirical caricature, and prototypes have been discovered for most of its major figures. Petr Verkhovensky is clearly distilled from Nechaev, and the murder of Shatov closely follows the known facts of the Ivanov killing. Like Nechaev, Petr is a charismatic personality, quick to exploit the follies and weaknesses of others. He too pretends to represent a vast political organization, on the strength of which he dominates the other members of his group.[4] Like Nechaev's, his "socialism" is of a peculiar variety: he shows little love for his fellow men, but demonstrates an impressive capacity for duplicity and political intrigue. At heart he is a tyrant who chooses the political arena in which to show his strength. Strangely enough Dostoevsky depicts him as a menacing, but nonetheless comic figure. By no stretch of the imagination could the exploits of Nechaev be dismissed as comic, but by presenting his own Nechaev in a semibuffoonish guise Dostoevsky displays his determination not to submit to the man's charisma. Nechaev was after all a cynical murderer and a rogue; such men could not, in Dostoevsky's view, merit heroic stature.

Several other members of Petr's group have recognizable prototypes: the fanatical Erkel, for instance, suggests N. Nikolaev, a coldblooded assassin and Nechaev's righthand man. The ridiculous Virginsky, who proclaims his enlightened views by encouraging his wife's sexual indiscretions, is clearly based upon a character in Chernyshevsky's well-known *roman à thèse, What Is to Be Done?* Shatov is the Ivanov to Petr's Nechaev, but he also stands as a fine, ironic caricature of the fanatical Slavophile for whom empty nationalism takes the place of a real faith in God. Shatov rejects Europe and its values, and regards the Russians as the only God-bearing people. He believes that Christ's second coming will be among the Russian people, who will then bring about the spiritual rebirth of the rest of the world. The fatal flaw in Shatov's position—a flaw exposed by Stavrogin—is that, despite his fanatical religious chauvinism, he does not believe in God. Shatov's dilemma is possibly all the more poignant in that critics have persistently seen in this character a painfully honest self-portrait of Dostoevsky himself. Certainly the writer shared Shatov's intense nationalism and populism and his view of the importance of Russian Christianity. Whether he also shared Shatov's paradoxical lack of faith, however, is questionable.

Shatov is ideologically counterbalanced by his neighbor Kirillov, whose Westernism is suggested by the fact that he is an engineer, a product of the West's technical expertise. His estrangement from his Russian roots is symptomized by his inability to speak Russian correctly, and the final flourish he adds to his suicide note—"de Kiriloff, gentilhomme russe et citoyen du monde" (X, 473)—anticipates Dostoevsky's description of the arch-Westernizer Herzen in *Diary of a Writer*.[5] Kirillov also embodies the militant atheism characteristic of the Westernizers: he advocates the apotheosis of man through will, and commits suicide as a gesture of strength. Yet ultimately Kirillov's convictions are as hollow as Shatov's, for beneath his defiant deification of man he is clearly tormented by profound and irrational faith in God. Shatov the Christian cannot find God; Kirillov the atheist cannot escape Him; and in their tragedies Dostoevsky exposes what he regarded as the failure of the extreme ideological positions adopted by Slavophiles and Westernizers in the middle decades of the century.

The figure of Stepan Trofimovich Verkhovensky was modeled on T.N. Granovsky, a professor of history and influential liberal of the 1840s, but he embodies features characteristic of many liberal Westernizers of that generation. His exaggerated use of French, his consignment of his native Russia to the dustbin of history, his love of romantic intrigue, his estheticism, his poetical idealism and loss of a sense of reality—all these features mark out Stepan Trofimovich as a generalized portrait of the "man of the forties," a type already familiar in Russian literature from Turgenev's *Rudin* and *Fathers and Sons*. Stepan Trofimovich stands as an indictment of the kind of romantic dreaming that had afflicted Dostoevsky himself in the 1840s, and which had colored Russian political thought for a whole generation. Although a genial and humane man, he is out of touch with Russian reality, and his otherworldliness leads him into moral and political duplicity. He preaches the brotherhood of man but abandons his own son; he advocates the abolition of serfdom but gambles away his serf, Fedka, at cards. The return of Petr and the murder of the Lebyadkins by the criminal Fedka are thus symbolic events: they allow Dostoevsky to indict the representative of the generation of the 1840s for the excesses committed by his "children." The naive and apparently harmless generation of idealists has bred a generation of monsters. For Dostoevsky the moral responsibility for the "sons" of the 1860s lay with the "fathers" of the 1840s, an interesting variation on the theme of Turgenev's novel.

This indictment of Stepan Trofimovich, as well as his eventual rebirth, is prefigured in the novel's epigraph from St. Luke, which describes how devils leave a possessed man and enter a herd of swine. The swine throw themselves into a lake and are drowned, while the possessed man is left cleansed and sitting at Christ's feet. Similarly the "swine" of the novel—Petr and his cohorts—take from Stepan Trofimovich's generation the revolutionary instincts which destroy them, and Stepan, no longer possessed, dies by a lakeside within sight of a village called Spasov (Village of Our Savior).

Dostoevsky's treatment of Shatov, Kirillov, and Stepan Trofimovich is on the whole goodnatured. The same cannot be said of his depiction of the writer Karmazinov, a spiteful caricature of his old enemy Turgenev. Dostoevsky had long despised Turgenev for his foppishness, affectation, wealth, Westernism, and ingratiating attitude toward the younger generation. He mocks these features mercilessly in *The Devils* as Karmazinov is revealed as a pretentious, written-out buffoon. Turgenev was bitterly offended by this caricature, and showed that he in turn had the measure of Dostoevsky by describing him as the nastiest Christian he had ever met.

The Devils contains many other examples of political caricature, but to discuss these further would be unproductive, for although they may excite our admiration of Dostoevsky's guile, malice, and satirical abilities, they do ultimately threaten to trivialize the novel's serious polemical design. For *The Devils* is not about the particular weaknesses of revolutionary personalities and their sympathizers, but about the moral failure of revolutionary ideals themselves. Revolutionary socialism purported to eliminate social injustice and create new social harmonies, but without first redeeming the sinful nature of man himself. For Dostoevsky such a dream was unrealistic; as Irving Howe remarks: "no political system which located salvation in the secular world could have been acceptable to Dostoevsky."[6] Man is unable to live in harmony not because his social institutions are wrong, but because he is morally incapable of so doing. The Old Testament tells of man's expulsion from paradise, and the New suggests that only his complete moral transfiguration through suffering and faith will allow him to return. Such a transfiguration cannot be achieved through social change, which is powerless to redeem a corrupt soul. In allowing the ideals of the Russian revolutionary movement to be disfigured by the criminal folly of Petr Verkhovensky and his followers, Dostoevsky points to the tragic gulf between man's highest aspirations and his nature. E.J. Simmons argues that Dostoevsky was maliciously unfair in his treatment of revolutionaries in *The Devils*, claiming that he "either did not know or willfully maligned the real Russian revolutionists of his time."[7] This comment misses the point. The Russian radicals may well have been better men than those Dostoevsky depicts (with one obvious exception in Nechaev himself,) but they are nonetheless *men*, and consequently in Dostoevsky's view condemned to debase every great ideal for as long as they fail to acknowledge their own sinful nature. The moral failure of individual radicals in *The Devils* is a device used by Dostoevsky to expose the moral bankruptcy of political revolution itself.

In the doctrines of Shigalev, the theoretician of Petr's group, Dostoevsky shows the attempt of a fanatical, but honest revolutionary to reconcile his dream of social order with the acknowledged reality of man's corrupt nature. Unlike Petr, Shigalev is not a rogue. Neither is he the fool that his paradoxical view of socialism might incline us to believe. He is an ardent social dreamer—a "Fourier," as Petr describes him—who has grasped the flaw in the foundations of the socialist ideal. He describes his system at the group's clandestine meeting at Virginsky's, but only Petr recognizes the subtle truth of his conclusions. The others ridicule him. Like most social dreamers Shigalev starts from the ideal of a society of equality, freedom, and justice, but his line of reasoning leads him to a paradoxical conclusion: "I have become rather confused by my data," he confesses, "and my conclusion is a direct contradiction of the idea from which I start. Starting with the ideal of unlimited freedom, I arrive at the ideal of unlimited despotism. I must add, however, that there can be no other outcome of the social problem than mine" (X, 311). This catastrophic reversal of Shigalev's ideals is the result of his insight into human nature. He recognizes what many other social dreamers have overlooked: that man is not by nature good; that his immediate actions are dictated not by idealism, but by egoism; and that the ideals of brotherly love, justice, and equality are all too readily sacrificed to man's self-will, the most characteristic manifestation of which is the will to power. Even in the most well-ordered human society the strong personality will in time come to the fore and the weak will recede. Shigalev's system attempts to regularize this fact of human nature, and incidentally anticipates the sort of societies described in such twentieth-century antiutopian novels as Evgeny Zamyatin's *We*, George Orwell's *Animal Farm* and *1984*, and Aldous Huxley's *Brave New World*. Shigalev envisages a two-tier society, wherein a relatively small elite of powerful men exercise their despotic will over the timid majority. Shigalev argues that such a society would be both stable and in an odd way just, for it would conform to human nature and guarantee harmony and equality for the majority, albeit the equality of servitude. What Shigalev overlooks is that the Darwinian clash of wills must continue to operate even within the strong minority until only one reigns supreme and the tyranny is complete. This point is not lost on Petr Verkhovensky, however, who makes it the core of his political philosophy.

Shigalev's system is extremely farsighted, and the twentieth-century reader will recognize uncomfortable similarities between it and the rise of Nazi Germany and the general principles of totalitarian states. Such systems acknowledge the need for a stable hierarchy to regulate, and at times suppress, personal freedom. *The Devils* deals with the breakdown of old hierar hies and the destruction of order. The revolutionaries secede from the political order and exercise their emancipated wills in acts of social chaos. On another level of the novel, Stavrogin secedes from the moral order and tests his freedom in wanton, unpredictable, and amoral personal behavior. In both the political and moral spheres Dostoevsky thus stresses the destructive capacity of the human will when it is not subject to a stable authority. But Shigalev's theory demonstrates that when such an authority derives from a secular or institutional source tyranny must be the final result. Free will and chaos, or tyranny and order: for Dostoevsky no secular solution to human problems could avoid one or the other of these alternatives. The ideal equilibrium of freedom and order is attained only when all men submit freely and equally to a unifying moral authority which is not imposed but rather experienced in each individual; in other words, when mankind regains its faith in God. Without God all politics lead to the devil, all moral authorities are sham, and all hierarchies established by men are wrong. In an interview with Stavrogin, Petr Verkhovensky ridicules an old army captain who in his simplicity has recognized this truth. The old man is upset to hear young atheists proclaiming that God does not exist, and in his despair he asks a question the wisdom of which only Stavrogin understands: "If there is no God then what sort of captain can I be after that?" (X, 180). Without God there is nothing more powerful than the individual human will, which in clamoring to assert itself sweeps away all frail human hierarchies and all pretense at social order. Without God there are no moral certainties, and the world disintegrates as in W.B. Yeats's apocalyptic and appropriate warning to a later age:

> Things fall apart; the center cannot hold;
> Mere anarchy is loosed upon the world,
> The blood-dimmed tide is loosed, and everywhere
> The ceremony of innocence is drowned;
> The best lack all conviction, while the worst
> Are full of passionate intensity.
>
> ("The Second Coming," 1921)

II   The Devils *and the Apocalypse*

In a previous chapter we noted that Dostoevsky's absence from Russia and consequent distance from political events imparted to *The Idiot* and *The Devils* a distinctive, urgent tone. The urgency of *The Idiot* was maintained by a network of apocalyptic references, suggesting the imminence of the day of reckoning. The climate of *The Devils* is also unmistakably apocalyptic. As in Revelation, a series of catastrophes presages the final disaster of the fete and its aftermath. The outbreaks of incendiarism and cholera in the district call to mind the scourges of fire and plague which accompany the Last Judgment. The apocalyptic mood is sustained by Karmazinov, who compares the decline of western Europe with the fall of Babylon (X, 287), and by Kirillov, who confesses that he reads the Apocalypse at night to Fedka the convict (X, 282). Moreover, the warning of the Apocalypse that "there will be time no more" and that the old heaven and earth will yield to the new is grotesquely echoed in Kirillov's belief that at the moment he takes his own life and proclaims the deification of man, time will be frozen and a new era in human life will begin (X, 187–89).

This apocalyptic note is struck not just by those characters and situations at the center of *The Devils*. The general climate of Russia in the novel is apocalyptic, and moral confusion is the dominant feature of an age which lacks a unifying faith. Petr Verkhovensky details this moral confusion and the spiritual rootlessness of contemporary man when he describes to Stavrogin his plans for utilizing them in his drive for power. He explains, in terms comparable with the lines from Yeats cited above, how in the present age even the best men lack conviction, how people no longer think for themselves and are consequently the slaves of any man of strong will:

Listen . . . . Do you realize that we are very powerful already? It's not just those who kill and burn . . . who belong to us. Listen, I've reckoned them all up: the teacher who laughs with his children at their God and at the home which nurtured them is already ours. The lawyer who defends an educated murderer by pleading that he is more developed than his victim and had no choice but to kill in order to get money, he too is already ours. Schoolboys who kill a peasant for the thrill of it are ours. The juries who acquit criminals without distinction are ours. The prosecutor who trembles in court because he is not liberal enough is ours, ours. Administrators, writers—oh, there are lots and lots of us, and they don't know it themselves! On the other hand the readiness of schoolboys and fools to obey has reached the highest point . . . . Do you realize how many we shall win over with just a few shabby, ready-made ideas? (X, 324)

In another passage from the Apocalypse, cited in *The Devils*, God rejects the Laodiceans for being "neither cold nor hot." Petr intends to take advantage of a similar ethical halfheartedness among contemporary men by creating and spreading the legend of Stavrogin as a mysterious and majestic figure, who is at present in hiding, but who will in time emerge and rescue his people from chaos. Petr is convinced—and perhaps justifiably—that in times of uncertainty people will cling to the most unlikely of myths if it promises a return to order. At the right moment Petr will spring his protégé into a position of supreme power.

Here again Dostoevsky's debt to Revelation is unmistakable. Chapter XIII of the Apocalypse describes a time to come when the earth will be ruled by a beast with supreme power, who is worshiped for his mystery and majesty. The way is paved for this beast by a false prophet who "exerciseth all the power of the first beast before him, and causeth the earth and them which dwell therein to worship the first beast" (verse 12). The false prophet, moreover, "maketh fire come down from heaven on the earth in the sight of men," deliberately deceives, inflames the myth of the beast, and destroys all who do not believe his fabrications. It is difficult not to see in these figures the "wild beast" Nikolay Vsevolodovich Stavrogin and his false prophet Petr Verkhovensky. The notions of supremacy and power are contained in their names—*verkhovenstvo* means supremacy; *Nikolay* suggests conqueror of nations; and *Vsevolod* means master of all. Petr's first appearance in the novel is to announce the arrival of Stavrogin, whom he plans to make men worship. On the night of the fete he too makes fire come down to earth by organizing the incendiarism which claims the lives of Lebyadkin and his sister. He too is a master of deceit and duplicity, which he practices most successfully on the Governor's wife and the members of the discussion circle. And finally he too disposes most adroitly of Shatov and whoever else rejects his deceptions. Symbolism such as this enlarges the significance of Petr and Stavrogin, the two main sources of chaos and destruction in the novel. They outgrow their functions as political intriguers and acquire metaphysical characteristics. They are indeed the devils, reaping their due in the spiritual wilderness of nineteenth-century Russia.

As in *The Idiot*, the apocalyptic coloring of *The Devils* is deepened by the use of minor symbols and references which, although of limited intrinsic interest, do nevertheless sustain an even apocalyptic texture throughout the novel. Proper names derived from birds—which in *The Idiot* pointed to the biblical description of Babylon as "the habitation of devils and a cage for every unclean and hateful bird" and suggested that Russia was doomed to a similar fate—recur in *The Devils*. Indeed, the Stavrogin estate, from which so much of the novel's discord originates and where the murder of Shatov takes place, is named Skvoreshniki, suggesting *skvorechnik*, a sort of birdcage. The surnames Drozdov, Lebyadkin, and Gaganov all derive from the names of birds: *drozd* ("thrush"); *lebed'* ("swan"); and *gaga* ("eider"). Maria Lebyadkina expresses her disappointment in Stavrogin by describing him as a falcon (*sokol*) who has changed into an owl (*filin*) (X, 218); and when at the end of the novel Varvara Petrovna rushes to be with the dying Stepan Trofimovich, she offensively dismisses his Bible-seller companion, Sofia Matveevna, as an "odd bird" and a "crow" (*vorona*). Only after recognizing her as a good woman does she address her more respectfully.

Stavrogin and Petr are at the center of the novel's apocalyptic design, yet, as we have seen, neither's name fits into the tradition of bird references. Stavrogin's name does have apocalyptic connotations, however: his surname is constructed around the word *rog* (horn), with its clearly diabolic implications, and a form of his first name, Nikolay, is actually found in Revelation as the Nicolaitans, a heretical sect practicing immorality and idolatry, condemned by John in II:6, 15.[8]

III *Stavrogin*

So far the arguments of this chapter have only occasionally touched upon Stavrogin. He seems of tangential relevance to the politics of the novel and avoids all activity himself, his political importance being confined to his place in Petr Verkhovensky's schemes. In a sense this chapter has followed the pattern of the novel, for, apart from a few strange rumors, Stavrogin does not enter *The Devils* until quite late, at a point when Stepan Trofimovich seems destined to be its central hero. The reader might well be forgiven for regarding Stavrogin as an intruder in the novel's established gallery of characters, almost an afterthought on Dostoevsky's part. Yet the working drafts and notebooks show that Stavrogin had ousted the Verkhovenskys as hero even at the planning stage and had led Dostoevsky to recast the novel completely. Certainly the later notebooks sketch an unambiguously central role for Stavrogin: he is to be the dark heart of the novel. "Everything is contained in the character of Stavrogin," wrote Dostoevsky. "Stavrogin is *everything*" (XI, 207). Yet Stavrogin is an unstable, reticent center; he seems to haunt the novel rather than live in it, and for much of the time he takes no part in events. Ralph Matlaw has given a memorable description of him as "an empty, disappearing center."[9] And if Stavrogin does not dominate the novel with his actions, neither does he fill it with his consciousness, as Raskolnikov fills *Crime and Punishment*. On the contrary, we rarely penetrate his soul, and he remains an enigma to us. This is how it must be, for Stavrogin's centrality in *The Devils* flows from his great mystery. Whereas the lesser devils—the Verkhovenskys, the Kirillovs, the Shigalevs, and the rest—can cavort freely in the novel's footlights, Stavrogin, the arch-demon, must remain in the darkness of the wings, for in him lies the mystery of evil itself. He is the life-denying principle, the spirit of negation, the vacuum left by a totally free will which has tired of its freedom and has consumed itself.

The dramatic requirement that Stavrogin remain an enigma must have been a major factor in Dostoevsky's decision not to replace the omitted chapter "At Tikhon's" in the later edition of his novel. The value of Stavrogin's self-revelation is undermined by its dramatic inconsistency. The principle of uncertainty was as important in the creation of Stavrogin as of Raskolnikov, and without the omitted chapter Stavrogin's outline remains blurred, which increases his suggestiveness. He is clearly a highly artificial character, rich in literary allusion. The rumors which introduce him suggest he is an anachronistic figure, a Byronic nobleman who has strayed from the pages of Romantic literature into the more prosaic reality of mid-nineteenth-century Russia. His world-weariness, unpredictability, amoralism, and the ritual testing of his strength all call to mind the exploits of Lermontov's heroes, and in particular Pechorin. Indeed, at one point in the novel Stavrogin is scorned as a "Pechorin-ladykiller" (X, 84), a comparison which Dostoevsky reinforces on other occasions. Shortly after Stavrogin's arrival there is a long passage in which the narrator concludes that Stavrogin has far outstripped the malice and ennui of Lermontov and other Byronic Russian noblemen of the early decades of the century (X, 165), an assertion borne out by Stavrogin's subsequent treatment of women and his actions during the duel with Gaganov. Moreover, when Petr Verkhovensky visits Stavrogin in his room to suggest the elimination of the Lebyadkins, he notices that Stavrogin has been reading an expensive volume of illustrations of *The Women of Balzac* (X, 180). The reader familiar with Lermontov's *A Hero of Our Time* will recall that at one point Pechorin himself is likened to "a thirty-year old Balzacian coquette."[10]

There are many other points of contact between Stavrogin and his Romantic counterpart,[11] but these only serve to draw our attention to the spiritual affinity between the two characters. In his lukewarm malice, his stuttering gestures of will, his aching emptiness, his indifference and loss of all conviction, Stavrogin represents the horrifying end of the quest for moral freedom pursued by the Byronic hero. Stavrogin's tragedy is that of a man who has sacrificed his personality to freedom. In his dedication to totally unfettered self-will he has liberated himself from all spiritual, emotional, and intellectual bonds, but he has found the freedom thus attained to be a sterile deceit. A man without convictions, without warmth, without enthusiasm no longer has a use for freedom, for there is no longer meaning in his life. At the end of *A Hero of Our Time* Pechorin has acknowledged that freedom is a burden, and he sets off on his travels in order to fill the emptiness of his existence. At the end of Part I of *Notes from Underground* the hero's perverse drive for total freedom has diluted his being to such a point that he cannot even construct a coherent sentence: how can one express oneself when there is no longer a self to express? Stavrogin has surpassed them both: in him total freedom becomes total nonbeing. He has no belief in himself upon which to base his existence. He has no interests and is incapable of loving, or indeed hating, anyone or anything. If he resorts to debauchery, it is to dissipate his boredom, but this serves only to emphasize it. He dulls his sense of ennui through scandalous acts such as biting the Governor's ear, marrying a cripple, and fighting the duel with Gaganov. These actions provide short-term interest and incentive, and temporarily distract him from his permanent sense of purposelessness. But Stavrogin knows that in the long term he must find some basis to his existence, or he will, as Shatov warns, "disappear like rotten mildew" (X, 203). Kirillov, too, recognizes that Stavrogin is seeking a burden (X, 227), that he is searching for a commitment or undertaking which will restore meaning to his life. It is a measure of the moral freedom Stavrogin has attained that he does not care whether hiŝ undertaking is a great noble deed or a foul criminal act. As Shatov observes, the totally free man can no longer distinguish between good and evil (X, 201–202), for if he did his freedom would be incomplete.

As Richard Peace has remarked, the chapters entitled "Night" represent Stavrogin's attempts to rediscover existential certainty among the ruins of his past.[12] He visits Shatov and Kirillov, who now expound ideas which Stavrogin himself has long since discarded. We learn that they each derived their philosophy from Stavrogin, and the fact that the latter was able simultaneously to inspire two such different personalities with two mutually exclusive ideologies suggests that he himself believed in neither. Indeed, both Kirillov and Shatov bring to their convictions that quality which Stavrogin lacks above all else—fanatical enthusiasm. But Stavrogin's pilgrimage on that damp, drab, and dirty night—the weather neatly corresponds with the state of his soul—is in vain. He is bored by both Shatov and Kirillov, just as he later scorns Petr and his political dreams. His subsequent confession to Tikhon and his love affair with Liza represent further attempts to bring purpose into his life; but his confessed violation of the young girl, Matresha, fails to kindle guilt, just as his affair with Liza fails to kindle love. A single genuine feeling would save Stavrogin, but to arouse such a feeling is the one feat beyond his superhuman power.

So Stavrogin remains empty and inactive, a hole at the center of the novel. His wearisome freedom condemns him to such inertia that he is incapable of returning Shatov's slap, of killing Gaganov, or of arranging the murder of his wife. In the disposal of the Lebyadkins Petr acts as Stavrogin's will and Fedka as his proxy; Stavrogin's part is entirely passive. He is a collapsed character, a dead sun, emitting neither light nor heat but nevertheless trapping all the other characters in his gravitational field. He is spiritually dead, as the description of him alone in his study makes dramatically clear (X, 182), but all are drawn to him, only to meet disappointment or their own destruction. The explanation of Stavrogin's fatal attraction is to be sought in his very emptiness: he illustrates the principle that nature abhors a vacuum. Each character sees in Stavrogin not the void that he really represents, but a reflection of his own personality. Each character invents his own Stavrogin, as Petr Verkhovensky acknowledges (X, 326). Kirillov sees in him confirmation of his ideas on the metamorphosis of man through will: "Remember what you've meant in my life, Stavrogin" (X, 189). Shatov, too, needs Stavrogin's blessing in his search for God: "I can't tear you out of my heart, Nikolay Stavrogin!" (X, 202). Petr Verkhovensky finds in Stavrogin the legendary force through which his political ambitions are to be realized: "You're just what we need. I . . . I particularly need someone like you. I know of nobody quite like you. You are my leader, my sun, and I am your worm . . ." (X, 324). The unfortunate Maria Lebyadkina considers Stavrogin her prince, her savior, although she alone finally sees into the vacuum of his existence; the philanthropic Dasha Shatova sees only his potential for salvation; and Liza is drawn to him as a focus for her own unhealthy preoccupation with evil.

In the end, however, Stavrogin disappoints them all. In spurning Kirillov and Shatov he leaves them to empty ideologies, for no idea bequeathed by Stavrogin can be fertile. The convictions of both Kirillov and Shatov, although fanatically held, are corrupted by their origin in Stavrogin's being. Like their creator, these ideas are arranged around an empty center: Shatov's religious fervor fails to disguise his lack of faith, and Kirillov's militant atheism and intoxication with man's freedom are negated first by his love of God and God's creation and second by his own intellectual servitude. Kirillov fails to see that in feeling *compelled* to proclaim his freedom through suicide he has relinquished that very freedom.

Stavrogin also fails to live up to the expectations of his women: he is no more capable of serving Liza's fascination with evil than he is of satisfying Dasha's hopes for his rebirth, for he is outside morality. His sexual impotence during the night he spends with Liza is symptomatic of the sterility of his whole existence. Other characters draw inspiration from him and rush to their destruction, thus affording another way of looking at the novel's epigraph, but he remains lukewarm, consumed by boredom and his own superfluousness. His shabby and apathetic suicide—he hangs himself on a greased rope

from a nail in the back of a door—is an empty ritual, a final acknowledgment of what he and the reader have known all along: that he is
devoid of life.

IV   *Beauty and Salvation*

Dostoevsky's great novels and his notebook material suggest that
the most persistent artistic problem confronting the author in the
later part of his life was that of depicting the mystery of salvation. This
was the task Dostoevsky explicitly set himself in *Atheism* and *The Life
of a Great Sinner*, but he had also attempted it on several previous
occasions. As early as 1864, in *Notes from Underground*, he had
envisaged the acquisition of faith as a means of escaping both the
constraints of reason and the chaos of self-will, but on that occasion his
designs had been frustrated by the censor. The Epilogue of *Crime
and Punishment* returns to the problem, but provides only a schematic and unconvincing account of Raskolnikov's return to life. Prince
Myshkin in *The Idiot* is already "the positively good man," but it
seems from the novel's drafts that here again Dostoevsky first intended him to be an egocentric, self-willed character who undergoes
a change of heart. The early sketches for Stavrogin have much in
common with the figure of Myshkin as Dostoevsky originally envisaged him, and it is clear that he meant Stavrogin to come to a more
positive end than the greased rope that is his fate in the completed
novel. Like the possessed man in the parable of the Gadarene swine,
Stavrogin was to be cleansed and sit at the feet of Christ, but instead it
is the comic figure of Stepan Trofimovich Verkhovensky who finds the
salvation originally planned for Stavrogin. This displacement of Dostoevsky's design leads to some interesting conclusions.

Much of the chaos in *The Devils* is indirectly attributable to Stepan
Trofimovich. He is the neglectful father of Petr and the careless
ex-master of Fedka. His generation must take responsibility for the
political indiscretions of the nihilists, for it first proclaimed liberalism
and godlessness. Stepan was, moreover, a powerful influence in the
formation of the young Stavrogin's character: we learn that he tutored
the boy and first awakened in him that aching dissatisfaction which
launched Stavrogin on the path of Byronic disillusionment. The
narrator confides his suspicion that Stepan "was responsible for up-
setting his pupil's nerves" (X, 35). Like Stavrogin, although to a far
lesser degree, Stepan is morally lukewarm; his convictions find expression in rhetoric, not in action. Yet he finds salvation because,

unlike his protégé, he retains humanity and emotional warmth. He does not sink into the complete ethical and esthetic indifference of Stavrogin. He is vain, petty, irascible, petulant, weak, and self-pitying, but he never loses the capacity to be genuinely moved by the noble and the beautiful. He remains convinced that humane liberalism is a nobler principle than rational egoism, even though he himself may fall short of its ideals. He defends his devotion to beauty in the face of the esthetic barbarism of a younger generation which proclaims that a good pair of boots is worth more than the Sistine Madonna. It is perhaps above all his sense of beauty that allows his salvation, just as in *Crime and Punishment* Raskolnikov's monstrous ethics were countered by his esthetic sense.

Indeed, Stepan is keenly aware that although the men of the sixties have inherited the ideas of their fathers, a vast esthetic distance nonetheless separates the ways these ideals have been realized by the two generations:

"Oh, my friends," he sometimes cried in moments of inspiration, "you can't imagine the sadness and anger that seize your soul when a great idea which you have long considered sacred is taken up by bunglers and dragged out into the street to fools like themselves, and you suddenly come across it in the second-hand market, unrecognizable, covered in filth, clumsily set up at an angle, without proportion, without harmony, a plaything for stupid children! No, it was different in our time; that wasn't what we strove for . . . . (X, 24)

Stepan thinks that between the two generations there has arisen what he calls "a displacement of aims, the substitution of one beauty for another," but in fact the difference is more radical than that. The men of the 1860s have denied altogether the value of that beauty without which Stepan finds life impossible. His defense of beauty at the Lembkes' fete echoes exactly the sentiments expressed in Dostoevsky's essay "Mr.——bov and the Question of Art":

I declare that Shakespeare and Raphael are higher than the emancipation of the serfs, higher than national feeling, higher than socialism, higher than the younger generation, higher than chemistry, higher almost than the whole of humanity, for they are the fruit of all mankind, and perhaps the highest fruition there can be! A form of beauty already attained, without the attainment of which I perhaps would not consent to live . . . . Do you realize that without the Englishman mankind would still be able to exist, without Germany too, and most certainly without the Russians. It could continue without science, and without bread; but the only thing it cannot do without is beauty, for then there would be nothing left to do in the world! The whole mystery is here, the whole of history! Even science would not last a minute without beauty—don't you realize that, you who are laughing at me? It would sink into loutishness—you wouldn't be able to invent a nail! (X, 372–73)

Stepan and Dostoevsky proclaim the primacy of the esthetic principle, not with the *précieux* fastidiousness of the decadent, but because they realize that ugliness can kill the noblest idea and that a man's capacity for esthetic response is a measure of his ethical perfectibility. These motifs find expression in Stavrogin's long conversation with Tikhon, and on these grounds at least the exclusion of "At Tikhon's" is to be regretted. Tikhon's elegant and well-furnished quarters betray a refined sense of form which Stavrogin finds suspiciously worldly in a man of his profession. Throughout their conversation Tikhon's measured and elegant Russian emphasizes the surprising ugliness of Stavrogin's written confession. Indeed it is the ugliness of Stavrogin's document that Tikhon finds most loathsome, for it condemns the man and lays bare the hollowness of his pretense at repentance. Stavrogin's monstrously deformed esthetic instincts are harnessed to his craving for intensity. He lacks the fixed sense of ideal beauty upon which Raskolnikov's salvation was founded, and only occasionally is he visited by the image of a golden age, inspired by his viewing of Claude Lorrain's painting *Acis and Galatea*. Stavrogin's dream of a golden age, in which mankind lives in harmony in an earthly paradise undefiled by egoism, represents a pinnacle of ethical and esthetic perfection, but Stavrogin cannot sustain the image, for it is always eclipsed by the image of the spider he observed at the moment Matresha took her life (XI, 22). In the whole of Dostoevsky there is nowhere to be found a more compelling symbol of man's exclusion from paradise.

Stavrogin's lukewarm and perverted esthetic responses are thus far inferior to the keen sense of beauty which illumines Stepan Trofimovich's idealism, and they preclude his resurrection. His suicide is itself a denial of beauty, for its casual shabbiness betrays a disinterest in form. In this respect Stavrogin's death contrasts significantly with the imaginary suicide of the hero of "The Dream of a Ridiculous Man," who is himself a Stavroginesque spiritual cripple and contemplates suicide as a retreat from the insufferable ennui of his existence. He, however, makes preparations which suggest that he possesses a strong sense of form or occasion. He is capable of esthetic response: he chooses his moment carefully to maximize the effect and uses a fine new revolver, bought especially for the event. Like Stepan Trofimovich, the Ridiculous Man finally finds the salvation denied Stavrogin.

Petr Verkhovensky also illustrates how man's natural attraction to beauty can be deformed in a corrupt soul. Petr is guilty of idolatry: he worships not ideal beauty, but the counterfeit beauty of his appointed master, Stavrogin. "Stavrogin, you're beautiful!" he cries. "I love beauty. I am a nihilist, but I love beauty. Is it true that nihilists don't love beauty? It's only idols they don't like, but I love an idol! And you are my idol!" (X, 323). Here *The Devils* looks back to *Crime and Punishment* and Raskolnikov's sterile, destructive adulation of Napoleon. But it also looks forward to *The Brothers Karamazov*, which contains Dostoevsky's final and greatest affirmation of the redeeming power of beauty, as well as—in the figure of Smerdyakov—a grim repetition of Tikhon's warning that ugliness kills even the noblest ideal, and that ethical values cannot be judged in isolation from the esthetic principle.

V   A Raw Youth

Throughout 1875 the journal *Notes of the Fatherland*, a progressive publication edited by the distinguished poet Nikolay Nekrasov, serialized the long novel *Podrostok* [A Raw Youth], generally considered the weakest of Dostoevsky's mature works. It takes the form of a chronicle narrated by Arkady Dolgoruky, the adolescent illegitimate son of a nobleman, Andrey Versilov, by the wife of Makar Dolgoruky, a peasant. The chronicle records the youth's ambiguous attitude toward Versilov, and his mixed fascination and revulsion as he witnesses his father's tragic love for two women, Arkady's mother and the enigmatic beauty Katerina Akhmakova. The novel is confused, but many critics have testified to its importance for the student of Dostoevsky,[13] and indeed it does deal more explicitly than the other, greater novels with several important Dostoevskian themes. Perhaps the greatest question raised by *A Raw Youth* is that of how the modern writer should respond in his art to the disordered texture of contemporary life, a disorder convincingly depicted in *The Devils*.[14] This aspect of *A Raw Youth* will be discussed in a wider context in the conclusion of this study. Yet despite its claims to importance, *A Raw Youth* lacks the compulsive readability of Dostoevsky's other major fiction, and for this reason it will be treated only briefly in this chapter. It does at the very least represent an interesting transition between *The Devils* and Dostoevsky's final novel, *The Brothers Karamazov*.

At the root of *A Raw Youth*, as in *The Idiot* and *The Devils*, is Dostoevsky's view of contemporary Europeanized Russia as a civilization lacking a unifying principle. The novel discusses how the erosion of the aristocracy and the consequent collapse of the notions of aristocratic honor and class morality have left Russia in the latter half of the nineteenth century disoriented, unconfident, and without a binding idea. The historical decay of the aristocratic ideal is suggested in *A Raw Youth* by the moral failure of the young Prince Sikolsky, who is involved in fraud, and by the fact that the great aristocratic name of Dolgoruky, once borne by the founder of Moscow, is now shared by the self-centered, illegitimate Arkady. The note struck in *A Raw Youth* is one of discord, and such social disorders as spiritual and political nihilism, the dissolution of family bonds, the breakdown of respect and communion between fathers and sons, the spread of self-will, violence, and financial greed—all suggest the disintegration of the moral order. *A Raw Youth* examines this volatile situation through the eyes of an adolescent who is both narrator and protagonist in the fiction. Such involvement of the narrator in the narrated events, a technique characteristic to a greater or lesser degree of all Dostoevsky's major novels, ensures that the fragmented and uncertain quality of contemporary life is recreated in the texture of the narrative.[15] In his drafts for *A Raw Youth* Dostoevsky wrote: "THE MAIN IDEA . . . of the novel is that the youth is seeking a guiding idea of behavior, of good and evil, and there isn't one in our society. But he thirsts for it, seeks it instinctively, and in this lies the aim of the novel" (XVI, 51). The inability of Arkady as protagonist to find a center of moral order in the world is the real reason for the lack of esthetic order in the novel of discord[16] he narrates. As we have seen, this technique of allowing the moral and psychological state of the hero to determine the esthetics of the work had been adopted by Dostoevsky for *Crime and Punishment* and, indeed, for two of his short novels of the 1840s, *The Double* and "The Landlady."

Many of the concerns of *A Raw Youth* are retrospective in the context of Dostoevsky's literary career. Arkady's quest for an ideal of moral and esthetic order—*blagoobrazie* (seemliness, form or harmony), as he calls it—is a feature of many Dostoevskian heroes. Some of them attempt to satisfy this craving for order by harnessing their personalities to an idea which promises to make sense of the absurdities of life. Raskolnikov, Kirillov, and Shatov spring to mind as examples of characters whose personalities are arranged around an idea. Stavrogin, on the other hand, illustrates the despair of a spiritual nihilist who can find no stable idea in the shifting sands of his personality. When an idea occupies a position of such central importance in the life of a character, it ceases to be an idea in a simple sense and is transmuted into what in *A Raw Youth* is described as an "Idea-Feeling" (XIII, 46). Arkady is possessed by such an idea: offended by the "unseemliness" (*bezobrazie*) of his fellow men, he hopes to retreat behind a barrier of wealth. He intends, like Ganya Ivolgin, to become a Rothschild through sheer strength of will, to attain the power and freedom of financial independence and to live forever apart from other men, a tiny island of psychological calm amidst the discords of modern society. He has no intention of spending his wealth, but means to use it as a buffer to protect the order erected behind it. Arkady is aware that such order will not be constructed out of the material of life, but will be achieved at the expense of "living life." The events of the novel eventually wean him from his sterile idea and confront him with the complexities of reality. Arkady's idea is related to the behavior of Mister Prokharchin, but whereas for the earlier hero miserliness was the result of fear, for Arkady it represents a conscious, willful attempt to overcome the unseemliness of life.

This conflict between the *bezobrazie* of modern life and the individual's dreams of *blagoobrazie* is crucial to *A Raw Youth*, and Dostoevsky explores it through a familiar metaphor—that of the city. The role of St. Petersburg in Dostoevsky's fiction has been widely discussed by critics; it is of course only one aspect of a wider tradition of the city in the nineteenth-century novel.[17] Dostoevsky is the supreme poet of the city, and even his provincial novels (*The Devils, The Brothers Karamazov*) reek of urban neuroses. The rational order of St. Petersburg, which the Underground Man calls "the most abstract and premeditated city on earth" (V, 101), becomes a specter mocking the chaotic existences of its inhabitants. The St. Petersburg of Dostoevsky's novels is a haunting reminder of lost social harmonies. Its classical architecture speaks of eighteenth-century man's faith in rational order as a governing principle of human life, and tragically highlights the moral and esthetic disorder of his successor in the post-Romantic age.

Early in *A Raw Youth* Arkady's Rothschild idea recedes, and his expectations of *blagoobrazie* are explored in his complex relationship with Versilov. For the idealistic, illegitimate, and abandoned Arkady his absent father has always seemed to represent both the possibility of a more seemly existence and a focus for his humiliated pride, an object of both romantic admiration and underground resentment. In their developing relationship Dostoevsky explores a theme that occupied much of his thinking in the last decade or so of his life: the mutual responsibility of fathers and children. Dostoevsky drafted plans for a major novel on this theme and, although the project was not realized, the idea itself occurs in the three novels written between 1869 and the writer's death: *The Devils*, *A Raw Youth*, and *The Brothers Karamazov*. As with the Verkhovenskys in *The Devils*, the relationship between Versilov and Arkady emphasizes the discontinuity between generations, another aspect of the moral fragmentation of contemporary Russian society. No binding idea or sense of kinship is transmitted from one generation to the next. Such "haphazard families" (*sluchainye semeistva*, XIII, 455) are contrasted unfavorably at the end of *A Raw Youth* with the kind of family described by Tolstoy in *War and Peace*. Tolstoy's Rostov family is typical of an earlier historical period, when the organic links between generations testified to the emotional health and moral stability of society. But Versilov has transmitted nothing to Arkady; the youth's actual illegitimacy symbolizes the emotional rupture; Arkady is a spiritual orphan. It is precisely the lack of a spiritual bond between the generations that renders Versilov so enigmatic in the eyes of his son.

Despite Arkady's hopes, Versilov can offer him no firm foundations, for his own existence lacks a moral center. Versilov is a strange, composite figure. Another of Dostoevsky's charismatic self-willed men, he is the very essence of the Romantic hero, strongly reminiscent of Stavrogin. Like the hero of *The Devils*, he is the spring of other people's actions, the real center of events. And, like Stavrogin, he enters into an existential quest, a search for a spiritual base, during which he plays his destructive egoism against his dreams of a world of moral beauty. He is, as he remarks himself, the victim of a crippling spiritual dualism (XIII, 408), realized in his love for two women. For Arkady's mother he feels selfless, healing, Christian love—the sort of love upon which men have for centuries built their dreams of world harmony. But for Katerina Akhmakova he harbors a dark and selfish animal passion that promises only destruction. In a scene of central importance he confides to Arkady his cherished dream of a golden age when men will live in a harmonious paradise (XIII, 375), but at the same time he contemplates the sacrifice of Akhmakova to satisfy his fatal passion. Versilov's dualism is not specific: it represents the sin of all mankind, the legacy of the Fall. Man's dream of harmony will always vie with brutal passions as long as he is subject to Original Sin. Versilov himself seems to acknowledge this when he confesses that his visions of earthly paradise always conclude with the image of Christ, the Savior who came to redeem the sins of man (XIII, 379). There can be no paradise except through the example of Christ, through suffering and rebirth, in a transfigured world, not in this.

The dream of a golden age is another feature Versilov inherits from Stavrogin, but Versilov does differ from Stavrogin in one important respect, described by Mochulsky: "Versilov is not a corpse galvanized by devils, but a living man, doubting, tormented, loving and believing in an ideal."[18] The reality of Stavrogin always threatens to dissolve into the abstract elements he is intended to represent. His tenuous hold on the reader's credulity is weakened by the many occasions when, as a hero, he skirts the supernatural, appearing more demon than human. Versilov is a much more convincingly human restatement of Stavrogin, although it might be argued that what he gains in humanity he loses in melodramatic appeal.

The character of Versilov also owes much to that other pivotal figure in *The Devils*, Stepan Trofimovich Verkhovensky. Like Verkhovensky, Versilov represents a particular point in the history of the Russian intelligentsia: he is a man of the 1840s, and the roots of his personality lie in the Idealism, Romanticism, and historical bankruptcy of that generation. His time has by now passed, and he is a stranger in his own land, a shadow from the past, manifestly out of place in the new reality of post-Emancipation Russia. Dostoevsky skillfully builds up Versilov's historical identity by drawing attention to such features as his inability to translate his aspirations into action, his Pechorinesque rootlessness, his dilettantism, his superfluousness, his aristocratism, Westernism, and liberalism. We are even told that Versilov took part in the preparations for the Emancipation. On the basis of such details Leonid Grossman discusses the possibility that Alexander Herzen served as a model for Versilov.[19]

Versilov's precise location in a particular moment of Russia's intellectual history affords an alternative explanation of the failure of his relationship with Arkady, for father and son stand on opposite sides of the most chronicled generation gap in nineteenth-century Russia— that between the Idealists of the 1840s and the Nihilists of the 1860s, described so vividly in Turgenev's novel *Fathers and Sons*. Dostoevsky here returns to his message in *The Devils*: the explanation of the spiritual nihilism of the younger generation must be sought in the moral failure of its progenitors.

But if Versilov represents a failure of fatherhood, its ideal is embodied in the man whose name Arkady inherits, the pilgrim Makar Dolgoruky. Makar offers Arkady all that Versilov cannot: an ideal of moral beauty and an example of a life constructed around an unshakable core of religious conviction. Alongside the discordant *bezobrazie* of one father stands the calm *blagoobrazie* of the other. Makar might be a wanderer in the literal sense, but through him we see that it is modern man who is the real spiritual nomad. Makar alone in the novel possesses the ability to laugh innocently, without bitterness, irony, or malice. This, observes Versilov, is unusual in the present age (XIII, 285), a remark which suggests that Makar, like all Dostoevsky's saintly heroes (Sonya Marmeladova, Myshkin, Tikhon, and so on) and unlike his willful men, is not embedded in time, but stands as a permanent ideal of humanity among characters whose own humanity is variously disfigured by the pressures of their age. In the person of Makar Dostoevsky distills all his faith in the Russian peasant, whose tranquil moral certainty—the outcome of an unbroken tradition of adherence to permanent Russian values, uncorrupted by time—strikes a harmonious note in the dissonant chorus of contemporary life.[20]

In juxtaposing Versilov and Makar, Dostoevsky explores the nature of fatherhood; but if being a father carries responsibilities, so does being a son—as the example of that most famous son of all, Christ, implies. If Versilov fails as a father, Arkady fails no less decisively as a son. His longing to love his father is distorted by his resentment and lack of faith. He can forgive his father neither the sins of his past nor the unseemliness of his present life. Yet in turning against him Arkady only intensifies the disorder. His bitterness frequently disrupts family harmony, and it is indirectly responsible for the suicide of the young girl Olya, whose distrust of Versilov Arkady reinforces. A son's love for his father must be like Christ's—faithful, unconditional, and strong enough to overcome the apparent unseemliness of the father's actions. To demand an accounting from a father is to fragment the family and open the way to isolation and rebellion. Dostoevsky explored the full and dreadful implications of this idea in his final novel, *The Brothers Karamazov*.

CHAPTER 7

Harmony and Redemption:
The Brothers Karamazov

There is but one morality, as there is but one geometry.
Voltaire, *Dictionnaire Philosophique*

THE Brothers Karamazov was completed in October 1880, only
three months before Dostoevsky's death. It is, however, a work
distilled from ideas and projects that had occupied the author for
much of his life. The basic plot of a man mistakenly sentenced for the
murder of his father was suggested to him by the case of Ilinsky, the
victim of just such a miscarriage of justice, whom Dostoevsky had
encountered in Siberia and whose fate is related in *Notes from the
House of the Dead*. The plot also owes much to Dostoevsky's love of
Schiller, in particular to that writer's treatment of the themes of
parricide and fraternal rivalry in *The Robbers*, which Dostoevsky had
seen performed when he was a boy. Moreover, *The Brothers
Karamazov* develops many of the motifs Dostoevsky had projected in
his two related plans of the late 1860s, *Atheism* and *The Life of a Great
Sinner*, both of which had floated the themes of the existence of God
and the loss and reacquisition of faith. Aspects of Dostoevsky's biography also find their way into this last novel, particularly his love of
children and his visit to the Optina monastery, made in the company
of Vladimir Solovev in June 1879. During this visit Dostoevsky had
met the holy elder Tikhon Zadonsky, who impressed him greatly and
who appears in *The Brothers Karamazov* in the guise of Father
Zosima.

Despite this complicated parentage, *The Brothers Karamazov* is
arranged around a fairly lucid central plot. As in many of Dostoevsky's
earlier works, money and murder dominate the action. Fedor Pavlovich Karamazov, a corrupt and seedy provincial landowner, is the
father of three legitimate sons: Dmitry, a retired army officer; Ivan, a
brilliant intellectual; and Alesha, a novice monk and disciple of

Father Zosima. Dmitry is the child of Fedor Pavlovich's first marriage, Ivan and Alesha the sons of his second. Fedor is also the father
of an illegitimate son, Smerdyakov, the result of a liaison with a local
idiot girl, Liza Smerdyashchaya. Smerdyakov now works as a servant
in the Karamazov household.

When Fedor Pavlovich is found murdered, suspicion falls on
Dmitry, although we learn later that the crime was in fact committed
by Smerdyakov. Dmitry's violent nature and his conviction that he
has been cheated out of his inheritance have already led to furious
scenes between him and his father. What is more, father and son are
rivals for the affections of Grushenka, a local seductress, whose
charms have already alienated Dmitry from his betrothed, Katerina.
All this points to Dmitry's guilt, and he is arrested. At the trial things
go badly for him and he is sentenced to Siberia. Grushenka decides to
follow him and Katerina remains to look after Ivan, who has discovered Smerdyakov's guilt and the role played in his father's death by
his own conversations with the lackey. But nothing can be proved.
Smerdyakov commits suicide, Ivan has a breakdown, and the novel
ends with Alesha leaving the monastery and following Zosima's advice to go out into the world.

I   The Collective Hero

A striking feature of Dostoevsky's novels is their taut and dramatic
intensity. Their apparent waywardness, their tendency to dissolve
into incautious polemic, and their range of plot and character cannot
obscure the firm dramatic principles upon which they are erected.
George Steiner has examined these principles in his excellent and
daring contrastive study *Tolstoy or Dostoevsky*.[1] In this chapter we
must start from one of these dramatic devices: the tendency of the
Dostoevskian novel to deploy itself around a highly dramatic event
and an obviously central figure. Raskolnikov and the murder of the
pawnbroker hold *Crime and Punishment* together; Prince Myshkin
and the murder of Nastasya Filippovna are central to *The Idiot*; and
Stavrogin and the killing of Shatov have a similar function in *The
Devils*. Moreover, the subsidiary resources of the novels all reflect
their main concerns: aspects of the central character are reflected and
exaggerated in the minor figures; secondary events often echo or
comment upon the primary action. As a result the secondary characters and incidents, rather than widening the scope of the novels, as do
the many characters and incidents in, for example, *War and Peace*,

serve instead to confine the novels to their central concerns, thus
deepening their dramatic intensity.

The Brothers Karamazov utilizes the structural principles of the
earlier novels, with one obvious and much-discussed complication:
here the single central figure yields to a central brotherhood of Ivan,
Dmitry, and Alesha. But this departure need not detain us for long,
for the three brothers quite clearly combine to form the equivalent of
a single central hero. Each on his own represents only one of three
aspects of man: the intellect, the physical presence, and the soul. The
cold, enigmatic Ivan discharges only ideas; he is the builder of
systems, the inventor of paradox. His enthusiasm is confined for the
most part to concepts and dialectics; the risks to which he exposes
himself are intellectual ones; and the crisis he faces in the course of
the novel is a crisis of reason. Dmitry possesses warmth, physical
strength, and great emotional and sensual capacity, but these are
uncontrolled by either an intellectual or a spiritual bridle. The crisis
with which the events of the novel confront him is related to his
physical nature. Finally there is Alesha, a novice seeking spiritual
guidance in a monastery, who is apparently free of both the physical-
ity and the intellectualism of his two brothers. He too undergoes a
crisis in the novel, and this crisis is significantly a spiritual one.

The three brothers are clearly intended to be viewed, in at least
one light, as a collective symbol of man, although this in no way
means that they cannot be regarded as successful individual characters. In common with its predecessors, this Dostoevskian novel is
effective in both its psychological and its symbolic insight. But the
inseparability and interdependence of the brothers are emphasized
throughout: each is drawn into a crisis involving reassessment of his
life and each is responsible to some extent for the death of his father,
who is actually murdered by the fourth, illegitimate son,
Smerdyakov.

II *Harmony and Dualism*

The brothers Karamazov are united in another, no less revealing
way. Each suffers a dilemma of perception. Ivan knows the world
through his restless intellectual probings; Dmitry through his insati-
able physical appetites; and Alesha through the simplifying prism of
his naive, untested, ritualistic Orthodox faith. Yet all three brothers
also possess a developed sense of form, a capacity for esthetic rapture,
a craving for harmony which eludes them in all but their occasional

moments of esthetic insight but which makes them aware of the inadequacy of their particular outlook and of the beastliness and fractured, inharmonious nature of man himself. This, of course, is not a new idea in Dostoevsky's novels: for several of his previous heroes the revelation of God, truth, and meaning had been achieved through a refined sense of beauty, a feeling for harmony and proportion. Prince Myshkin had insisted that beauty would save the world and that man's esthetic capacity, his feeling for ideal beauty, offered him a means of redemption. It is precisely such an esthetic sense that rescues Raskolnikov from the nightmare of rational ethics, and it is the total failure of esthetic response that condemns Stavrogin to the desert of sterile will and finally to the shabbiest of suicides.

In this sense at least *The Brothers Karamazov* is an important synthesizing work. It is Dostoevsky's final statement of faith in the existence of some higher, absolute, unifying harmony, which lies beyond man's rational awareness and which promises the ultimate reconciliation of man's discords and moral despair in the "vale of tears" of earthly existence. The craving for this harmony cannot be satisfied by the logic of Ivan, the sensual experiments of Dmitry, or Alesha's conventional veneer of faith. None of the brothers can find a temporal equivalent or embodiment of this higher harmony. For Ivan the mathematical harmonies of rational analysis lead to a *cul-de-sac* where he is confronted with their inadequacy; for Dmitry the inharmonious, primitive formlessness of his physical urges brings despair; and the harmonious tranquility of Alesha's monastic retreat becomes increasingly incapable of withstanding the encroachment of worldly disorder. This last point is illustrated at the very start of the novel when the divided Karamazov family invades the reflective peace of Father Zosima's cell. Subsequently the introduction of Father Ferapont and his opposition to Zosima eloquently conveys the petty discords and squabbling hidden within the monastery itself. Zosima recognizes the frailty of monastic harmony when he sends Alesha out into the world. The young novice must experience moral chaos, he must face up to his "Karamazov nature" instead of concealing it beneath a cassock, before he can find a lasting harmony.

In the brothers' inability to discover a worldly form to accommodate their craving for harmony Dostoevsky confirms his lifelong view of the fallacy of all temporal harmonies. In the course of this study we have seen how man's rebellious and divided spirit cannot be contained within the ordered frameworks erected by neat minds. In the tales of the 1840s even the timid rebellions of Devushkin, Golyadkin,

Prokharchin, and Shumkov were enough to expose the inadequacy of a mechanical bureaucratic regime. Later Dostoevsky rejected the facile harmonies of idealism, the civic harmonies of socialism, the rational harmonies of the philosophic materialists of the 1860s, and of course the ecclesiastic harmonies of that "handmaiden of socialism," the Roman Catholic Church. It is in the nature of Dostoevsky's sternly Orthodox outlook that there should be no heaven on earth, no redemption or reconciliation for man in this world.

In *The Brothers Karamazov* Dostoevsky's analysis of absolute "suprarational" harmony and the attempts of men to create earthly equivalents accessible to their three-dimensional minds is couched in a mathematical analogy: he compares the "higher logic" of the modern non-Euclidean geometries, invented by the outstanding Russian mathematician Nikolay Lobachevsky (1792–1856) and subsequently elaborated by the German Bernhard Riemann, with classical Euclidean geometry. Riemann's work was begun at Göttingen in 1865 and it is unlikely that Dostoevsky was aware of it. But he certainly was familiar, even if only in a general sense, with the discoveries of Lobachevsky, who published most of his results at the end of the 1820s and during the 1830s, although they were not widely accepted until the latter half of the 1860s.[2] Dostoevsky almost certainly encountered his work during his time as a student at the St. Petersburg Academy of Military Engineering, and might well have discussed it further during his acquaintanceship with the great Russian woman mathematician Sofia Korvin-Krukovskaya (later Kovalevskaya), to whose sister, Anna, Dostoevsky contemplated marriage.[3] Certainly Dostoevsky speaks of Lobachevskian geometry in very revealing terms in notes and drafts for *The Brothers Karamazov*. Here is an extract from his notebook for 1880–1881, where he discusses the implications of parallel lines meeting, a situation conceivable in Lobachevskian geometry but possible only at infinity in Euclidean terms:

Parallel lines ought to meet at infinity, but this infinity will never be reached. If it were, there would be a limit to infinity, which is absurd. If parallel lines were to meet that would be an end to the world, the laws of geometry and God, which is absurd—but only for the human mind. If parallel lines were to meet, the laws of this world would come to an end. But at infinity they do meet, and the existence of infinity is beyond doubt. For if there were no infinity, the concept of finiteness would not exist, it would be inconceivable. But if there is infinity, then there is God and another world constructed on different laws than the real world.[4]

Of course, Dostoevsky is speaking ironically here: there is nothing absurd about non-Euclidean geometry or in the idea of parallel lines meeting. Euclidean geometry is a splendid hypothetical system, and we could build little without it, but it does assume the existence of hypothetical flat planes and hypothetical straight lines which do not correspond with a curved earth and a universe which we now know to be warped by gravitational fields. For example, if two strictly Euclidean draftsmen were carefully to draw two straight parallel lines at the earth's equator and crossing the equator at right angles, they would be horrified on extending those apparently straight and parallel lines to discover that they met at the north and south poles! The apparently "illogical" laws of Lobachevskian geometry yield a more complete picture of the universe.

Dostoevsky adduces non-Euclidean geometry in *The Brothers Karamazov* to counter the strictly Euclidean harmonies accessible to Ivan's classically rational mind, and to point out the possibility of other harmonies, of other ways of looking at things, which are no less valid. In the section entitled "Pro and Contra," for example, Dostoevsky challenges the Euclidean logic of Ivan's rebellion against God with the non-Euclidean "logic" of Father Zosima's faith.

The three brothers Karamazov all experience, however imperfectly, just such a "non-Euclidean" harmony, which is both compelling and liberating. It liberates insofar as it promotes in the brothers a sense of participation in some higher harmonious whole and offers a refuge from their base, fragmented, chaotic, and limited Karamazov natures, which even the childlike Alesha is aware of possessing.

III   *Dmitry*

Perhaps Dmitry embodies most clearly this conflict between higher and lower modes of being. He is conscious of some intangible harmony—something perhaps like Pascal's *agrément*—in which the whole of creation apart from man, and in particular himself, participates. He regards himself as a beast, an "insect with lust" (XIV, 100), and is ashamed of his body, his physical excesses, and his chaotic lack of self-control. These, he feels, debase the ecstatic harmony he sometimes senses, a harmony which stands in such tormenting contrast to the physical and moral squalor with which he surrounds himself. Dmitry's sense of esthetic alienation is, in some respects, at least, comparable to that of Prince Myshkin in *The Idiot*, who through a physical clumsiness occasioned by illness feels unable to participate in the harmonious chorus of God's world. The fact that Myshkin senses this harmony, but fears that he might debase it, makes his estrangement from it all the more poignant.

The existence of some higher purpose, of some cosmic consonance, behind the ugliness of earthly existence is revealed to Dmitry, as to his brothers, in moments of esthetic rapture. For Dmitry, the physical brother, this rapture accompanies a primitive pagan exultation in the physical joys of life. A profoundly sensual person, he is easy prey for drink, emotional excess, and the seductive curves of his beloved Grushenka. His very name points to his pagan nature: Demeter was the Greek goddess of the earth and agriculture, and Dmitry is a true child of the earth. In moments of intense exultation Dmitry's thirst for harmony is temporarily slaked by poetry, an evocative metaphor for the sense of life contained within a harmonious form. But even in his choice of poetry Dmitry confirms his pagan nature: he cites Schiller's "Eleusinian Festival," followed by his ode "To Joy" with its clearly pagan delight in nature and life:

> Joy eternal gives drink
> To the soul of God's creation,
> And enflames the cup of life
> With the secret force of fermentation.
> It has drawn the grass to the light,
> Has developed chaos into suns
> And scattered them out in the voids
> Beyond the astrologer's ken.
> At the bosom of bounteous nature
> All that breathes drinks of joy;
> All creatures, all nations
> Are drawn after her.
> In misfortune she has given us friends:
> The juice of grapes, the garlands of the graces;
> to the insects she has given sensualism . . .
> The Angel faces God.   (XIV, 99)

But Dmitry's primitive pagan receptivity to the joy of being, his intoxication with life, is not controlled by a moral form. For him the cup of life spills over equally easily into debauchery or adoration, into sensuality or spiritual ecstasy. The breadth and all-consuming nature of his appetite for life oppress Dmitry as a mystery: "There's an awful lot of mysteries! Too many enigmas oppress man on earth . . . . Yes, man is too broad, too broad indeed! I would narrow him down . . ."

(XIV, 100). The crown of this mystery is beauty, which for Dmitry
seems to possess a dreadful ambiguity. The breadth of his esthetic
instincts allows him to detect what he regards as beauty in both vice
and virtue, in Sodom as well as in the Madonna, and he is susceptible
to both types of beauty:

> Beauty is a terrible and terrifying thing! Terrible because it's indefinable, and
> it's impossible to define because God presents nothing but enigmas. Here the
> shores meet, here all contradictions live together . . . . Beauty! Besides I
> cannot bear it that a man, even though noble of soul and with a fine mind,
> should start from the ideal of the Madonna and end with the ideal of Sodom.
> It's even more terrible when a man with the ideal of Sodom already in his
> heart does not renounce the ideal of the Madonna . . . . What appears to the
> mind as shameful is sheer beauty to the heart. Is there beauty in Sodom?
> Believe me, for the vast majority of people it is indeed in Sodom—did you not
> know that? It is terrifying that beauty is not only a terrible, but also a
> mysterious thing. Here God and the Devil struggle for mastery, and the
> battlefield is the heart of man. (XIV, 100)

Dmitry's behavior reflects his devotion to the two ideals of beauty,
as spiritual joy and sensual joy combine to yield a totally amoral
ecstasy:

> If I am to fly into the abyss [of debauchery] then I shall do so precipitously,
> headlong, and shall even be pleased to find myself in such a degrading
> situation, shall consider it beautiful as far as I'm concerned. But in the very
> depths of that shame I shall suddenly begin a hymn. Let me be cursed, let me
> be low and base, but let me also kiss the hem of that garment in which my God
> is cloaked; even if I'm chasing after the Devil at that very moment, I am still
> your son, O Lord, and I love you, and I feel that joy without which the world
> could not be . . . . (XIV, 99)

Dmitry's sensitivity to "the beauty of the Madonna" seems to
derive from Dostoevsky's conviction that the need for ideal beauty is
as natural to man as eating or breathing, an idea which he elaborated
as early as 1861 in his essay "Mr.——bov and the Question of Art"[5]
and which is important in the subsequent conception of the characters of Raskolnikov (*Crime and Punishment*) and Myshkin (*The Idiot*).
Man, oppressed by the limitations, distractions, and formlessness of
his physical being, craves an absolute harmony, a fusion of his moral
and esthetic ideals, in which he can seek release, redemption, and
eventual reconciliation. The idea of finding an "esthetic" appeal in
the Sodom of deliberate self-abasement and the willful perversion of

one's higher instincts Dmitry derives, however, from his father, and indeed from a whole gallery of Dostoevskian characters, beginning with Golyadkin and the hero of "Polzunkov" in the 1840s and culminating with the civil servant Marmeladov from *Crime and Punishment*. Early in *The Brothers Karamazov* Fedor Pavlovich, Dmitry's father, confesses to Zosima that he abases himself largely to gratify his esthetic feelings: "Exactly, exactly! I've been offending myself all my life for pleasure, for the sake of my esthetic feelings, for it's not only pleasant, but sometimes even beautiful to be offended" (XIV, 41).

But Fedor Pavlovich is a lost soul, and he sees ideal beauty as merely a spice to enliven his taste for the beauty of Sodom, and vice versa. This explains his perverse, asexual attraction to the saintly mother of Ivan and Alesha as a foil to his sensualist nature. Dmitry is far less capable of accepting his disturbingly divided esthetic appetite. His moments of harmonious release do not allow him to live easily with his own moral chaos, and his quest for a definite moral form to contain his physical vigor is clearly revealed by his actions throughout the novel. He describes in desperate terms the degraded state of mankind in general by quoting Schiller's description of the horrors which confront Ceres, the Roman equivalent of the Greek Demeter, Dmitry's namesake, when she comes down to earth from the Olympian heights:

> The fruit of the fields and the sweet grapes
> Do not gleam at the feasts;
> Only the remains of corpses
> Smoke on the bloody altars;
> And wherever Ceres casts
> Her melancholy gaze
> She sees man everywhere
> Sunk in deepest degradation!   (XIV, 98)

In more personal terms, he professes his preoccupation with the degradation of man's earthly life and goes on, in a conversation with Perkhotin, a young civil servant to whom he pawns his pistols, to couch his craving for form and harmony in less oblique language. The conversation occurs after one of Dmitry's monumental orgies:

"You know, my friend," Dmitry said suddenly, with feeling, "I've never liked all this disorder."
"Who does! Fancy wasting three dozen bottles on peasants. That would make anyone's blood boil."

"No, I don't mean that. I'm speaking of a higher order. I have no order in
me, no higher order . . . . The whole of my life has been disorder, and I must
impose order . . .

> Glory to the highest on earth
> Glory to the highest in me!

That verse once burst from my soul; it's not a verse, but a tear . . . ." (XIV,
366)

Dmitry is prepared to destroy himself for the sake of a higher
harmony, for he feels that his own existence is an intolerable slight
upon that divine order. He obtains the opportunity for such a sacrifice
through his arrest for the murder of his father, but he does not acquire
the moral awareness needed to direct his sense of life until after his
arrest. He dreams during his interrogation of the apparently needless
sufferings of a starving child, and the barriers of self-absorption and
isolation are breached by a growing sense of responsibility for the
misfortune of others, in particular the child:

And he felt that his heart was touched in a way it had never been touched
before, that he wanted to cry, that he wished to do something in order that
neither the baby, nor its black, dried-up mother, would ever have to cry
again, so that there would be no further need for anyone's tears from that
moment on . . . . (XIV, 456–57)

This moment marks the start of Dmitry's transfiguration, as he
prepares to take the sufferings of others upon himself. He is prepared
to go to Siberia, not for the particular crime of parricide with which he
is charged, but for the crimes of humanity as a whole as distilled in the
image of a starving child. Dmitry's dream is a revelation which
transforms his joy from self-centered, directionless, pagan ecstasy to
a Christian religious and moral passion. He is transformed by the
Christian doctrine that "all are responsible."

A clear parallel to Dmitry's conversion is provided in Father Zosima's account of the final months in the life of his brother, who is dying
from consumption. The sick man's despair is relieved by a dawning
awareness of the beauty of the world and of the individual's complicity
in the life of all creation. In turn, his brother's example allows Zosima
himself to undergo the transformation from thoughtless, self-
centered, strutting army officer to the self-denying ascetic who accepts responsibility for all men, even his servant.

IV *Ivan*

Ivan Karamazov, too, experiences moments of release and self-sublimation, moments when his chronic self-awareness dissolves in a sense of the harmonious fusion of all God's creation, a state not dissimilar to Myshkin's ecstatic, albeit pathological, preepileptic experiences of a "higher mode of being." As with Dmitry, Ivan's craving for harmony originates in an awareness of the ugliness and disorder of human life. He cites Voltaire's well-known remark about the existence of God, "*s'il n'existait pas Dieu il faudrait l'inventer*," and then expresses the view that man has invented God in order to satisfy a craving for a higher harmony which dignifies him even in his squalor:

> But what is so strange and marvellous is not that God actually exists, but that such a thought—the idea of the necessity of God—should have crept into the head of so savage and wicked a creature as man; so holy is it, so touching and so wise, and so much does it redound to man's honor. (XIV, 214)

Such a redeeming need for harmony is present in Ivan himself. Surprisingly, perhaps, he confesses to Alesha something which clearly aligns him with Dmitry: his passionate, irrational, and undisciplined thirst for life. He even describes this thirst with the very image used by Dmitry: Schiller's "cup of life," which Ivan cannot renounce until he has drained it. Ivan's knowledge of Schiller, which surprises Alesha, is used by Dostoevsky as a form of shorthand to suggest the intellectual brother's sense of life and capacity for esthetic response, which is later confirmed in Ivan's admission that he suffers a duality of perception similar to Dmitry's. He is instinctively drawn by the beauty of God's world, as condensed in the image of the "sticky little leaves in spring" (XIV, 210), and this contradicts his intellectual disgust over God's ordering of creation. In other words, Ivan's arrogant intellectual confidence is shaken by an instinct for a higher order that is beyond his intellectual comprehension: "This isn't intellect; it isn't logic; it's something you love with your insides, from your belly . . . . I want to live, and I shall live, albeit in spite of logic . . . . Even if I've lost faith in the order of things; even if I'm convinced that, on the contrary, everything is disordered, damned and perhaps even chaos created by the devil . . . I nonetheless wish to live . . ." (XIV, 209–10).

But perhaps Ivan transcends the limits of his purely intellectual knowledge most radically in his *rapturous* anticipation of God's final harmonious reconciliation, when all chaos and anguish will be dispersed in the grace that will fill the universe: "And so I accept God; and not only willingly, but what's more I accept also His infinite wisdom and His purpose, which we are not given to understand. I believe in the order and meaning of life, I believe in the eternal harmony into which we are all supposed to flow, I believe in the Word towards which the universe is striving and which was 'with God and is God,' and so on . . ." (XIV, 214). Ivan is speaking here with genuine, if reluctant, ardor of a state of universal consonance where the will of man corresponds with the will of God, and which is defined in the Christian doctrine of synergism. The irony is that, although Ivan senses the inevitability of this reconciliation, he is compelled to reject it for two very important reasons which indicate his contrary impulse to pit his will against the divine order in an impressive metaphysical rebellion. First, the existence of this higher harmony is, for Ivan, an affront to the dignity and independence of rational man, whose understanding is confined to the three dimensions of Euclidean logic. Ivan is in this respect an archetypal victim of Original Sin: tormented by the memory of Eden in his moments of esthetic reconciliation, he cannot accommodate these experiences within the framework of strict, analytical logic. As a modern man, proud of his reason and enlightenment, Ivan is reluctant to deny his logical perception in favor of some intangible, indefinable sense of spiritual well-being. Surely, he argues, if God had wished us to participate in His mystical, suprarational reconciliation He should have allowed us to understand His "mysterious ways" by endowing us with minds capable of transcending the purely logical. Ivan construes His apparent refusal to do so not as the gift of freedom of faith to man, but as a slight upon that crown of all human endeavor—rational analysis. Ivan, a nineteenth-century European intellectual, is compelled to pledge his allegiance to logic rather than intuition, to place "the understanding of life" (*soznanie zhizni*) higher than "the sense of life" (*chuvstvo zhizni*). The understanding of life dignifies man; the mere sense of it debases him by reducing him to the status of the animals. Perhaps this accounts for Ivan's intense dislike of his brother Dmitry, whose behavior wantonly proclaims a base sense of life and an absence of all analytical understanding. Ivan's unwillingness to accept the love of life as more important than understanding its meaning differentiates him also from Alesha, who urges him to "love life regardless of logic, as you say; yes, most certainly regardless of logic, for only then will you grasp its meaning" (XIV, 210). Their different attitudes are neatly exposed in a comparison of Ivan's comments about Europe being a graveyard with Alesha's behavior after the Cana of Galilee episode. In his moment of sublime insight, Alesha falls to the ground and drenches it with his tears. This for him is a moment of ecstasy when the sense of life and harmony overcomes his inability to understand God's apparent refusal to crown the life of the deceased Zosima with a miracle. Previously, Ivan, too, had spoken of drenching the earth with his tears, but the earth he had in mind was that heaped upon the graves of his beloved European rationalist philosophers, the champions of skepticism rather than faith.

Moreover, Ivan's Euclidean mind cannot accept a harmony that can accommodate, without apparently *correcting*, the brutal moral discords introduced into this world by mankind's cruelty and inhumanity. Significantly in the context of Dmitry's conversion through the image of a suffering child, Ivan illustrates his hatred of moral ugliness by referring to the torture of children. The tears of these innocent victims of perverse inhumanity must, he demands, be avenged and injustice resolved; but Ivan's concrete, rectilinear mind can be appeased only by concrete, rectilinear justice and reconciliation, in this world rather than in the next. God's higher harmony, the inevitability of which Ivan is prepared to concede, is improper because man's brutish behavior *spoils it*, like an irritating blemish on a piece of fine porcelain. Ivan is therefore forced to the conclusion that temporal chaos must be countered not by God's redeeming non-Euclidean harmony, but by an imposed temporal order, represented most vividly in his unwritten poem "The Grand Inquisitor," but already implicit in an earlier article he had written on the relations between Church and State.

"The Grand Inquisitor" is the philosophical core of *The Brothers Karamazov*, providing as it does a fine dramatic confrontation between earthly and divine concepts of harmony. Ivan explains his idea to Alesha in what is perhaps the most compelling philosophical conversation in literature. "The Grand Inquisitor," set in sixteenth-century Spain, tells of Christ's returning to earth to revive the faith of his followers during the darkest days of the Spanish Inquisition, when heretics and enemies of the Roman Church are suffering in their scores in brutal autos-da-fé. Christ heals the blind and raises the dead, and is at once recognized by all, including the Grand Inquisitor, a shriveled old man of ninety, who orders his immediate arrest "as the vilest of heretics" (XIV, 228). That night the Inquisitor enters the prison where Christ is held and explains to his captive why he is to be burned. For the first time in his life he says aloud "what he has been thinking in silence for ninety years." He accuses Christ of returning to meddle in the affairs of the Church, which, although ostensibly acting in Christ's name, has in fact for fifteen centuries been engaged in the task of correcting His work. The Inquisitor argues that Christ was wrong to insist on man's freedom of faith by resisting in the wilderness the three temptations of Satan, "the terrible and wise spirit" (XIV, 229), who understood that man is a weak creature, unable to endure freedom. "There are three forces," he says, "the only three forces on earth, which are able to conquer and hold captive for ever the conscience of these weak rebels for their own happiness—these forces are: miracle, mystery and authority" (XIV, 232). The Devil's three temptations, the wisdom of which the In-quisitor regards as "miraculous," were perfectly matched to the weaknesses of human nature, and would have allowed Christ to impose unity and happiness upon his children forever through the exercise of the forces of miracle, mystery, and authority. Christ, however, wanted man's free love: "Instead of taking possession of man's freedom you multiplied it and burdened the spiritual kingdom of man forever with its sufferings" (XIV, 232). In order to relieve mankind of the burden of this freedom the Roman Church has accepted the three forces rejected by Christ, and out of love for humanity has set out to enslave it. The Inquisitor concludes his long monologue by insisting that Christ's return would only cloud the issue and set back the work of the Church by many centuries. He must therefore die.

The "poem" does not, however, end there; Christ, who has re-mained silent and impassive throughout the Inquisitor's confession, rises to his feet and kisses the old man gently on his lips. The Inquisitor is visibly moved and releases his prisoner with the warning that he must never return. "The kiss burns in his heart, but the old man clings to his idea" (XIV, 239).

The key to the meaning of "The Grand Inquisitor" is contained in Ivan's earlier remark to Alesha that "Christ's love for men is in its way a miracle that is impossible on earth" (XIV, 216). Christ's love is—in the opinion of both Ivan and the Inquisitor—pitiless, for it includes man's freedom to err, and "nothing has ever been more unbearable for man and human society than freedom" (XIV, 230). Loss of free-dom is for the Inquisitor the price mankind must pay for happiness on earth, and here we see the root of his disagreement with Christ, for it is precisely happiness *on earth* that he wants for men at the expense of joy in heaven. Like his creator, Ivan, the Inquisitor is prepared to deny the higher, non-Euclidean harmony of divine justice for the sake of temporal, Euclidean order. The Inquisitor's lineage is here clearly disclosed—he is Shigalev in ecclesiastical guise, concealing beneath his ardent concern for mankind a profound contempt for men, whom he sees as sheep to be shepherded by the few strong enough to endure the rigors of freedom. This too is a distortion of Christ's example. He suffered for the sake of man's happiness in the next world; the Inquisitor and his fellow custodians of the Roman faith suffer for the sake of harmony on earth.

Ivan shares the Inquisitor's contempt for his fellow men, and is equally aware of the discrepancy between abstract, theoretical love for mankind and Christian love for men. He had introduced his story of the Grand Inquisitor with a confession to Alesha that he could never understand how one could love one's neighbors: "It is precisely one's neighbors, in my view, that one can't possibly love, but only those who live far away . . . as soon as a man shows his face love disappears" (XIV, 215). The section on Father Zosima's life, which follows shortly after "The Grand Inquisitor," reaffirms the importance of Christian love as the answer to the monstrous abstract philanthropy of the Inquisitor's loveless utopia. But the ending of "The Grand Inquisitor," where the Inquisitor is touched by his victim's kiss of forgiveness, suggests that even Ivan is keeping his options open, and this discloses his moral ambiguity. Ivan the cosmic rebel is—like his brother Dmitry—a desperately split victim of a dual perception: his rational rebellion, despite its impeccable logic, is persistently confounded by his esthetic love for God's creation. This conflict of intellect and esthetic sense is suggested in the very nature of "The Grand Inquisitor": Ivan confesses that he has never been able to write it down. His esthetic sense denies form to the horror created by his intellect. Ivan's later hallucinatory confrontation with the devil echoes this conflict, as he recoils in esthetic disgust from that ultimate rebel against God's order.

V Alesha

The youngest brother, Alesha, possesses neither the gross physical appetite of Dmitry nor the isolating intellectual arrogance of Ivan, so we might expect his perception of universal harmony to remain unclouded by either sensual or intellectual self-awareness. And indeed, despite both his youth and Dostoevsky's unsatisfactory deline-

ation of his character, he does appear to share his brothers' capacity
for esthetic rapture, particularly in the scene following the reading of
the biblical passage on the wedding at Cana of Galilee, when his faith
returns after the challenge of Zosima's death and unseemly decompo-
sition. But, as his father points out and as Alesha himself is aware, he
is nonetheless tarred with the Karamazov brush. Dostoevsky intended to show Alesha's decisive fall from grace in a subsequent, and
of course unwritten, part of the novel; but even in the completed
portion Alesha displays both potential sensualism (he passively yields
to his surly friend Rakitin's attempts to arrange his seduction by
Grushenka) and the capacity for the same kind of intellectual revolt as
Ivan displays. In the chapter "Rebellion" Alesha is drawn by Ivan into
complicity, albeit momentarily, in his brother's revolt. Ivan's critique
of an "irrational" God is consonant with Alesha's incomprehension of
the events following Zosima's death and helps to compound his loss of
faith.

Still, Alesha's subsequent experience of mystical ecstasy is the
most detailed description we have in the novel of that higher harmony elusively perceived by the other brothers. I have tried in this
chapter to describe this "indescribable" rapture and define it by
analogy, but Alesha's experience provides a more concrete account:

His soul, filled with rapture, craved freedom, room, space. The dome of
heaven was inverted above his head, vast, boundless and studded with silent,
shining stars. The Milky Way, still elusive, ran from zenith to the horizon in
two arms. The night, fresh, silent and still, enfolded the earth. The white
towers and golden domes of the cathedral gleamed against the sapphire sky.
The luxuriant spring flowers in the beds around the house fell asleep till
morning. The stillness of the earth seemed somehow to merge with that of
the heavens. The mystery of the earth came into contact with that of the stars
. . . . Alesha stood and looked, and suddenly he fell to the ground as if he'd
been cut down.

He didn't know why he was embracing it; he was not aware of why he
longed so irresistibly to kiss it, to kiss it all, but he kissed it, weeping, sobbing
and drenching it with his tears; and vowed in a frenzy to love it, to love it till
the end of time. "Water the earth with the tears of your joy and love those
tears," this rang out in his heart. Why was he weeping? Oh, in his rapture he
was weeping even over those stars which shone on him from out of the abyss,
and "he was not ashamed of his frenzy." It was as if threads from all those
innumerable worlds of God came together at once in his soul, and it was all
a-tremble "as it touched other worlds." He wanted to forgive all men for all
things and to beg forgiveness—oh, not for himself, but for all men, for
everyone and everything. "And others will plead for me"—this rang out in

his soul again. And with each moment he felt clearly and in a way almost tangibly that something firm and immovable, like that heavenly vault, was entering his soul. Some sort of idea was taking possession of his mind—and would rule it for the rest of his life, for all time. He had fallen to the ground a weak youth, but he rose from it a resolute fighter for the rest of his life, and he realized and felt this suddenly at the very moment of his rapture . . . . (XIV, 328)

VI *The Brothers and Original Sin*

The dual perception of each of the brothers Karamazov confirms the dualistic nature of man as revealed in the book of Genesis: he is created from both the Holy Spirit and the dust of the earth. His participation in some higher harmony, revealed to the brothers in moments of esthetic rapture, is counterbalanced by weaknesses of the flesh and the intellect which rupture the sense of harmony. The human weaknesses of the three brothers assume metaphorical significance when it is seen that, as well as being individual failings, they also contain overt echoes of three aspects of Original Sin, the fall of man from Grace. In the biblical account of the Fall, man's experience of the forbidden fruit from the tree of knowledge leads, as in Ivan's case, to intellectual arrogance and rebellion as Adam and Eve seek to *know for themselves* the nature of good and evil, which had hitherto been the prerogative of God alone. They become as God, just as Ivan demands to know the ways of God, and place what Ivan calls "the understanding of life" (*soznanie zhizni*) higher than the joy of life. This consciousness alienates man from the rest of creation. The acquisition of knowledge also leads in Genesis to the acquisition of self-consciousness and a sense of bodily shame. When the Lord asks Adam why he has concealed his nakedness behind a figleaf, Adam replies: "I was afraid, because I was naked" (Genesis 3:10). This is clearly echoed in *The Brothers Karamazov* by Dmitry's physical disgust over himself and particularly by his overwhelming sense of shame after his arrest as he stands naked before *his* prosecutors. Interestingly enough, both Adam and Dmitry display this bodily shame when confronted with the accusation that they have turned against their "fathers": Adam by betraying the trust of the Lord; Dmitry by apparently having killed Fedor Pavlovich. Yet another link is established between Adam and Dmitry when we remember that as a punishment for tasting the forbidden fruit Adam is banished from Eden with Eve and told to till the soil. Dmitry and Grushenka also contemplate expurgating their sins by a life of exile in America, where they intend to work the soil. Dmitry's name, suggesting as it does the goddess of agriculture, adds further weight to this interpretation.

But Alesha, too, is guilty of metaphorical complicity in Original Sin, when man turned in his pride against his heavenly father. Adam's decision to eat the fruit of the tree of knowledge must be seen as a temptation and a failure of faith in God. Alesha yields to a comparable temptation, though proffered not by Satan but by that other advocate of metaphysical rebellion, his brother Ivan. Ivan's arguments conspire with Alesha's disappointment at the lack of a miracle to dignify Father Zosima's death to promote in the young novice a severe, if temporary, crisis of faith. This diverts him from his all-important duty of watching over both his father and his brother Dmitry, a duty imposed earlier by Alesha's spiritual father, Zosima. It is during this crisis that the murder of Fedor Pavlovich takes place.

All three brothers, therefore, combine to form a collective symbol of mankind tainted by Original Sin. Within the context of the Christian faith it is axiomatic that the sins of mankind are to be redeemed through the sacrifice of Christ. Christ has shown man how to overcome the legacy of the Fall, and in *The Brothers Karamazov* this idea, too, is demonstrated and related to the particular sins of the three brothers. Ivan's unwritten poem "The Grand Inquisitor" deals with Christ's experiences in the wilderness, where he rejected the three temptations of Satan, and argues that the Son of God was wrong to reject the serpent's blueprint for temporal harmony in favor of allowing suffering mankind freedom of choice. The importance of Ivan's poem lies in the fact that in the wilderness Christ resisted, and showed man how to redeem, the same three sins to which the brothers yield in the course of the novel. The first of Christ's temptations is that of transforming the stones of the desert into loaves, in order to win the allegiance of man by guaranteeing him bread, or the gratification of his physical appetites. Christ refuses, asserting that man does not live by bread alone and that the satisfaction of his physical needs is meaningless unless his spiritual needs are also met. This relates directly to the particular problem of Dmitry, whose physical appetites are chaotic and destructive in the absence of a guiding moral principle. Before his conversion Dmitry tries to live by bread alone, seeking oblivion in sensual gratification.

In the next temptation the Devil suggests that Christ leap down from a pinnacle of the temple, so that God might save him and men might be converted by the miracle. Christ again refuses, this time on the grounds that men must come to him of their own free will and not be compelled by the force of miracle. Moreover, Christ recognizes that by precipitating himself from the temple he would be tempting God and testing his faith, when faith in God must be stronger than any miraculous proof. The significance of this temptation is revealed by Alesha's loss of faith when God fails to crown Zosima's life with the miracle all had been expecting. Christ builds his church on the same grounds that cause Alesha to lose his faith—the absence of a miracle.

Finally, Christ is offered direct dominion over all the kingdoms of the earth—the sword of Caesar—with the opportunity to create a tangible, temporal "Euclidean" harmony by direct rule, in order to overcome—by authority and not by love—the bestial discords of human existence. Christ refuses, insisting again that men should be free to exercise choice between good and evil, but Ivan longs for a concrete, secular harmony apparent to his Euclidean mind and is prepared to sacrifice his intuitive knowledge of a higher harmony in its cause.

The failings of the three brothers—the Karamazov strain—are thus the hallmarks of human nature, the legacy of the Fall. Christ could overcome similar temptations because he was divine, but the brothers can redeem this legacy only by following the path taken by Christ himself—that of suffering and rebirth. The importance of this idea for the novel is suggested by the epigraph from St. John: "Verily, verily, I say unto you, Except a corn of wheat fall into the ground and die, it abideth alone: but if it die, it bringeth forth much fruit." All must be redeemed through suffering, and for the brothers the nature of their suffering neatly corresponds to the nature of their sins: Dmitry has to undergo the *physical* torments of penal servitude and exile; Ivan—the *mental* anguish of a nervous breakdown and the disintegration of his reason; and Alesha—the *spiritual* agonies and degradation of his life in the world outside the monastery. All must find their heaven along the road to Calvary.

VII   *Parricide and Smerdyakov*

We have seen how the rational arrogance, the failures of faith, and the bodily shame of the brothers Karamazov implicate them symbolically in Original Sin. In the novel this Original Sin is represented by the particularly apt metaphor of parricide. Man's revolt against his heavenly father is miniaturized in the murder of the despicable Fedor Pavlovich, a murder actually committed by the bastard son Smerdyakov but for which, as Richard Peace argues,[6] each of the brothers is in some measure responsible. The idea of equating in this metaphor the repulsive Fedor Pavlovich with the Lord strikes one initially as horrifically inappropriate, but it is important for the purposes of the novel that the father of the Karamazov family be as difficult to love as God is for Ivan. Any man can serve a benign father, divine or otherwise, but love for a father whose benevolence is not apparent—whether because he indulges in distasteful sensualism or permits the sufferings of children—is a much more refined test of faith and character. The Public Prosecutor at Dmitry's trial explores this parallel further in terms which in the reader's mind link a son's demand that his father should earn his love to Ivan's demand that God should account for his actions: "But what would become of us if parricide were merely a prejudice and if every child were to ask his father: 'Father, why should I love you?' What would happen to the foundations of our society? What would become of the family?" (XV, 174). The answer to the Prosecutor's final question is that the harmony of the family would be ruptured in the same way that the harmony of Eden was by man's insistence that he *know*. And the harmony of the Karamazov family has been irrevocably shattered, as the sons first recoil in distaste from their father and then conspire, through their sins either of commission or omission, to cause his death. Professor Peace has described the complicity of the brothers in the murder of their father in great detail, so there is little need to dwell upon the matter here. But it is worth reaffirming that the balance of the novel is maintained in the guilt of the brothers, in that the nature of their individual responsibility derives from the dominant features of their personalities. Ivan's guilt is intellectual, for he provides the "ideology" that motivates Smerdyakov in his belief that if there is no God "all is permitted." Dmitry's guilt is emotional and physical, in that he creates the emotional climate for violence by his repeated threats and provides a physical dress rehearsal of the murder in his bodily attack upon his father's person. Alesha's guilt is spiritual, for he cannot bring himself to love his father, and by falling into despair during his crisis of faith he fails to watch over the tensions of the family.

But the most compelling pledge of the collective guilt of the sons is provided in the shadowy figure who actually commits the crime—the lackey Smerdyakov, their disowned half-brother. The dark and disgusting Smerdyakov is the last of Dostoevsky's great melodramatic specters, haunting both the pages of the novel and the minds of the brothers in the same way that Svidrigailov haunted *Crime and*

Punishment and its hero, Raskolnikov. He is a composite double, the external projection of all the ugliness and baseness hidden within the brothers Karamazov; he is the agent of the dark aspects of their natures. He stands before the brothers like a hideously distorting mirror, reflecting back at them their own failings in a fashion that compels recognition of the ugliness of these failings. For example, Ivan out of a sense of pride and human dignity concludes that if God does not exist or is rejected, then "all is permitted"; human beings are their own masters, responsible for their own actions, and should base their behavior not on the promise of redemption or the threat of damnation in the afterlife, but on a morality of their own making founded upon the freedom of choice in the face of good and evil. For Ivan this is a noble idea, which liberates man from superstition and compels him to exercise his own moral discretion in a rational choice between good and evil. But Smerdyakov, in acting upon this idea, exposes its fallacy by using it as a justification for murdering Ivan's father. Through him Ivan is forced to recognize that the morality embodied in the statement "all is permitted," far from dignifying man, allows him to exercise his dark and criminal instincts without fear of divine retribution. The figure of Dmitry too may be discerned behind Smerdyakov's outline, albeit in a grotesquely distorted form. Indeed, the very existence of Smerdyakov as a brother is an affront to the poetry-loving, physically vigorous Dmitry. For example, the sensuous and lyrical confessions of Dmitry to Alesha, in which he recounts his passionate love for life, for Grushenka, and for Schiller, are followed and debased by the scene in which the asexual, life-denying, eunuchlike Smerdyakov ironically and passionlessly serenades his neighbor, Maria Kondratevna. Dmitry's startling and uninhibited extracts from Schiller are lifelessly echoed in Smerdyakov's high-pitched intoning of a trivial love song, and monstrously inverted in the lackey's insistence that he dislikes all poetry (XIV, 204). The symbolic links between Dmitry and Smerdyakov are established again in the scene where Dmitry scales the wall of his father's property with murder in his mind. Ultimately, of course, he refuses to murder his father, but by attacking his surrogate father, the old retainer Grigory, who had looked after him as a child, he does open the way for Smerdyakov. The complicity thus established between the two half-brothers is anticipated in Dmitry's recognition of the fact that he has climbed his father's garden wall at exactly the same spot where years earlier the idiot girl, Liza Smerdyashchaya, had come to give birth to Smerdyakov.

Finally, to complete the symmetry, there are tenuous but revealing links between Smerdyakov and the brother who apparently least resembles him, Alesha. Their mothers, for instance, were both saintly fools, and both were seduced by Fedor Pavlovich. Alesha's association with the monastery and the Orthodox faith is parodied in Smerdyakov's apparent association with an extremist sect of religious schismatics, the Castrates, who supply certain unsettling motifs in a great number of Dostoevsky's works.[7] But the most convincing parallel is provided in chapter 7 of Book III, "The Controversy," where Smerdyakov declares that if he ever fell into the hands of heathens he would renounce his Christian faith if by doing so he could save his life. The manner in which he develops his argument grotesquely anticipates Alesha's subsequent fall from faith, when it is not his life that is at stake, but his devotion to the memory of Father Zosima. Smerdyakov, too, bases his hypothetical renunciation of faith on the absence of a miracle. He explains, in terms which the reader will recall during Alesha's later crisis, how if God refuses to answer his plea for a mountain to move and crush his tormentors he is perfectly justified in denying God in order to save his skin:

> But if at precisely that moment I'd tried all that and deliberately cried out to that mountain to crush my tormentors, and if it hadn't crushed them, then tell me, how could I not have doubted at such a dreadful hour of great and mortal terror? Knowing, moreover, that I should never fully attain the Kingdom of Heaven (for if the mountain didn't move at my word, it must mean that they didn't think much of my faith up there and that I wouldn't be in line for much of a reward in the next world), why therefore should I give them my skin to flay and to no good purpose? (XIV, 121)

Alesha, too, is tempted by the unexpected turn of events after Zosima's death to conclude that his faith has not been rewarded or highly thought of in heaven, and temporarily renounces it.

In conclusion, if each of the brothers Karamazov senses in the course of the novel the existence of some higher redeeming harmony to which all must eventually be reconciled, each is also obliged to recognize in the repulsive figure of Smerdyakov an echo of his base and discordant human weaknesses. In his rudimentary rationalism, his debasement of poetry and sensualism, and his easy renunciation of faith under duress, Smerdyakov strikes chords in the hearts of all three brothers. But the novel's promise of redemption ultimately overcomes even the existence of Smerdyakov, for the same sense of form and harmony that beckons the brothers to reconciliation allows them also to deny Smerdyakov. The ingratiating, slippery, sly lackey—the novel's most effective incarnation of the spirit that seduced man from Eden—offends against the esthetic sense of the collective hero, the three aspects of man, and allows Ivan, Dmitry, and Alesha to take the first steps along the road that leads first to Calvary, but ultimately to the promise of salvation.

CHAPTER 8

Conclusion

IN the hundred years since Dostoevsky's death his work has meant many things to many people. Each generation and school of thought has brought to the examination of his novels new and occasionally startling insights. This continuous process of reassessment, which shows no sign of abating, is in itself a measure of the importance and vitality of Dostoevsky's achievement. It is not confined to academia; each new generation of intelligent readers discovers his great novels with the same sense of intellectual excitement and emotional commitment. Dostoevsky appears to be in no danger of becoming a "classic," a literary fossil respected for his historical achievement but of limited relevance to modern thought. His works speak directly and with urgency in the present age, and have contributed greatly to the shape and psychology of modern fiction. This presumably is what Steiner has in mind when he argues that "Dostoevsky has penetrated more deeply than Tolstoy into the fabric of contemporary thought."[1] But the continuing significance of Dostoevsky's work, and the colorful variety of critical interpretation that it has engendered, can in itself prove a deterrent to the reader approaching Dostoevsky for the first time. The shelves of libraries sag with often-conflicting accounts of Dostoevsky the Christian, Dostoevsky the Existentialist, Dostoevsky the psychologist, Dostoevsky the great thinker with little regard for artistic technique, and Dostoevsky the superb literary craftsman whose derivative and second-rate thought is worth little or nothing. In addition there are innumerable comparative accounts of Dostoevsky's relationship to other great writers and philosophers. To juxtapose so crudely such various interpretations is not to belittle them, for they have all contributed to our understanding. But perhaps the real significance of Dostoevsky lies in his ability to draw from twentieth-century intellectual life such a wide variety of responses. The ease with which his work accommodates such sustained, diverse, and occasionally partisan critical interest suggests that Dostoevsky is indeed "an artist who was supremely representative of his age,"[2] and that this age is by no means over. His novels, which tend toward plurality and discord in both their techniques and the image they project of modern man, correspond so perfectly to the complex texture of modern life as to engage the interest of all readers, no matter how diverse their outlooks. The twentieth century has done everything possible to confirm the accuracy of Dostoevsky's chaotic vision.

Yet, ironically, Dostoevsky was constantly obliged to defend that accuracy, and the realism of his work, from the persistent accusation of his contemporaries that his novels were strange, exaggerated, and improbable. Belinsky's distaste for the grotesque qualities of *The Double*, "The Landlady," and "Mister Prokharchin" infected many of Dostoevsky's subsequent critics. The social philosopher Nikolay Mikhailovsky (1842–1904), in his remarkable essay "A Cruel Talent" (1882), suggested that Dostoevsky had invented improbable characters with unlikely psychological dilemmas solely in order to satisfy his own sadistic tastes, and even Tolstoy criticized what he considered to be a lack of verisimilitude in Dostoevsky's novels.[3] The reaction of Dostoevsky's early foreign readers, familiar with the gentler Russian novels of Turgenev, was equally outraged. George Moore considered him a cheap melodramatic novelist "with psychological sauce," and *The Spectator*, in its review of *The Idiot* (1887), remarked upon "the so-called realism which consists in a display of deformities, more or less hideous, dragged forth and paraded for the public to gloat over."[4]

It is easy to sympathize with these views, for Dostoevsky's works do challenge the limitations of the conventional realistic tradition, with its emphasis on verisimilitude. They lack the preoccupation with manners, social detail, physical reality, and naturalistic description we find in the novels of Dostoevsky's great Realist contemporaries Tolstoy, Turgenev, and Goncharov. They do not suggest the qualities of normality and ordinariness, but present instead a sensational, exaggerated, and contrived picture of reality, concentrating always on extreme characters in extreme situations. The world of *The Devils*, for example, seems far removed from the world of *Anna Karenina*, but both novels describe broadly comparable social groups at more or less the same time in Russian history. Yet *Anna Karenina* strives toward stability and continuity with its underlying affirmation of the enduring powers of normality, which absorbs and softens the individual tragedy of Anna, whereas *The Devils* denies normality and depicts a world catastrophically torn apart by its extremes, eccentricities, and contradictions.

Dostoevsky always defended his status as a Realist, but the terms in which he did so are interesting. In seeking inspiration for his novels, and indeed confirmation of the truthfulness of the reality they depict, he often turned not directly to the normal ebb and flow of life itself, but instead to the intensified reality of the newspapers. He did in fact claim that his "Realism" was of a "higher" kind, and that "what strikes others as fantasy is for me the very essence of reality."[5] The implications of his remarks are that conventional Naturalism, capturing and stabilizing in artistic form the world of appearances, is no longer adequate for the presentation of the complex and shifting realities of the modern age, and that his own "higher realism"—often exaggerated, contrived, symbolic, and interpretative—yields a more complete picture of the forces which drive the contemporary world. The conclusion of *A Raw Youth* provides a rare elaboration of these ideas. Arkady Dolgoruky receives a letter from Nikolay Semyonovich, in whose family he had lived while at school, and to whom he has sent a copy of his autobiographical memoir for comment. Nikolay remarks that the disorder of Arkady's life is entirely characteristic of contemporary life. He observes that in the past there was an established moral order, "completed forms of honor and duty" (XIII, 453) derived from the aristocracy, which, however imperfect, provided stable moral certainties capable of reclaiming even the most rebellious individual for society. But in the present age there is, as Arkady's memoir suggests, no longer a unifying moral or intellectual center, and consequently society fragments. Nikolay then goes on to justify the "disorder" of Arkady's memoir by remarking that the artist, whose duty it is to create from the material of life permanent and stable images, "beautiful forms," cannot draw harmony and beauty from the chaos of contemporary life: "The position of our novelist in such a case would be quite definite: he could not write in any form other than the historical, for there are no longer any beautiful types in our time" (XIII, 454). "If I were a Russian novelist and had talent, then I would definitely take my heroes from the Russian ancestral gentry, because only in that type of cultured Russian can one find even the semblance of beautiful order" (XIII, 453).

In a thinly disguised reference to Tolstoy, Nikolay then points out that the artist of outstanding talent "can so distract the reader that the latter will accept an historical picture as a reality possible even in the present. Such a work, if executed by a real talent, would belong not so much to the realm of Russian literature as to the realm of Russian history. It would be a portrait, artistically perfect, of a Russian mirage" (XIII, 454). Here Dostoevsky, the poet of the contemporary age of uncertainty, dismisses as artistic anachronisms the stable world and the confidence in the survival of normality depicted in the novels of Tolstoy. Works such as *War and Peace* and *Anna Karenina*, in creating "beautiful forms," transfigure the material of life, suggesting stability where there is only discord through the historical redundancy of their artistic vision. They belong firmly to the past, and if no new "beautiful forms of life" emerge, then "the future Russian novel is impossible" (XIII, 454). At best the passing of time will put our age in perspective and allow the artist of the future to "find beautiful forms even for the depiction of present disorder and chaos" (XIII, 455). Meanwhile the novel (and Nikolay cites Arkady's memoir as an example) must utilize esthetic disorder and uncertainty in order to capture the texture of contemporary life—"a thankless task, without beautiful forms" (XIII, 455).

In the course of this study we have seen how Dostoevsky's novels respond to the spirit of the age as described by Nikolay, creating forms of esthetic uncertainty to match the moral chaos of life. The ultimately monologic nature of Tolstoy's novels, his use of a narrator outside the fiction to objectify, reconcile, and stabilize the discords of the world he describes, is replaced in Dostoevsky's artistic world by polyphony and an unstable, relativistic point of view which perfectly correspond to the plurality of reality.

Tolstoy would have made an impressive *philosophe*: certainly his esthetic and moral vision was far closer to that of the great eighteenth-century thinkers than to that of his contemporary Dostoevsky. History, however, has left behind the confidence of the Enlightenment in the objectivity of truth and its accessibility to the rational mind. The last century and a half have seen another revolution in European intellectual life, one which has complicated the reality observed by artists, philosophers and scientists alike, and suggested that man's understanding of, and relationship to, that reality will always be an imperfect one. It seems that Dostoevsky intuitively understood this, and the finest testimony to the modernity of his vision is provided by the man who has most comprehensively understood and described the uncertainty and relativity of physical reality in the modern age: Albert Einstein. "Dostoevsky gives me more than any other thinker,"[6] he wrote, and the fact that the founder of modern physics should affirm the central importance of Dostoevsky's thought, rather than that of, say, Newton, in his own intellectual development is a remarkable, if initially puzzling accolade. The question of the interdependence or mutual influence of the worlds of science and art has always aroused strong feelings, and there are those—George Steiner, for example—who would insist that the language of one is inappropriate to the discussion of the other.[7] In a strict sense this is, of course, true, but science has always shared with art one striking characteristic: the picture it yields of the world and the answers it provides depend largely on the outlook of him who practices it and the questions he asks. But the kind of questions men ask and the outlook to which they adhere are indissolubly related to the current state of their knowledge and the dominant intellectual climate of their age. It seems hardly coincidental that in the eighteenth century science, art, and philosophy by and large combined to suggest a picture of reality which emphasized its stability, rationality, and accessibility to the mind of man, and that subsequently all three have by contrast disclosed the difficulties of perception, and the uncertain, relativistic nature of reality. The homogeneous and rational laws of Newton's clockwork universe, and his faith in the absolute nature of space and time, derive from the intellectual confidence of his age, which allowed him to assume an omniscient, "God's eye" point of view from which he could observe the universe objectively. Two hundred years later Einstein understood the "arrogance" of Newton's assumption and realized that man grasped "humbly and only imperfectly" the nature of the universe.[8] He recognized that man was a participant in the universe and consequently unable to assume a detached and omniscient vantage point. His adoption of a participating observer and a relativistic, subjective point of view necessarily complicated our perception of the universe, and cast doubt on the previously accepted absoluteness of space and time. When Dostoevsky obstructs Ivan Karamazov's quest for a precise, mathematical, absolute, and Euclidean harmony, and suggests instead the existence of some higher harmony, non-Euclidean and apparently irrational; when he locates his narrative point of view within Raskolnikov's consciousness and casts doubt on the nature of objective reality—then he achieves in art something like "the emotional, psychological and esthetic equivalent"[9] of Einstein's relativity.[10] The lasting significance of Dostoevsky's achievement lies in his role as the Einstein to Tolstoy's Newton, and in the highly appropriate moral vision and novelistic techniques he bequeathed to the post-Einsteinian age of uncertainty.

Notes and References

Chapter One

1. E.H. Carr, *Dostoevsky* (London, 1962), p. 13.
2. A.S. Dolinin, ed., *F.M. Dostoevskii v vospominaniiakh sovremennikov* [Dostoevsky in the Memoirs of His Contemporaries], 2 vols. (Moscow, 1964), I, 97.
3.. Ibid., I, 106.
4. F.M. Dostoevskii, *Pis'ma* [Letters], ed. A.S. Dolinin (Moscow-Leningrad, 1928), I, 56.
5. Ibid., I, 73.
6. *F.M. Dostoevskii ob iskusstve* [Dostoevsky on Art], ed. V.A. Bogdanov (Moscow, 1973), p. 300.
7. *F.M. Dostoevskii v vospominaniiakh sovremennikov*, I, 172.
8. *F.M. Dostoevskii ob iskusstve*, p. 349.
9. *F.M. Dostoevskii v vospominaniiakh sovremennikov*, II, 429–30.

Chapter Two

1. See, in particular, V. Terras, *The Young Dostoevsky, 1846–1849* (The Hague, 1969); J. Frank, *Dostoevsky, the Seeds of Revolt* (Princeton, 1976); and V. Ia. Kirpotin, *F.M. Dostoevskii, tvorcheskii put'* [F.M. Dostoevsky and His Literary Work] (Moscow, 1960).
2. N. Hampson, *The Enlightenment* (Harmondsworth, Eng.: Penguin, 1976), p. 18. Hampson's work was a source of many of the ideas used in this introduction. I should like also to acknowledge the value of R. Grimsley, ed., *The Age of Enlightenment, 1715–89* (Harmondsworth, Eng.: Penguin, 1979), and P. Gay, *The Enlightenment, an Interpretation*, 2 vols. (London: Wildwood House, 1970).
3. See T. Proctor, *Dostoevskij and the Belinsky School of Literary Criticism* (The Hague: Mouton, 1969), and V. Ia. Kirpotin, *Dostoevskii i Belinskii* [Dostoevsky and Belinsky] (Moscow, 1976).
4. R. Neuhäuser, "Social Reality and the Hero in Dostoevskij's Early Works," *Russian Literature* 4 (1973): 18–36.
5. For details see Frank.
6. Neuhäuser, p. 24.
7. E. Wasiolek, *Dostoevsky, the Major Fiction* (Cambridge, Mass., 1964), p. 6.
8. Terras, p. 22.

9. Wasiolek, pp. 8–9; and T. Pachmuss, *F.M. Dostoevsky, Dualism and Synthesis of the Human Soul* (Carbondale, Ill., 1963), p. 24.

10. K. Mochulsky, *Dostoevsky, His Life and Work*, trans. M. Minihan (Princeton, 1967), p. 50.

11. R.B. Anderson, "Dostoevsky's Hero in *The Double*: A Re-examination of the Divided Self," *Symposium* 26 (1972): 104.

12. F.M. Dostoevskii, *Pis'ma*, I, 100.

13. *Dostoevsky's Occasional Writings*, trans. D. Magarshack (London, 1964), p. 37.

14. Ibid., p. 33.

15. Ibid., pp. 29–38.

16. *Pis'ma*, I, 106.

17. Terras, pp. 195–96.

18. A.L. Bem, "Gogol i Pushkin v tvorchestve Dostoevskogo" [Gogol and Pushkin in Dostoevsky's Work], *Slavia* 7–8 (1929–30): 60–100 (vol. 7) and 297–311 (vol. 8).

19. A.L. Bem, "Dramatizatsiia breda" [The Dramatization of Delirium], *O Dostoevskom* [On Dostoevsky], ed. A.L. Bem (Prague, 1929), pp. 77–124.

20. V.G. Belinskii, *Polnoe sobranie sochinenii* [Complete Works], 13 vols. (Moscow, 1953–59), XII, 467.

21. For further details see my article "Dostoevsky's Treatment of the Theme of Romantic Dreaming in *Khozyayka* and *Belyye nochi*," *Modern Language Review* 69 (1974): 584–95.

22. Mochulsky, p. 95.

23. R.L. Jackson, *Dostoevsky's Quest for Form* (New Haven, 1966), p. 21.

24. F.M. Dostoevskii, *Polnoe sobranie khudozhestvennykh proizvedenii* [Complete Artistic Works], 13 vols. (Moscow-Leningrad, 1926–30), XIII, 158–59.

25. Mochulsky, pp. 29, 31.

26. J. Bayley, *Pushkin, a Comparative Commentary* (Cambridge, Eng.: Cambridge University Press, 1971), p. 41.

27. I have written on this in further detail in "Pushkin and the Early Dostoyevsky," *Modern Language Review* 74 (1979): 368–85.

28. *F.M. Dostoevskii ob iskusstve*, p. 55.

29. Mochulsky, p. 51.

30. J. Bronowski, *The Ascent of Man* (London: B.B.C., 1973), p. 180.

31. M.M. Bakhtin, *Problems of Dostoevsky's Poetics*, trans. R.W. Rotsel (Ann Arbor, 1973).

32. Bakhtin, p. 4.

Chapter Three

1. *Pis'ma*, I, 142.

2. Mochulsky (p. 229) remarks that Karamzin's sentimentalism is also parodied in *Winter Notes*, where the narrator is a travesty of Karamzin's

sentimental traveler in *Pis'ma russkogo puteshestvennika* [Letters of a Russian Traveler].

3. L'Abbé Prévost, *Manon Lescaut*, trans. L. W. Tancock (Harmondsworth, Eng.: Penguin, 1951), p. 22.

4. See, for instance, Frank; N.F. Bel'chikov, *Dostoevskii v protsesse Petrashevtsev* [Dostoevsky and the Petrashevsky Trial] (Moscow, 1971); and my own essay "Idealism and Utopian Socialism in Dostoyevsky's *Gospodin Prokharchin* and *Slaboye serdtse*," *Slavonic and East European Review* 58 (1980): 524–540.

5. For details of Dostoevsky's anxiety see Mochulsky, pp. 56–58.

6. See M. Slonim, *Three Loves of Dostoevsky* (London: Alvin Redman, 1957).

7. See F.M. Dostoevskii, III, 523.

8. Mochulsky, p. 216.

9. E.J. Simmons, *Dostoevsky* (London, 1950), p. 106.

10. W. Kaufmann, *Existentialism from Dostoevsky to Sartre* (Cleveland: World Publishing Co., 1956), p. 14.

11. D.S. Mirsky, *A History of Russian Literature* (London: Routledge & Kegan Paul, 1964), p. 278.

12. See D. Offord, "Dostoyevsky and Chernyshevsky," *Slavonic and East European Review* 57 (1979): 509–30.

13. A.D. Nuttall, *Dostoevsky's Crime and Punishment* (Sussex: Sussex University Press, 1978), p. 22.

14. M. Holquist, *Dostoevsky and the Novel* (Princeton, 1977), p. 64.

15. Ibid.

16. *Pis'ma*, I, 353.

17. See Bakhtin, pp. 190–99.

Chapter Four

1. See, for example, F.M. Dostoevskii, VII, 141.

2. P. Rahv, "Dostoevsky in *Crime and Punishment*," in *Dostoevsky, a Collection of Critical Essays*, ed. R. Wellek (Englewood Cliffs, N.J., 1962), p. 21.

3. Ibid., p. 20.

4. I have discussed this aspect of Raskolnikov's crime in more detail in my article "Raskolnikov and the Enigma of his Personality," *Forum for Modern Language Studies* 9 (1973): 153–65.

5. For a fuller discussion of such "doubles" in Dostoevsky see E.J. Simmons.

6. G. Rosenshield, *Crime and Punishment, the Techniques of the Omniscient Author* (Lisse, Holland: Peter de Ridder Press, 1978), pp. 26–37.

7. Rahv, pp. 17–18.

8. R.P. Blackmur, "Crime and Punishment, a study of Dostoevsky's Novel," *Chimera* 1 (1943): 26–27.

9. Wasiolek, p. 70.

10. R.A. Peace, *Dostoyevsky, an Examination of the Major Novels* (Cambridge, 1971), p. 45.

11. R.L. Jackson, *Dostoevsky's Quest for Form*, p. xi.

12. M. Iu. Lermontov, *Polnoe sobranie sochinenii* [Complete Works] (Moscow-Leningrad, 1937), V, 306.

13. *F.M. Dostoevskii ob iskusstve*, p. 81.

14. Peace, p. 173.

15. N.N. Strakhov, *Biografiia, pis'ma i zametki iz zapisnoi knizhki F.M. Dostoevskogo* [Biography, Letters, and Notes from F.M. Dostoevsky's Notebook] (St. Petersburg, 1883), p. 372.

16. *F.M. Dostoevskii ob iskusstve*, p. 379.

17. N.A. Dobroliubov, *Izbrannye sochineniia* [Selected Works] (Moscow, 1948), p. 103.

18. Mochulsky, p. 312.

19. V. Ia. Kirpotin, *Razocharovanie i krushenie Rodiona Raskol'nikova* [Rodion Raskolnikov's Disillusion and Downfall] (Moscow, 1970), pp. 382, 385.

Chapter Five

1. M.V. Jones, *Dostoyevsky, the Novel of Discord* (London, 1976), p. 97.

2. Peace, p. 101.

3. A.I. Gertsen, *Sobranie sochinenii* [Collected Works], 30 vols. (Moscow, 1954–66), XI, 402.

4. R. Hollander, "The Apocalyptic Framework of Dostoevsky's *The Idiot*," *Mosaic* 7 (1974): 123–39.

5. *Pis'ma*, II, 71.

6. See E. Wasiolek, ed., *The Notebooks for The Idiot* (Chicago, 1967).

7. See F.M. Dostoevskii, IX, 396–99.

8. Peace, p. 69.

9. *Pis'ma*, II, 71.

10. *F.M. Dostoevskii ob iskusstve*, p. 520.

11. For a full discussion of sectarianism in Dostoevsky's novels see Peace.

12. Peace, ch. 5.

Chapter Six

1. Peace, pp. 146–50, gives a clear account of the Nechaev affair.

2. *Pis'ma*, II, 257.

3. The description "Westernizers" (*zapadniki*) was applied to Russian intellectuals of the 1830s onward who believed that Russia's political and cultural isolation from the West had distorted the nation's historical development. They urged that Russia should learn from the West's technical

and cultural superiority. The Westernizers were opposed by the "Slavophiles" (*slavianofily*), who argued that Russia's isolation had allowed her to follow a uniquely national line of development, superior to that of the West, and which would be compromised by the wholesale adoption of Western attitudes.

4. Petr's devotion to Stavrogin has led Grossman to conclude that Stavrogin was modeled on Bakunin, Nechaev's mentor. See L.P. Grossman, *Dostoevsky*, trans. Mary Mackler (London, 1974), p. 473.

5. See *F.M. Dostoevskii ob iskusstve*, p. 187.

6. I. Howe, "Dostoevsky, the Politics of Salvation," in *Dostoevsky, a Collection of Critical Essays*, ed. R. Wellek, (Englewood Cliffs, N.J., 1962), p. 56.

7. Simmons, p. 229.

8. G.A. Buttrick, ed., *The Interpreter's Dictionary of the Bible* (New York: Abingdon Press, 1962), III, 547–48.

9. R.E. Matlaw, *The Brothers Karamazov, Novelistic Technique* (The Hague, 1957), p. 37.

10. M. Iu. Lermontov, *Polnoe sobranie sochinenii* [Complete Works], V, 224.

11. See E. Stenbock-Fermor, "Lermontov and Dostoevskij's Novel *The Devils*," *Slavonic and East European Journal* 17 (1959): 215–30.

12. Peace, p. 185.

13. See, for example, Grossman, *Dostoevsky*; M.V. Jones, "Dostoyevsky and an Aspect of Schiller's Psychology," *Slavonic and East European Review* 52 (1974): 337–54.

14. A working title for *Podrostok* was *Besporiadok* [Disorder].

15. Grossman writes (p. 525): "With his usual boldness of innovation, Dostoevsky set himself an extremely difficult task—to depict the chaos prevalent all over Russia in a fittingly chaotic manner."

16. A phrase borrowed from M.V. Jones, *Dostoyevsky, the Novel of Discord*.

17. An excellent account of the city motif is to be found in D. Fanger, *Dostoevsky and Romantic Realism* (Cambridge, Mass., 1965).

18. Mochulsky, p. 494.

19. Grossman, pp. 510–20.

20. Dostoevsky's populist views are developed most forcefully in his journalism, and are consequently largely outside the concerns of the present study. The interested reader is advised to consult *Dnevnik pisatelia*, which has been well translated by B. Brasol as *The Diary of a Writer* (New York, 1954).

Chapter Seven

1. G. Steiner, *Tolstoy or Dostoevsky* (London, 1959).

2. See F.M. Dostoevskii, XV, 551.

3. C.M. Woodhouse, "Dostoevsky," *Listener*, 22 October 1970, p. 543.

4. I.S. Zil'bershtein and L.M. Rosenblium, eds., *Neizdannyi Dos-toevskii* [Unpublished Dostoevsky] (Moscow, 1971), p. 699.

5. *F.M. Dostoevskii ob iskusstve*, pp. 80–81.

6. Peace, ch. 8.

7. Again, see Peace for a full and stimulating discussion of this theme.

Chapter Eight

1. Steiner, *Tolstoy or Dostoevsky*, pp. 346–47.

2. A. de Jonge, *Dostoevsky and the Age of Intensity* (London, 1975), p. 1.

3. See H. Troyat, *Tolstoy* (Harmondsworth, Eng.: Penguin, 1970), pp. 554–55.

4. G. Phelps, *The Russian Novel in English Fiction* (London: Hutchin-sor, 1956), p. 157.

5. *Pis'ma*, II, 169. See also *Pis'ma*, II, 150–51; S. Linnér, *Dostoevskij on Realism* (Stockholm: Almqvist & Wiksell, 1967), p. 203.

6. B. Kuznetsov, *Einstein and Dostoevsky* (London, 1972), p. 7.

7. G. Steiner, *Language and Silence. Essays 1958–1966* (London: Faber, 1967), p. 34.

8. B. Hoffmann, *Albert Einstein* (St. Albans, Eng.: Paladin, 1977), p. 95.

9. Kuznetsov, p. 12.

10. The twentieth-century Russian novelist Evgeny Zamyatin, who com-bined the roles of scientist and artist and whose debt to Dostoevsky is beyond doubt, suggested that "after the geometrical-philosophical earthquake pro-duced by Einstein space and time as previously understood were finally destroyed. But even before Einstein this earthquake had been recorded by the seismograph of the new art." E. I. Zamiatin, *Litsa* [Faces] (New York: Inter-Language Literary Associates, 1967), p. 238.

Selected Bibliography

PRIMARY SOURCES

Polnoe sobranie sochinenii v tridtsati tomakh [Complete Works in 30 Volumes] Leningrad: Nauka, 1972–. At the time of writing publication is still in progress, having reached volume 19.

Polnoe sobranie khudozhestvennykh proizvedenii [Complete Artistic Works] in 13 vols. Moscow-Leningrad: GIZ, 1926–30.

Sobranie sochinenii v desiati tomakh [Collected Works in 10 volumes], Moscow: Goslitizdat, 1956–58.

F.M. Dostoevskii ob iskusstve [Dostoevsky on Art]. Ed. V. Bogdanov. Moscow: Iskusstvo, 1973.

Pis'ma [Letters] in 4 vols. Ed. A. Dolinin. Moscow-Leningrad: GIZ, 1928–59.

The standard translations of Dostoevsky's works are still those of Constance Garnett, published in a uniform edition by William Heinemann, London, 12 vols., 1912–20.

Readable translations of the major novels have been published by Penguin Books. These translations are by David Magarshack and Jessie Coulson.

English translations of the notebooks and draft material for the major novels have been prepared by Edward Wasiolek. Chicago and London: University of Chicago Press, 1967–71.

The Diary of a Writer has been translated by Boris Brasol. New York: George Braziller, 1954.

Dostoevsky's Occasional Writings, translated by D. Magarshack and published by Vision Press, London, 1964, contains a selection of Dostoevsky's journalistic writings.

Dostoevsky: A Self-Portrait, by J. Coulson, published in London by Oxford University Press, 1962, contains a helpful selection of Dostoevsky's letters.

SECONDARY SOURCES

1. Bibliographies

F.M. *Dostoevskii, Bibliografiia proizvedenii F.M. Dostoevskogo i literatury o nem 1917–65*, [F.M. Dostoevsky: A Bibliography of His Writings and Works About Him, 1917–65]. Ed. A.A. Belkin, A.S. Dolinin, and V.V. Kozhinov. Moscow: Izdatel'stvo Kniga, 1968.

S.V. Belov, "Bibliografiia proizvedenii F.M. Dostoevskogo i literatury o nem, 1966–69," [A Bibliography of F.M. Dostoevsky's Writings and Works About Him, 1966–69] in *Dostoevskii i ego vremia* [Dostoevsky and His Time], ed. V.G. Bazanov and G.M. Fridlender, Leningrad: Nauka, 1971, pp. 322–56. (Also contains a supplement to the bibliography of Belkin, Dolinin, and Kozhinov).

S.V. Belov, "Proizvedeniia F.M. Dostoevskogo i literatura o nem 1970–1," [F.M. Dostoevsky's Writings and Works About Him, 1970–1] in *Dostoevskii, materialy i issledovaniia*, [Dostoevsky: Materials and Investigations] Vol. 1, ed. G.M. Fridlender, Leningrad: Nauka, 1974, pp. 305–38.

There is a useful current bibliography compiled by Rudolph Neuhäuser and others, published regularly in the *Bulletin of the International Dostoevsky Society*.

Two works by Vladimir Seduro afford useful bibliographical information: *Dostoyevski in Russian Literary Criticism 1846–1956*. New York: Columbia University Press, 1957; and *Dostoevski's Image in Russia Today*. Belmont, Mass.: Nordland Press, 1975.

2. Biographical and Critical Works

BAKHTIN, MIKHAIL. *Problems of Dostoevsky's Poetics*. Translated by R.W. Rotsel. Ann Arbor: Ardis, 1973. Pioneering study of polyphony in Dostoevsky's novels, first published in 1929.

BELKNAP, ROBERT. *The Structure of "The Brothers Karamazov."* The Hague: Mouton, 1967. Stimulating discussion of structural principles.

BERDIAEV, NIKOLAI. *Dostoevsky*. Translated by Donald Attwater. New York: Meridian, 1957. Contentious analysis of religion in Dostoevsky's works.

CARR, EDWARD H. *Dostoevsky*. London: George Allen and Unwin, 1962. Sensible and well-written biography.

CATTEAU, JACQUES. *La création littéraire chez Dostoïevski*. Paris: Institut d'études slaves, 1978. Appeared during the preparation of this work. A brief examination suggests that it is a very important work indeed.

CHIRKOV, NIKOLAI. *O stile Dostoevskogo* [On Dostoevsky's Style]. Moscow: Nauka, 1967. Brief but perceptive analysis of Dostoevsky's work.

DALTON, ELIZABETH. *Unconscious Structure in "The Idiot."* Princeton: Princeton University Press, 1979. Interesting application of psychoanalytical methods to *The Idiot*.

DOLININ, ARKADII, ed. *F.M. Dostoevskii v vospominaniiakh sovremennikov* [Dostoevsky in the Memoirs of His Contemporaries], 2 vols. Moscow: Khudozhestvennaia literatura, 1964. A revealing selection of memoirs.

DOSTOEVSKAIA, ANNA. *Vospominaniia* [Memoirs]. Moscow: Khudozhestvennaia literatura, 1971. The memoirs of Dostoevsky's second wife.

FANGER, DONALD. *Dostoevsky and Romantic Realism*. Cambridge, Mass.: Harvard University Press, 1965. A comparative study of Dostoevsky, Balzac, Dickens, and Gogol, and an important analysis of the role of the city in Dostoevsky's fiction.

FRANK, JOSEPH. *Dostoevsky, the Seeds of Revolt 1821–49*. Princeton: Princeton University Press, 1976. The first volume of Frank's intellectual biography. Sure to become a standard work, it is meticulously researched.

FRIDLENDER, GEORGII. *Realizm Dostoevskogo* [Dostoevsky's Realism]. Moscow-Leningrad: Nauka, 1964. Valuable work by a leading contemporary Soviet scholar.

GROSSMANN, LEONID. *Dostoevsky*. Translated by Mary Mackler. London: Allen Lane, 1974. English translation of a splendid critical biography by an outstanding Soviet Dostoevsky specialist.

HOLQUIST, MICHAEL. *Dostoevsky and the Novel*. Princeton: Princeton University Press, 1977. A difficult and adventurous work of formal criticism which has many persuasive insights.

IVANOV, VYACHESLAV. *Freedom and the Tragic Life*. London: Harvill, 1952. English translation of a classic study which has stood the test of time very well.

JACKSON, ROBERT L. *Dostoevsky's Underground Man in Russian Literature*. The Hague: Mouton, 1958. A study of the impact of Dostoevsky's hero on other Russian writers.

———. *Dostoevsky's Quest for Form*. New Haven: Yale University Press, 1966. A very important work, devoted to Dostoevsky's esthetic views but yielding many broader insights.

———, ed. *Twentieth Century Interpretations of "Crime and Punishment."* Englewood Cliffs, N.J.: Prentice-Hall, 1974. A useful collection of essays and extracts for students.

JONES, MALCOLM. *Dostoyevsky, the Novel of Discord*. London: Elek, 1976. A study of the compositional principles of Dostoevsky's major work. Well researched, and with useful notes and bibliography.

JONGE, ALEX DE. *Dostoevsky and the Age of Intensity*. London: Secker and Warburg, 1975. Rhetorical, incautious, but undoubtedly stimulating discussion of Dostoevsky's responsiveness to the texture of the modern age.

KIRPOTIN, VALERII. *Dostoevskii-khudozhnik* [Dostoevsky as Artist].
Moscow: Sovetskii pisatel', 1972. An important work by a leading Soviet
scholar.

———. *F.M. Dostoevskii, tvorcheskii put'* [F.M. Dostoevsky and His Literary Work]. Moscow: Goslitizdat, 1960. A solid account of Dostoevsky's
early career.

———. *Razocharovanie i krushenie Rodiona Raskol'nikova* [Rodion Raskol-nikov's Disillusion and Downfall]. Moscow: Sovetskii pisatel', 1970.
Detailed examination of *Crime and Punishment*.

KUZNETSOV, BORIS. *Einstein and Dostoevsky*. Translated by V. Talmy.
London: Hutchinson, 1972. Highly provocative work by a leading Soviet
physicist. Kuznetsov has uncovered a highly significant area of comparative study.

LORD, ROBERT. *Dostoevsky, Essays and Perspectives*. London: Chatto and
Windus, 1970. Uneven collection of essays, at times stimulating, at
others contrived.

MATLAW, RALPH. *The Brothers Karamazov, Novelistic Technique*. The
Hague: Mouton, 1957. Brief but interesting analysis of structural principles of Dostoevsky's novels.

MOCHULSKY, KONSTANTIN. *Dostoevsky, His Life and Work*. Translated by
Michael Minihan. Princeton: Princeton University Press, 1967. Widely
regarded as the best critical biography on Dostoevsky in any language.
Essential reading for all students.

PACHMUSS, TEMIRA. *F.M. Dostoevsky, Dualism and Synthesis of the Human
Soul*. Carbondale: Southern Illinois University Press, 1963. Perceptive
analysis, with a broader range than its title suggests.

PEACE, RICHARD. *Dostoyevsky, an Examination of the Major Novels*. Cambridge: Cambridge University Press, 1971. A remarkably good close
reading of the major novels, and an interesting account of religious
sectarianism in Dostoevsky's major fiction.

SHKLOVSKII, VIKTOR. *Za i protiv, zametki o Dostoevskom* [For and Against:
Notes on Dostoevsky]. Moscow: Sovetskii pisatel', 1957. Important
work by a founder of Russian Formalism.

SIMMONS, ERNEST J. *Dostoevsky, the Making of a Novelist*. London:
Lehmann, 1950. One of the first reliable critical studies of Dostoevsky in
the West, and still of great value.

STEINER, GEORGE. *Tolstoy or Dostoevsky*. London: Faber, 1959. Scintillating contrastive study of Dostoevsky as a "dramatic" novelist and Tolstoy
as an "epic" novelist. The argument is aggressively clear-cut, but the
work is undoubtedly valuable.

TERRAS, VICTOR. *The Young Dostoevsky, 1846–1849*. The Hague: Mouton,
1969. Detailed, sensible examination of the early works. A useful adjunct
to Frank's study, which is weak in literary analysis.

VETLOVSKAIA, VALENTINA. *Poetika romana "Brat'ia Karamazovy"* [The Poetics of *The Brothers Karamazov*]. Leningrad: Nauka, 1977. Persuasive analysis of *The Brothers Karamazov*, affording a rare polemic with Bakhtin's views.

WASIOLEK, EDWARD. *Dostoevsky, the Major Fiction*. Cambridge, Mass.: MIT Press, 1964. Sensible criticism, particularly good on *Notes from Underground*, and with a full and useful bibliography.

WELLEK, RENE, ed. *Dostoevsky, a Collection of Critical Essays*. Englewood Cliffs, N.J.: Prentice-Hall, 1962. A valuable anthology of critical opinion.

Index

Alexander II, 24

Allegory. *See* Dostoevsky, Fedor Mikhailovich: allegory in his works

Anderson, R., 42

Apocalypse. *See* Dostoevsky, Fedor Mikhailovich: apocalyptic vision

Bakhtin, Mikhail, 52, 81–82

Bakunin, Mikhail, 119, 120, 175n4

Balzac, Honoré de, 16, 17, 37, 46

Beketov, Alexey, 20

Belinsky, Vissarion, 19, 20, 21, 22, 29, 32, 33, 36, 37, 38, 39, 40, 42, 44, 47, 48, 53, 57, 59, 167

Bentham, Jeremy, 35, 64

Bergson, Henri, 78

Blackmur, R.P., 79

Blanc, Louis, 20

Bronowski, Jacob, 51

Byron, Lord, 84, 89

Carr, E.H., 13

Cervantes, Miguel de, 106

Chermak, Leonty, 14

Chernyshevsky, Nikolay, 64, 71–72, 86, 122

Citizen (Grazhdanin), 29

Corneille, Pierre, 16

Crimean War, 24

Darwin, Charles, 126

Dickens, Charles, 37, 46, 59

Dobrolyubov, Nikolay, 86

Dostoevskaya, Anna Grigorevna *neé* Snitkina (second wife), 26, 27, 28, 30

Dostoevskaya, Maria Dmitrievna *neé* Constant (first wife), 23, 25, 26, 63

Dostoevskaya, Maria Fedorovna (mother), 13, 14, 15

Dostoevsky, Fedor Mikhailovich: allegory in his works, 97–98, 101–103, 105–108, 112–14, 128–29, 145, 159–61; apocalyptic vision, 54, 98–103, 127–29; arrest and exile, 22–24, 32; association with discussion groups in 1840s, 20–21; at St. Petersburg Academy of Military Engineering, 14–17; attitude to nihilists and radicals, 24, 55, 64, 71–72, 86–87, 120, 122–27; attitudes to Western Europe, 54–55, 99–101, 119, 138–39; Christian views, 24, 56, 57, 62, 67–68, 118, 123, 126–27, 134, 156–57; death and funeral, 30–31; death of daughter, Sonya, 27, 96; death of father, 17, death of son, Alexey, 30; early life, 13–15; enters military service, 17; epilepsy, 17, 22, 30, 96, 110; esthetic views, 84–87, 94–95, 135–37, 146, 150–51; financial difficulties, 17, 26, 96; first marriage, to Maria Dmitrievna Isaeva (*neé* Constant), 23; gambling compulsion, 26, 96; influences of Pushkin and Gogol, 49–51; journalistic experiences, 24–26, 29; literary debut, 18–20, 32; made corresponding member of Academy of Sciences, 29; mock execution, 22, 115; money in works of, 45, 103–104, 139; parricide in life and works of, 17, 143, 161–62; perfectibility of man, views on, 33–36, 106, 110–11, 118, 125–26, 146–47; point of view in works of, 43, 51–53, 71, 76–83, 138, 169–70; populist attitudes, 22, 24, 55, 123, 142, 175n20; Pushkin celebrations (Moscow 1880), 15, 27, 30, 55; realism in his works, 167–70; retreat from early romanticism and utopianism, 18–19, 23, 46, 55, 58–59, 60, 62, 118; return from exile, 24; St. Petersburg and theme of city, 16, 61, 139; second marriage, to Anna Grigorevna Snitkina, 26; translates Balzac's *Eugénie Grandet*, 17–18; travels abroad, 25, 27–28, 54; utopian socialism, 20–21;

182